THE COWBOY

THE
COWBOY

Representations of Labor in an American Work Culture

BLAKE ALLMENDINGER

New York   Oxford
OXFORD UNIVERSITY PRESS
1992

Oxford University Press

Oxford   New York   Toronto
Delhi   Bombay   Calcutta   Madras   Karachi
Kuala Lumpur   Singapore   Hong Kong   Tokyo
Nairobi   Dar es Salaam   Cape Town
Melbourne   Auckland   Madrid

and associated companies in
Berlin   Ibadan

Published by Oxford University Press, Inc.,
200 Madison Avenue, New York, New York 10016

Library of Congress Cataloging-in-Publication Data
Allmendinger, Blake.
The cowboy : representations of labor in an American work culture
Blake Allmendinger.
p.   cm.   Includes bibliographical references and index.
ISBN 0-19-507243-X
1. American literature—West (U.S.)—History and criticism.
2. Cowboys' writings, American—History and criticism.
3. Western stories—History and criticism.   4. West (U.S.)—Popular culture.
5. Cowboys in literature.   6. Work in literature.   7. Cowboys in art.
8. Work in art.   I. Title.   PS271.A43   1992
810.9'3278—dc20   91-36256

Portions of Chapter 2 first appeared in *Western Humanities Review* and are reprinted here with permission.
The Autobiography of Will Rogers, edited by Donald Day. Copyright 1949 by Rogers Company.
Copyright © renewed 1977 by Donald Day and Beth Day.
Reprinted by permission of Houghton Mifflin Company.
"Bucking Bronco," reprinted from *Songs of the Cowboys,* compiled by N. Howard Thorp.
Courtesy of University of Nebraska Press, Lincoln, NE.
"The Cowboy's Dream" and "Poor Lonesome Cowboy," collected, adapted,
and arranged by John A. Lomax and Alan Lomax. TRO. ©
Copyright 1938 (renewed) Ludlow Music, Inc., New York, NY. Used by permission.
"The Oyster," reprinted form *Croutons on a Cow Pie.* © Baxter Black 1988.
"Reincarnation," by Wallace McRae, from *It's Just Grass and Water,* published by the Oxalis Group.
Copyright 1986, Wallace McRae.
Transcript from ABC News, reprinted by permission.
Copyright 1987. All rights reserved.

2 4 6 8 9 7 5 3 1

Printed in the United States of America
on acid-free paper

To
Rose Mary Allmendinger
and

Acknowledgments

Now, when I look back, it seems hard to isolate the most traumatic event in my career as a teenager. But of all the many, mostly imagined, nightmarish episodes, moving with my family from town to a cattle ranch and exchanging my identity as a city-dweller for that of a rancher's son probably represented the low point in My Adolescence from Hell. Having to learn to brand livestock and to castrate calves with a pocketknife, while our dog gulped down thrown-away scrotums as though they were bloody, flea-infested hors d'oeuvres . . . Having to take the engorged penis of our half-blind, three-legged stud and aim it for him as he mounted a quarterhorse mare . . . Having to stand in a barnyard, knee-deep in mud, while my sister preg-tested cows . . . (She casually informed me that cows have free-floating, unattached wombs and made her point by corralling a cow, sticking her hand up its rectum, and pushing its empty uterus back and forth, as though she were dribbling a decompressed basketball. Feeling weak, I clutched a fence post for strength, but while my sister rearranged its internal cavities, the cow stood there complacently, chewing its cud, swatting flies with its tail, and staring off at the horizon, dreamy-eyed.) . . . None of these sexual-initiation rites made the on-slaught of my own teenage puberty seem like something to celebrate.

Nor did these life lessons seem to help me understand ''literature,'' which I was just beginning to think of and care about. One night, after I had finished my homework, I went into the family room, sat down in a La-Z-Boy, and commenced telling my parents about *A Farewell to Arms,* which I had just read for my tenth-grade English teacher, Ms. Phillips. Somewhere in the middle of my interpretive monologue, my mom got out of her rocking chair, picked up a rifle that lay near her feet, cocked it, walked toward me, and, after pausing to aim, shot out an open window behind me, killing a coyote that had been prowling around, unbeknownst to me, outside the house. As a young critic and lecturer, I worked a lot of tough joints. And like the coyote, another endangered species, I often found myself peering up the unfriendly end of some firearm.

Not surprisingly, when I went off to college, I still didn't feel that ranch life had prepared me for reading and writing about literature. On the other hand, though, I fancied that other undergraduates, who had grown up back East, admired me be-cause of my difference, my ''westernness.'' I could never rupture the silence of the library reading room by striding across its polished floors in my squeaky, rubber-soled, high-heeled cowboy boots without causing other students to look up and stare—signs, I thought, of my long overdue social acknowledgment, examples of the rude but welcome gaze of idolatry. Maybe such delusions were good for me.

What I mistook for the flattering curiosity of city folk actually made me reexamine myself and take an interest in my own background and heritage. Over the years, that interest broadened as I tried to combine what I already knew about western literature, culture, and history with the critical-thinking skills that a formal East Coast education had given me. In a roundabout way, this book is the product of efforts to unite my ranching and academic identities—to explain where I came from, where I went, and what happened.

My mom made most of "what happened" take place. She paid my bills for the first twenty-two years of my life, read everything I wrote, and, when this book wasn't going well, kissed it and tried to make it get better. Today she runs the Hitch Rack Ranch by herself. In winter, she puts on her ex-husband's overalls and a loud hat with ear flaps and goes out to chop ice from the stock's frozen water tanks. In summer, she bounces across the pastures in a beat-up orange pickup, with Spot—her unspotted black Labrador—running ahead of her, every now and then stopping to point out her way. A pitchfork-packin' mama, she shoots straight from the hip and never talks out of both sides of her mouth unless she's juggling a filter-tipped cigarette.

When my mom stopped paying my bills, institutions began doing so. The University of Pennsylvania gave me a Dean's and a Mellon Dissertation Fellowship, nonteaching grants that enabled me to get through the dissertation phase of the English Department's Ph.D. program. Between 1989 and 1991, the Academic Senate at UCLA offered me money for purchasing photographs. Institutions located and lent or sold me archival photographs. Men and women, some of whom live on farms and ranches in rural parts of the West, volunteered—at their own expense—to drive into towns where their antique bridles, halters, and spurs could be photographed, knowing that there was nothing "in it" for them. Darrell Arnold and others are acknowledged in credits that accompany the book's sixty-eight photographs.

As it turned out, *The Cowboy* was the first book that Liz Maguire approved when she became the literary studies editor at Oxford University Press. I'd like to thank her and Bill Sisler for taking a chance on the book, and Irene Pavitt for catching and editing mistakes I made in the manuscript. (Whatever they pay you, it isn't enough.) I'd also like to thank David Rahmel, a computer wiz in the English Department at UCLA. I'm a computer illiterate who, until recently, thought that the TAB key was named after a soda pop. To give some idea of what David had to put up with when he worked with me, suffice it to say that, on one occasion, I called him, after having spent many fruitless hours hunting and searching, and asked him where the on–off switch was on my printer. (It's on the back . . . I think.) And this, after I'd been using the printer for two or three years.

While I was writing the manuscript, faculty members and friends in various English Departments advised and morally supported me. Between 1984 and 1989, it was my privilege to study at Penn and to profit from comments made by two members of its unsurpassed faculty. To Paul Korshin and Betsy Erkkila: thank you for treating me like your peer when I wasn't. To Steve Tatum and Barry Weller at the University of Utah: thank you for reading and championing the manuscript. To Hilene Flanzbaum, to Jenny Green (my barbed-wire muse), and to a woman at

UCLA known as Deborah Garfield, known as ''Deb Girl'' to me: thank you for just being my friends.

And to Elaine Scarry, my Garbo. With love.

Los Angeles   B. A.
July 1992

Contents

THE COWBOY

INTRODUCTION

I

A *cowboy* is defined by the work that he does. Any man lays claim to that name if he lives on a ranch and works—drives, brands, castrates, or nurtures—a cattleman's herd. In addition, working accounts for ways in which cowboys portray themselves in their art: in nineteenth-century poems that they orally composed and sang on the range, in twentieth-century poems that they write, in books that they publish, and in art objects that they fashion, cowboys always represent themselves as engaging in some form of labor. This book's threefold purpose is, first, to look at art that cowboys produce—art that has never been studied before—and, second, to demonstrate that cowboy art values historically documented labor routines that cowboys have traditionally acted out in their work culture.

I use the term *work culture* not only to suggest that cowboys are defined by *work* that they do, but also to argue that they are self-represented in *culture* by poems, prose, and art that all reveal cowboys to be men who are culturally unified by engaging in labor routines that they think of as cowboy work. Art deals with cowboy work, as well as with concerns about economics, gender, religion, and literature, even though these thoughts sometimes express themselves as concerns about cattle branding, livestock castration, and other tasks. The book's third and most important function is therefore to show that artistic self-representations of labor also formulate systems of thought in which cowboys use work as a metaphor for discussing economics, gender, religion, and literature, sometimes equating branding with religious salvation, at other times representing livestock castration as beefing up sexual potency, elsewhere defining spur making as freedom, and so on.

The rest of this section outlines four systems of thought that operate in the cowboy's work culture.

Religion and the Branding Myth

Two members of the Reagan administration were either injured or killed by horses in the process of illustrating their political ties to the cowboy's work culture. In 1989, on the Fourth of July, former President Ronald Reagan went to a Mexican ranch, rode on and fell from a horse, and injured himself in the fall. In facetiously declaring that he had just prematurely completed his first cowboy "rodeo,"[1] Reagan did not seem to recall that a similar mishap had previously taken the life of a friend and former associate. On July 25, 1987, Secretary of Commerce Malcolm Baldrige had accidentally been killed by a rearing horse while practicing for a California rodeo's steer-roping contest. At the subsequent memorial service held in Washington's National Cathedral on July 29, and attended by close "cowboy" friends of the family, Reagan had acknowledged his cabinet member's recent induction into the prestigious Cowboy Hall of Fame and had praised Baldrige's good fortune to die doing "what he [had] loved most."[2] During the funeral on the following day, Vice President George Bush had joined the audience in reciting a cowboy poem that promises eternal salvation for God's chosen frontiersmen.[3] Theodore Roosevelt and Lyndon B. Johnson had already borrowed the cowboy's image to make their public personas and political policies clear: one had commanded the Rough Riders, the other had made use of his ties to the Texas frontier, and both had appealed to the American public by describing their administrations in terms of the cowboy's rugged and individualistic work ethic. Now the Reagan administration reemphasized the link that connected frontier culture with national government by equating cowboy poetry with religious and political discourse—by using a poem about the cowboy's perpetuation in heaven to illustrate the legacy left by a government officer.

Baldrige's steer roping and reenactment of a cowboy labor routine inspired the reading of a cowboy poem that concerns itself with the Christian myth of salvation, just as the cowboy's performance of other work-related historical functions motivated his oral composition and writing of holy discourse and contemplative poetry. Before fencing transformed the public space of the open range into a series of privately controlled segments of land, cattlemen let their livestock graze with other ranchers' wandering herds; hence animals could easily mix and become confused with one another in promiscuous groups that roamed the unfenced frontier. Ranchers used brands to distinguish their stock from that of other cattlemen and to protect their possessions from outlaws who could rustle and sell unbranded mavericks. Ranchers invented hieroglyphic economic inscriptions, or forms of language, to inform readers that no one could take ranchers' cattle or mistake their bulls, heifers, calves, and castrated steers for other men's real estate.

But although they authored language by inventing brands, ranchers did not inscribe brands or write brands themselves. They hired cowboys to imprint the cattlemen's signs on the animals' hides and to act out the cowboys' economic subordination and literary disenfranchisement. Cowboys imprinted brands on the livestock of their employers, but they did not own the "texts" that they wrote. Cattle hides were like manuscript pages, and cattle brands were like pens: ranch hands penned texts on pages, but ranch owners owned both the "books" and the "signatures" that cowboys inscribed on them. Hence branding acted out the notion that cowboys were economically and literarily destitute, by indicating that ranchers (not cowboys) owned cattle and that ranchers (not cowboys) owned language. Ranchers invented brands, used them to signify ownership, and employed manual laborers who worked for menial wages to function as go-betweens. Put between brands, on the one hand, and stock, on the other, cowboys simply placed one on the other, but never owned either.

As a way of denying their disenfranchisement, cowboys invented a branding myth in which they interpreted branding as a form of empowerment. In poems about branding, ranch hands stated that they took brands from ranchers and gave them to God, who then branded cowboys in order to illustrate that cowboys were God's chosen race or ''livestock'' in the Lord's ''herd'' in heaven. Cowboys subverted cattlemen, translating branding into an act of religious naming and claiming in heaven, not accepting it as a means of economically and textually empowering ranchers on earth. Branding cowboys as members of God's chosen race and, at the same time, excluding ranchers from the Lord's privileged group permitted workers to redress an economic imbalance and to do so by assessing the significance of language in a western cattle economy. Cowboys used brands to witness the fact that they had been religiously saved, and they orally composed or wrote poems about branding to contest representations of their subordination in workplaces.

Historical acts and inventions attempted to nullify the language that empowered cowboys as branders. But the invention of barbed wire and the building of barbed-wire fences, while making branding unnecessary and cowboy branders therefore expendable, only served to make cowboy branders more important in poetry. Barbed wire, invented in the 1870s and strung across the West extensively in the 1880s and afterward, enabled cattlemen to define and distinguish their stock not by branding their herds on the open range, but by confining them within fenced-off enclosures. It led ranchers to fire cowboys who were no longer needed in such large numbers to watch over and round up livestock that barbed-wire fences, instead, could incarcerate. Cowboys complained that ranchers, in a sense, fenced them out of employment. But in their religious poems, they continued to state that God gave them shelter. Branding cattle on earth, they acted out what God did in heaven when He saved men, branded them, and then turned them loose to roam in the unfenced open ranges of heaven. Fencing open ranges, cattlemen therefore not only displaced cowboys, but attempted to overthrow God by challenging His right to brand men-as-livestock. As a result, ranchers could never hope to find places in heaven. Only cowboys who did God's will on earth could save themselves: losing jobs when ranchers fenced open ranges on earth, cowboys knew that they were still destined to enjoy rewards in the afterlife.

Sexuality and the Castration Myth

Cattle branding and livestock castration typically occurred at the same time—when newborn calves were rounded up on the ranch in the spring and when late arrivals were caught in the fall and worked over before being shipped off to market. Cowboys indicated that ranchers had legal rights to possess—and to sell, kill, or alter—

animals' bodies not only by burning brands into hides, but by cutting into bodies and by surgically assigning certain physical functions to animals. Castration ensured that neutered bull calves became fattened steers and therefore sold for higher prices at auction, and that spayed heifers became immune to the remaining adult bulls and hence served as convenient nonreproductive devices for preventing the otherwise unpredictable growth and mismanagement of cattle herds. If the cattlemen's ownership of brands denied cowboys an access to language, then the ranchers' castration of cattle provided ranch hands with a metaphor for their own denied access to social and sexual forms of engagement, for in addition to supervising the castration of livestock, ranchers socially and sexually deprived cowboys who worked for them. In the nineteenth century, ranchers hired only unmarried cowboys. Married men required higher wages to support wives and children and tended to own homes in town. Commuting to work and dividing their loyalties between employers and families, married men devoted only part of their lives to ranching, unlike single men. Bachelors could subsist on lower wages, live on ranches, and share cramped quarters in bunkhouses. They could always be counted on, for they were always there when cattlemen needed them. Working on predominantly male ranches or going away on all-male cattle drives, cowboys almost never met women, except on paydays when they went to town, got drunk, and met prostitutes, or when they entered cowtowns at the end of cattle drives. Geographically isolated and socially cut off, unmarried cowboys were temporarily and metaphorically castrated in that they were forced to abstain from engaging in relations with women for great lengths of time. They were hired because they were already unattached, deprived single men, and they were forced to stay that way or risk being fired for moving to town, getting married, and fathering offspring. Therefore, the logic that compelled ranchers to castrate animals also tempted ranchers to employ unmarried cowboys: castrated steers realized more cash flow, since they sold for higher prices at market, and single men maximized profits, since they worked for less money and lived on the spot in cheap and convenient single-sex housing.

Cowboys often contested their representation as castrated workers. As they fought their denied access to language, turning the cattlemen's branding signs into texts that promised cowboys religious salvation in heaven, so they fought their denied access to women, turning the cattlemen's castration of livestock into symbolic acts that made cowboys seem sexually "masculine." After castrating bulls, cowboys ate the bulls' castrated testicles and took on the bulls' roles as breeders. By consuming organs that are anatomical indications of maleness, they enhanced their *own* sense of maleness. Ingesting organs that are able to generate sex drives in bulls, they metaphorically increased their own potency, empowered by these aphrodisiacs. Therefore, the castration myth argued not that the act of castration signified the cowboys' social deprivation, geographical isolation, or sexual abstinence, but that castrating livestock could undo the cattlemen's castration metaphor, paradoxically reconfirming the cowboys' virility and sexual stamina.

Noncowboy society tried to shield women from "sex-hungry" cowboys by using its square dances to deny the force of the cowboy's castration myth. Square-dance callers referred to dancers as "herds," to women as "heifers," and to cowboys as "steers" when they could not find women to dance with, or "heifers" to couple with. Because men outnumbered women out West, and because cowboys constituted the bulk of these men in cowtowns where most dances took place, ranch hands at dances therefore, more often than not, ended up single, acting out roles as castrated "steers" and ironically finishing right where they started. Metaphorically castrated at ranches, where they almost never met women, ranch hands went to town and tried to meet women, only to wind up cast in roles as nonpollinating wallflowers at square dances.

Even today, noncowboy cultures (in America, Europe, and Asia) still think of cowboys as sex-hungry predators. In the nineteenth century, western societies thought of ranch hands as sex-starved men who came to cowtowns on payday with the purpose of indiscriminately seducing decent women, prostitutes, or anyone else they could lay their hands on and ravage. In the twentieth century, both American political structures and foreign governments exploit cowboys as metaphors, equating men on horseback with satyrs and describing them either as real stalkers of women or as symbolic rapists of noncowboy cultures. In 1987, for instance, American journalists and newspaper cartoonists compared Senator Gary Hart to a cowboy, both because he had made his home in a place called Troublesome Gulch and because pundits had later understood the western place name to signify, by foreshadowing, Gary Hart's downfall. As Colorado's "cowboy" senator, Hart had first "troubled" other Democratic presidential contenders by representing himself as a youthful political maverick and by threatening to win the Democratic presidential nomination away from older, non-"cowboy" statesmen. But then he had seemingly self-destructed by allegedly aligning himself with Donna Rice and by reconfirming the castration myth, which suggests that cowboys can never become part of the social or political mainstream precisely because they conduct themselves as sexually undisciplined or morally outlawed outsiders. In 1989, representations of the castration myth carried over into foreign configurations of American politics when the Soviet Union distributed copies of a propaganda piece entitled *American Cultural Invasion of Europe*. The book argued that America's "'bourgeois ideology and culture' [were] overrunning the Old World," and it advertised that premise on the illustrated book jacket, which showed "a satyr wearing a cowboy hat." The mythological figure was in the process of raping a "naked woman," or a personification of Asia and Europe, which had been victimized by bourgeois America.[4] Hence the book reaffirmed the castration myth by suggesting that a cowboy's metaphorical violation of women was brought about by his invasion of noncowboy cultural sites.

Economics and the Drifting Myth

If cultural invasion is envisioned in the castration myth as a violation of the opposite sex, then it is also portrayed in the drifting myth as a theft of goods from noncowboy society's economy. Cowboys have always been rendered as threats to society's propertied class—as unmonitored cattle thieves who roam through the land on the prowl and who rustle the cattlemen's stock, as unskilled and unemployable vagrants who drift through the West on the loose, and as outlaws on horseback who wreak havoc on men as they ride through towns on the rampage. Even before the decline of the cattle kingdom in the late 1880s and the 1890s, cowboys frequently moved from one job at a cattleman's ranch to another position at a different location, never living long enough in one place to acquaint themselves with townspeople or to challenge their own status as social outsiders, and never working long enough at one ranch to make themselves indispensable to a rancher or foreman. Coupled with drifters who wandered by choice were cowboys who involuntarily left cattlemen's ranches at the end of each season. Hired in the spring to brand and castrate the stock, in the summer to graze the meandering herds, and in the fall to drive them to market, cowboys were then dismissed in the winter by ranchers who had no more use for a cheap and expendable labor force that had, in effect, worked itself out of a job by engineering the transfer of cattle from ranches to cowtowns and meat-packing plants. If this seasonal unemployment led some cowboys to feed and support themselves by stealing the livestock of their former employers—even during the years when the cattle industry prospered—then the chronic unemployment that resulted from the industry's decline in the late 1880s and the 1890s encouraged even more men to practice rustling full-time.

Some cowboys found gainful employment by consenting to work for the Pinkerton Detective Agency or for ranchers' local livestock associations, which hired otherwise unemployable cowboys to protect cattlemen's property. Ironically, a depressed economy ended up pitting cowboy detectives against former peers who illegally rustled the stock that other cowboy detectives defended. It also engendered a drifting myth that justified the work of parapolicemen and cattle thieves. Horseriding cowboys, who were defined by their freedom of movement, could continue to drift by illegally working or "rustling" (a word that suggests exaggerated or audible motion). They could also reenact their nomadic lives by sleuthing as livestock detectives, signing on with loosely run organizations that permitted them to ride on the range by themselves and to answer to no one for great lengths of time. Unlike policemen, who worked for the city or state, cowboy detectives functioned as free agents and vigilante patrols. They were employed by independently and privately run investigative agencies that allowed them to roam the range and to embody an informal version of justice, as it benefited only the cattleman-employer's economic self-interest.

In their representations of frontier American life, fiction and film have overemphasized the role that the cowboy detective has played. While exploiting the dramatic potential for violence inherent in any clash between cattle thieves and their captors, and while ignoring the economic foundation of the class struggle between cowboys and ranchers, they have neglected to point out two important historical facts. First, cattle thieves did not always voluntarily prey on the cattleman's stock because they refused to look for proper or lawful employment, as Owen Wister's *The Virginian* (1902) and other novels and films insinuate. Some rustlers were formerly hard-working hired hands who turned to dishonest labor only after they had been fired by ranchers and forced to fend for themselves. Second, cowboy detectives were not simply abstract symbols of justice: they were friends and former associates of men whom they apprehended out West. The cattleman's *economic* decision to discharge his cowboys had the *cultural* effect of dividing the cowboy group into warring factions that incited unemployed and scavenging cowboy vagrants to face off against newly reemployed and respectable livestock detectives. The cowboy's temptation to drift facilitated the dispersal of an earlier, more culturally unified cowboy group. But the cowboy's drifting myth also reaffirmed the indestructible cultural bonds that tied together convicts and cowboy detectives, even during times of depression and widespread economic confusion. In prison, convicted rustlers artistically reconstructed their nomadic lives by making and engraving spurs and by weaving horsehair bridles, halters, and ropes—by creating art objects that articulated the drifting cowboy's continuing desire to move, even inside his cell. At the same time, cowboy detectives wrote autobiographical works in which they confessed to preferring a life of unlimited motion and to understanding the rustler's reluctance to settle down to a joyless, sedentary career.

Literature and the Orphan Myth

The branding myth, castration myth, and drifting myth often found their most effective forms of artistic expression in oral poems that early cowboys produced. Composed by many men, each of whom contributed a word, a line, or a verse to a text that the cowboy group then agreed to embrace as an authentic portrait of frontier American life—and of religious, social, and economic concerns—each poem can therefore be said to have reflected the group members' consensus: not an outsider's perception of culture or a single cowboy insider's artistic summation of life, but every cowboy's acceptance of myths that mutually consenting and interacting singers composed. The orphan myth first appeared in the oral verse that cowboy insiders created to distinguish their artistic representations from those of noncowboy, book-writing outsiders. Cowboys suggested that they had metaphorically orphaned themselves by physically moving away from the geographical sites of reproductive civilization, or from cities and towns in which their parents and families had lived.

In traveling out West and in deciding to work on the underpopulated frontier with other bachelors, or essentially celibate men, the outcasts believed not only that they had made themselves absent from social life, but that they had adopted an *invisible* art form that made their *absence* from reproductive communities manifest. Literate reproductive societies perpetuated themselves by procreating and by creating (writing, publishing, and distributing) knowledge in book form, hence preserving knowledge, tradition, and culture for the sake of posterity. Orphans, however, had no biological heirs and no book culture to connect them to men and women outside their circle. They maintained their social autonomy by literally separating themselves from the wellsprings of civilization. And they preserved their cultural purity by symbolically engaging in a version of "invisible" discourse—by passing their group myths from mouth to mouth, or from one singer to the next member of the insider's select circle of "orphans." In such a way, they prevented noncowboy outsiders from hearing, writing down, and distributing works that insiders composed, or from appropriating a culture that took pride in independently asserting itself.

The decline of the cattle economy in the 1880s and 1890s affected the cowboy's social position, economic condition, and artistic self-representation. Escalating unemployment rates on the range led many cowboys to vacate the orphan group: to move to town, marry, and look for jobs in noncowboy society. Displaced cowboys, determined to find new forms of employment and forced to support families, abandoned the cowboy's oral tradition as well as his work culture. Now when they sought to remember their roles in the West, they did so by *writing* poems that preserved their past on printed pages of published anthologies. Writing texts in isolation from the rest of the group, individual authors no longer necessarily thought and spoke for other cowboys with whom they had lived: they wrote for themselves and for a new audience of noncowboy outsiders. Hence the disbanding of the cowboy group was followed by the fragmentation of a frontier culture that had once cohesively gathered together the conflicting opinions of various men; that had reconciled those opinions, refined them in myths, and distilled them in verse poems that ranch hands had recited at cowboy group gatherings. The literary marketplace encouraged cowboys to relinquish their ties to the cowboy group by publishing and by competing with other publishing cowboys, each of whom had retired from cowboy life and had begun to look for fame in the marketplace. No longer professional ranch hands, men became professional poets and made money by writing exclusively for readers in a consumer-oriented noncowboy society.

This economic situation explains why the relationship between work and culture has changed in the twentieth-century cowboy's *work culture*. In the nineteenth century, *work* was the inspiration for producing *culture*, or artistic representations of cowboy life: animal branding, livestock castration, trail driving, cattle rustling, western prison labor programs, and cowboy detective work functioned as metaphors for analyzing religious, sexual, and economic concerns in prose, poems, and art. In the twentieth century, however, these tasks have either disappeared or decreased in frequency, for the consolidated cattle economy and the technology of a new urban frontier have made the anachronistic work functions of the cowboy dispensable. Hence it is now fair to say that the phrase *work culture* connotes something different from what it did in the past. It means that *culture* is *work*, or that the relationship between the two words in the phrase has reversed itself: the composition of poetry, or the production and propagation of culture, is one of the only forms of labor that exists to support cowboys in urban, book-reading societies. Like rodeo performers who market themselves to noncowboy spectators, theatrically reenacting such cowboy skills as roping and riding for profit in staged noncowboy environments, so cowboy writers publish poems and receive fees for reciting verses on lecture circuits and talk shows, on records and videos. They fill the void left by the absence of real working cowboys and satisfy society's nostalgic craving for what is absent by manufacturing artistic renditions of cowboy life and by aiming those renditions at a noncowboy audience in the mainstream American marketplace.

II

The branding and castration myths indicate ways in which cowboys separated themselves from noncowboy society. In the first two chapters, when I use the term *noncowboy society* I refer to *western groups not made up exclusively of ranch hands*, including cowtowns that depended on cattle raising for their continued economic survival, square dances and other social events that occurred in those towns and

distinguished between social dancers and nonsocial cowboys, and ranchers who lived with cowboys outside towns, but functioned as the cowtowns' wealthiest and most visible, respected, powerful, and influential constituents. The first two chapters of this book show that cowboys cut themselves loose from noncowboy society by subverting codes that sustained ranchers and people living in cowtowns. Rereading the ranchers' economic language of branding, overturning the cattlemen's notion of male human and livestock castration, and reacting against the cowtowns' square dances, cowboys distanced themselves from the mainstream and formed an ideologically autonomous group by reinterpreting the dominant branding and castration codes of noncowboy society.

The drifting and orphan myths examine ways in which cowboys dealt with the alternative problem of returning to noncowboy society. In the last two chapters, when I refer to *noncowboy society* I mean *all social groups, western or otherwise*. These include local rural groups such as livestock associations, which were run by ranchers and employed men who assimilated into them, leaving the cowboy's work culture, and local urban sites such as western prisons, which "reformed" cowboys and then, after the cowboys had finished serving their sentences, sent them back into noncowboy society. In addition, *noncowboy society* refers to marketplaces in western and nonwestern cities in which urban commerce, technological progress, and noncowboy economies prosper and dominate. Today, cowboys market themselves in noncowboy economies, taking advantage of newly discovered technologies to publish poems and to market them on television, video, record, and radio. How they wrestle with the dilemma of "selling" themselves in noncowboy society while defining themselves as antisocial cowboy outsiders is an important issue that I address in the book's final chapter.

But to suggest that cowboys first isolated themselves from and then sold themselves back to noncowboy society is clearly too facile. For cowboys, poaching on the codes of the mainstream in order to fashion a distinct marginal and autonomous cultural group and then allowing the mainstream to poach on the art that cowboys made out of those new marginal codes are back-and-forth ongoing processes.[5] In addition to analyzing the myths and art that the cowboy produced, the book moves out of the margins and into the worlds of popular and canonical novels, short stories, and plays to illustrate that while cowboys were crafting their "difference" in artistic renditions of four cowboy myths, the mainstream was poaching on those four myths and incorporating them into the dominant texts of noncowboy society. The play back and forth between branding in cowboy poems and in prose works by Steinbeck and Twain, and between livestock detection as a historically documented labor activity and as an act represented in the novels of Wister and Cather, indicates that sometimes surprising patterns weave in and out of the tapestry made up of mainstream and marginal literatures.

This interdisciplinary study is the first work of its kind to combine four earlier approaches to cowboy life. The folkloric approach was first undertaken by N. Howard Thorp, whose *Songs of the Cowboys* (1908) introduced readers to cowboy poems that the author had come across while working as a cowboy in the late nineteenth century. *Cowboy Songs and Other Frontier Ballads* (1910) and later annotated collections of verse published by John Lomax complemented Thorp's book and provided more data for scholars to work with. The second and third approaches to understanding the cowboy were utilized by such authors as Douglas Branch in *The Cowboy and His Interpreters* (1961), Don D. Walker in *Clio's Cowboys* (1981), and William W. Savage, Jr., in *The Cowboy Hero* (1979). Branch and Walker examine the cowboy from a historical distance, while Savage moves from history to popular culture in tracing the North American cowboy's influence. The fourth and most recent approach has grown out of the need to explicate contemporary poems written by cowboys and cowgirls. As a result, a literary analysis of texts is undertaken in a section of the book's final chapter. For the most part, however, each chapter tries to combine folkloric, historical, pop cultural, and literary approaches to the literature and labor of an American work culture that began in the mid-nineteenth and continues as we head into the twenty-first century.

Even interdisciplinary studies neglect to examine some sources, and I have chosen not to focus on dime novels, pulp fiction, and film. In *Virgin Land* (1950), for example, Henry Nash Smith wrote about the role that dime novels played in representing the West in the late nineteenth century (90–120). More recently, Jane Tompkins has dealt with the way in which the West is represented as being gendered, using Zane Grey's and Louis L'Amour's pulp fiction and Hollywood's films as examples.[6] Smith, Tompkins, and others have used *noncowboy* texts—novels written by Zane Grey, a New Jersey dentist, and films made in Hollywood—as sources for their investigations of "cowboy" film and literature. Their works exploit cowboys as metaphors: not interested in "real" cowboys, the work that they did, or the art that they made, the books use cowboys only as symbolic springboards for diving off into discussions of wide-ranging issues, most of which have little or nothing to do with real working cowboys. Because I am interested in cowboys first and foremost, I have therefore chosen to focus on cowboy history, culture, and literature, and on cowboy *self-representations* found in them, looking only secondarily and selectively at portraits of cowboy life found in the works of noncowboy writers and filmmakers.

Unfortunately, the cowboy's own art does not always provide a full sense of what life was like for each man who worked on a cattle ranch. We know that Native Americans, Hispanics, and African Americans hired on as vaqueros, or cowboys, although they seldom left written records or trustworthy statistics to indicate the extent to which they influenced history.[7] For example, *The Life and Adventures of Nat Love* (1907) is the only autobiography that a black cowboy is known to have written, but, because it does not concern itself with the issues that I have set forth in this book, I have chosen to look at it separately in a forthcoming article. Scholarship has not done a sufficient job of illustrating the labor that black cowboys enacted,[8] and nineteenth-century oral poems—because they were collectively and anonymously composed by groups of men, none of whom left written records of authorship—have not yielded clues to suggest what roles blacks played in composing songs that cowboys recited on trail drives, around campfires, and in bunkhouses at ranches. Men of color, unlike their white peers, don't tend to write cowboy poetry in the twentieth century either, for whatever reason, nor do noncowboy black authors tend to write about black men and women out West, with the exception of Ishmael

Reed, whose novel *Yellow Back Radio Broke-Down* (1969) speaks out against this odd silence.

Native Americans often took jobs as vaqueros or were sometimes enslaved by Spaniards and Mexicans and forced to tend mission livestock in what is now California. *Two Years Before the Mast* (1840) mentions this fact, but, with the exception of Richard Henry Dana's account, few nineteenth-century texts dwell on the vaquero's history or literature. Indians usually remained in their tribes instead of becoming part of the cowboy group, but when cowboys and Indians encountered each other they seldom interacted as depicted in "westerns." Shoot-'em-ups argue that white horsemen protected the prairies and plains from attacks that were initiated by red men or savages. In fact, the cowboys' contact with Indian tribes most likely occurred when cowboys drove livestock to market, crossing reservations and paying Indians tolls for storming across what was left of their land, or when cowboys raped or seduced Indian women living in tribes on reservations out West. Contemporary Native American literature seldom depicts cowboys or Indians who become cowboys, although James Welch's *Winter in the Blood* (1974), Leslie Marmon Silko's *Ceremony* (1977), and a handful of other texts portray Indians ranching, herding, and engaging in labor traditionally thought of as "cowboy" work.

Finally, mention of the cowboy's cross-dressing might suggest that homosexual or homoerotic behavior was common out West. However, cross-dressing cannot be *equated* with these forms of behavior in the absence of textual historical proof. While it is tempting to speculate, it is also important to note that due to stigmas attached to such behavior or to a sense of decorum that may have led to self-censored omissions, no cowboy writer or poet whom I have read mentions same-sex relations. The reader will have to decide whether I have gone too far or not far enough in investigating the extent to which cross-dressing and dancing influenced the cowboy's real sense and artistic formulation of maleness.

Inadequate data may prevent us from ever completely understanding the roles that cowboys have played or from fully grasping the meaning that cowboys have attached to those roles. But it doesn't prevent us from tentatively outlining certain conclusions. First, cowboys have been responsible, in the last hundred years, for producing a vast amount of oral and written poems, prose work, and art. Second, cowboy texts and art objects engage, voice, and criticize issues that scholars of high and low culture don't give cowboys credit for dealing with. In *West of Everything* (1992), Jane Tompkins speaks for most critics, who think that the phrase *cowboy culture* is a contradiction in terms. The word *cowboy,* she writes, "posits a world without God, without ideas, without institutions, without what is commonly recognized as culture, a world of men and things, where male adults in the prime of life find ultimate meaning in doing their best together on the job" (37). Without debating whether or not this statement is true of cowboys in western pulp fiction and film (the media that most interest Tompkins), one must acknowledge that the conclusion doesn't ring true if one looks at the cowboy's own poems, prose, and art. Cowboys work "on the job," but the job itself generates meditations on a world more complex than the one that Tompkins describes—a world *with* God, *with* ideas, *with* institutions, and *with* (what Tompkins calls) "culture." Too many of us take Hud at face value when he says, in Larry McMurtry's *Horseman, Pass By* (1961), that cowboys "just work from the shoulders down" (77). The notion of ranch hands writing about Christian salvation, for example, therefore strikes us as ludicrous, since most of us imagine cowboys not as thinkers, but as doers—stereotypical strong, silent men whose silences indicate that they have nothing of substance to think, speak, or write about. This book voices a correction and indicates otherwise.

CHAPTER ONE

SKIN GRAMMAR
Cattle Branding and Symbolic Wounds

I

Today, if one were to look at the West from an aerial view one would see a series of tortuous but well-reasoned labyrinths: branding chutes surrounded by metal holding pens, metal holding pens enclosed by wooden corrals, and wooden corrals encompassed by miles of barbed-wire fences, all of which chart the mazes through which the livestock must pass as it moves around, across, or through a cattleman's property. In the early and mid-nineteenth century, however, ranching took forms that were less physically rigid. Pastures were unfenced, and ranchers were apt to let their herds mix with one another, using only cattle brands to mark and define moving objects that strayed and intermingled with other ranchers' animals. Inscribed, branded herds moved like floating texts across open ranges, but no matter how far they roamed, they always bore signs of ownership, enabling ranchers to identify and reclaim their cattle (from the word *chattel*, meaning "property"). Fencing open ranges in the late nineteenth century, ranchers later penned in their herds, preventing their cattle from escaping or being stolen by demarcating their land and the livestock that grazed on it. Now, in the twentieth century, even though branding still ensures ownership, cattle brands no longer play an important role in parceling out property—fences do. Even before cattlemen textualize property, branding and encoding it with hieroglyphic signs of possession, they distinguish their land and the living chattel that inhabit it by erecting strongly built fortifications that barricade herds and keep them from wandering. Transferring animals from large, faraway pastures into smaller corrals built close to home, herding them out of these smaller corrals into holding pens, pushing them out of these holding pens into channels that feed into branding chutes, squeezing them out of these branding chutes into caged cells, pulling levers that flip these cells over and that, in rotating from the vertical to the horizontal position, convert cells into tables, ranch owners operate like surgeons, using operating tables to brand, castrate, and vaccinate property. But by the time that branding as a dramatic gesture occurs, it is anticlimactic. Ranch owners act out their ownership prior to branding, moving cattle through labyrinths, each smaller than the last and therefore better able to witness that cattle are "owned," whether they are allowed to migrate in large but fenced-in enclosures or forced to lie, like inmates, in cells and holding pens.

In the nineteenth century, branding took place on open ranges in public, with many ranch owners and their cattle herds present, not on privately owned ranches where ranchers now ritually reenact ownership each year at branding time. Men assembled on ranges in roundup districts in the spring, after cows had given birth to their calves, and again in the fall, when ranchers gathered together their strays and prepared to ship their herds to market or auction in cowtowns. Governors in western states and territories established roundup districts and appointed commissioners who determined roundup days. Roundup commissioners, in turn, subdivided their districts and chose roundup captains to supervise the roundups that took place in each separate section.[1] Cattlemen met here, collected their cattle, and divided them according to the distinguishing brands of each owner, identifying strays by matching each with a mother that wore the correct ranch owner's cattle brand. Roping them and working in groups, cowboys branded unmarked calves by pinning their necks and forelegs down to the ground and by extending their hind legs while pressing brands into cattle hides.[2]

The calves were then released, and the range became a floating text whose meaning shifted with the migration of cattle and the movement of marks on their flanks. As objects, cattle had written histories that evolved with the incision of additional hieroglyphics or brands. When a rancher acquired a new calf, he ordered the cowboy to burn a symbol of ownership on its skin, and when he sold the calf or cow at a later date he directed that a second brand be placed on its side. The vent brand acknowledged that the stock had been sold to another ranch, whose brand appeared next to the first and second ones.[3] If the new owner drove the livestock to market, he used a fourth mark, the road brand, to distinguish his cattle from others that were driven on the road or down the trail to market, and to group together the disparate stock that he had bought from other ranchers and cattlemen.[4] Cattle rustling and subsequent brand alterations resulted in the further revision of written texts: rustlers stole cattle, changed brands, and tried to convince any brand reader that they were the real authors and owners of reinscribed cattle herds. Rustlers invented illegal brands that canceled out or reconstructed legal ones. To reclaim a rustler's purloined stock, for instance, a cattleman read its skin as though it were a palimpsest manuscript. In his book *The XIT Ranch of Texas and the Early Days of the Llano Estacado* (1929), J. Evetts Haley notes that the more recent brand of a nineteenth-century rustler left a white scar on cowhide and refused to "hair over." A cattleman unable to find such a scar would kill a cow, skin it, and read the skin, knowing that his older brand would show through clearly on the opposite side of the hide, unlike a rustler's more recent brand. Soaking the skin and holding it up to the light, or letting it dry until the original brand stood out, provided a cattleman with incontestable evidence that his own cow had been stolen, rebranded, falsified, and transferred to a fictitious owner's cattle herd (123).

The quest for knowledge provoked and the act of reading fulfilled a need that was greater at times than the mere desire to possess the meat of an animal. Hence the important and sometimes difficult task of reading and interpreting cattle brands ironically meant that killing property (skinning and reading it) was the price that one might pay for owning a now useless (because wasted and sacrificed) animal. Brands were read according to semantic guidelines that also made the interpretation of cattle texts difficult. The constituent parts of a cattle brand were like alphabetic letters in a western system of language, and only ranchers who created those brands or that language and cowboys who worked for them knew how to read brands on animals.

Rules teach nonranchers and noncowboys how to *read* brands, but they do not teach novices how to *interpret* the meaning of brands that they read. For instance, the brand

would read from left to right. One would call it "The Circle T" brand.[5] If a brand were written vertically instead of horizontally, one would read it from top to bottom, so that the brand

would take the name "The X Over Heart." And if a sign in the brand were combined with an encompassing mark

one would read it from the outside in and identify it as "The Box Two" cattle brand.

Rules for reading brands are established by time-honored conventions. But following one of three guidelines—tracing signs in brands from left to right, from top to bottom, or from the outside in—does not help one interpret the *names* of brands. How does one know, for instance, that the first brand should read as the brand of "The Circle T" ranch? A reader could also call it "The Zero T" brand, or read the first sign in the sequence alphabetically instead of numerically and call it "The O T" with seemingly equal assurance. And what about the second example, "The X Over Heart"? J. Evetts Haley contends that the "XIT" brand referred to the fact that the XIT Ranch was larger than all the ranches surrounding it. The first sign ("X"), according to Haley, was a symbol for the Roman numeral ten; the last two signs ("IT"), abbreviations for the ranch's location "in Texas." Hence the brand alluded to the size of the ranch, which was larger than *ten* counties *in Texas* (77). However, a reader would misread "The X Over Heart" by following Haley's example and by referring to the brand as "The *Ten* Over Heart," just as one would misinterpret the third brand if one called it "The *Square* Two," instead of "The Box Two" cattle brand.

If these three examples seem like instances of semantic hairsplitting, then consider another brand that indicates just how greatly (mis)readings and (mis)interpretations of livestock brands vary. The brand

could be read as "The Running M," referring to the lines of the letter being fluid. How does one know, then, that the brand is actually a representation of two mountain peaks, specifically a crude rendering of two peaks in the Rocky Mountain range as they appear to a rancher who lives in the foothills near Colorado Springs, Colorado? The rules lead one to believe that one can read brands, when in fact they allow one only to follow the *sequence* of signs—as they move from the outside in, from left to right, or from top to bottom—in complicated notational frameworks. Sometimes one can piece signs together and approximate accurate readings of cattle brands if the brands use letters or numbers. But letters and numbers sometimes combine with cryptic traces and pictures, all of which refer back to objects (mountains), places, or things with which one may or may not be acquainted because they are selectively chosen, subjectively rendered, and therefore meaningless to non-ranchers, noncowboys, and other nonmembers of interpretive communities that exist in the ranching world.[6] The ideational content of "The Rocky Mountains" brand, for instance, makes sense only to people who live near the mountains, know them, and print them on herds with a cattle brand that only they have invented.

In the middle and late nineteenth century, ranch owners began filing and registering cattle brands with local western county officials, who annually published registered cattle brands as a way of warning other county residents not to infringe on trademarks that ranch owners had registered. However, the first brand books in Colorado (1867), Montana (1872), and Wyoming (1882), as well as early books in other western states and territories, reproduced and described each ranch owner's registered brand without ever telling readers how to translate, pronounce, or interpret it—without ever naming it. "The Spinning Wheel" brand

Jany 4, 1855 Barbara Carton
Marks an Over Bitt in Each Ear
Brands thus **B1**

an. 1st 1855 ‡ Jas. C. Cade's Mark & Brand
Mark on hogs & Cattle &c. An un-
der bit and slit in each ear.
Brand on Cattle, horses &c   C2

Febry 6th Josh Carters
1855   Mark a Smooth Crop
off the right Ear a nick or
saw set in the left
Branded Trowel

Miss Eliza Crawford's Brand

April
4th
1855. D. A. Carothers
April mark Crop & under & upper bit
23   in the Left Ear & crop of
1855   the other Branded thus   C3

Ap. 23 George J. Carothers mark
1855   Crop & under half crop in each
Ear   Brand

Early brand books listed the owners of registered brands, the locations of brands on the stock, and the pictures of what brands looked like after they were marked on cattle, horses, and hogs. But brand books seldom named signs that appeared on their pages, making the processes of reading and interpretation almost impossible. (From the 1855 Cattle Brands and Marks Records of Texas. Barker Texas History Center, University of Texas at Austin)

G

May 9th 1866 O.H. P Garrett Mark crop off the right & half crop in the left Ear. Branded thus — P.G

1866, May 19th J.T. Gunnell a Gingleboh on each Ear, Branded thus — Ⓖ

Sept. 25 James Graves (F.M.C) Brand thus — 2

Geo. W. Gilmore oct 4. 56 Marks Crop & Saw Lett. in Each Ear. Brand thus. — ◇G

1867 Feb. 25 Hal & C. Graves (F.M.C) mark under Bit in each Ear Brand thus — C. G

Godfrey Whiten (F.M.C) Mark under & over Bit in the Right Ear April 15 & over Bit in the Left. Brand thus — G.W

Lett Robinson (F.M.C) April 15 marks under & over Bit in the Left Ear and over Bit in the Right. Brand thus. — L.8

Dec 21 Thomas Glover Mark One Split in each ear Brand. — T C

Even without knowing how to "read" brands, one can ferret out the sense of signs that make use of numbers and letters. But how does one add up or spell out the meaning of a brand such as the third one from the top? (From the 1866–67 Cattle Brands and Marks Records of Texas. Barker Texas History Center, University of Texas at Austin)

B

19. 1870. Brown Bryant,
  √   Mark: Smooth crop *o over slit in each Ear
      Brand thus: 3.B

April 19. 1870. Bell Si
  √   Mark: Smooth crop and hole in each Ear.
      Brand thus: ℬ̃

May 9. 1870. Bostick George.
  √   Mark: Under slit and Swallow fork in
              each Ear.
      Brand thus: ⊢B

27 1870. Abram Brown
  √   Mark: Swallow fork and over slit in the
      right Ear. Half under crop. Half off
      and Over slit in the left.
      Brand thus: A.5.

Aug 11 70 le Brandt
  √   Mark Split and over slit
      in the left ear
      Brand   ℬR

6. 1870. Pickles Henry
  √   Mark: Hole in the left & split in the right Ear.
      Brand: C.H.B.

Aug 24. 1870. Brown Oscar.
  √   Mark: Swallow fork in the right and Over
              slope in the left Ear.
      Brand thus: ⚭

How would one interpret and name the last brand on this page? (From the
1870 Cattle Brands and Marks Records of Texas. Barker Texas History Center,
University of Texas at Austin)

might therefore be described in a brand book as a "spiraling circle on the lower-left-hand side of the stock. Registered by John P. Doe, who lives on a ranch twenty miles south of Lincoln, Nebraska." But a name such as "The Spinning Wheel" would not appear next to the picture, making the process of naming and interpreting almost impossible.[7] Even such recent works as the *Colorado Brand Book* (1972), which transcribes brands that are recorded with the Colorado State Board of Stock Inspection Commissioners, never "reads," translates, or interprets cattle brands.

Brands seem to have "real" meaning—real physical presences that indicate real historical and economic necessities: to illustrate possession of "real" estate. At the same time, brands seem to appear in the same form and to operate in the same way that "fiction" does: they *are* texts, they appear in larger texts (brand books), and they have meanings that seem so uncertain and unstable that brand "readers"—like readers of fiction—can interpret them to mean whatever they think the brands signify. Not suprisingly, in the late nineteenth and early twentieth centuries, brands finally *became* symbols in fiction, taking on purely abstract meanings in literature. At the turn of the century, Andy Adams, a cowboy turned author, began writing fiction that dealt with aspects of western life. In order to prove that his cowboy fiction was authentic and trustworthy, Adams wrote about branding and other chores that he had once acted out as a real working cowboy. But Adams removed brands from real working contexts, placed them in fiction, and used them as symbols to stand for the real world of ranching, a world that the cowboy novelist and short-story writer had once worked in but now only wrote about.

Cattle Brands appeared as a short-story collection in 1906. An illustration of actual cattlemen's brands in the preface suggests that the signs have a historical referent—that each sign refers to the possession of stock on the early frontier—but no acknowledgment of this fact appears in the fiction that follows. Although each of the stories indicates what life on the range was apparently like, none of them concern cattle per se. As a writer and as a former cattle worker, Adams is concerned with authenticating his firsthand acquaintance with range life and with validating his claims to be a realistic, and therefore reliable, short-story writer. But in the preface, each brand stands, like an abbreviated table of contents, for a short-story that Adams has written. It is a sign indicating the author's fluency in the language of real working ranch operations, but it is also a marker showing that a short story or fiction grows out of each brand in the table. In *The Wells Brothers* (1911), Adams later has one of his cowboys associate the reading of brands with the interpretation and understanding of fiction. "Down here," the character says, "we have boys who read brands as easily as a girl reads a novel" (57).

Later writers wrestle overtly with brands and attempt to define them both as economic marks, which signify possession to their cattlemen owners, and as fictitious symbols, which may mean one or more things to each reader. Will Rogers, for instance, details three successive stages in which a reading of brands develops in a portion of his *Autobiography* (1949). In a section that attempts to explain the essence of nationhood, he turns a branded calf loose in a fictitious arena and then reads its brand to determine the marks of patriotic American citizens:[8]

After working as a cowboy in the late nineteenth century, Andy Adams earned a living by writing western novels and short-story collections such as Cattle Brands (1906). (Painting by Charles Craig. Barker Texas History Center, University of Texas at Austin)

[N]ow I am going to take up the subject [of patriotism] and see what I can wrestle out of it. Let's get our rope ready and turn [the calf] out, and we will watch it and see really what brands it has on it. Here it comes out of the Corral. We got it caught; now it's throwed and Hog Tied; and we will pick the Brands and see what they are.

The first thing I find out is there ain't any such animal. This American Animal that I thought I had here is nothing but the big Honest Majority, that you might find in any Country. He is not a Politician. He is not a 100 percent American. He is not any organization, either uplift or downfall. In fact I find he don't belong to anything. He is no decided Political faith or religion. I can't even find out what religious brand is on him. From his earmarks he has never made a speech, and announced that he was An American. He hasn't denounced anything. It looks to me like he is just an Animal that has been going along, believing in right, doing right, tending to his own business, letting the other fellows alone.

He don't seem to be simple enough minded to believe that EVERYTHING is right and he don't appear to be Cuckoo enough to think that EVERYTHING is wrong. He don't seem to be a Prodigy, and he don't seem to be a Simp. In fact, all I can find out about him is that he is just NORMAL. After I let him up and get on my Horse and ride away I look around and see hundreds and hundreds of exactly the same marks and Brands. In fact they so far outnumber the freakly branded ones that the only conclusion I can come to is that this Normal breed is so far in majority that there is no use to worry about the others. They are a lot of Mavericks, and Strays. (108)

Rogers attempts to capture the calf and to interpret its brand, but failing to find an objective meaning for the slippery animal's equally slippery sign, he opts instead for a subjective impression of it. Interpretation leads to argumentation or to hypothetical variations on the possible meanings of brands, and Rogers can only conclude with a rhetorical pose that denies the existence of brands as well as their ability to convey information. He invents the brand and defines the subject of patriotism only by *refusing* to do so: by negating a list of preconceptions in the second paragraph and by acknowledging a void or an absence of meaning in the succeeding one. He states that the American calf has no "religious brand," but then he contradicts himself by suggesting that the calf belongs to a herd of stock with similar spiritual "marks and Brands." These calves are "Mavericks, and Strays"—but *mavericks* and *strays* are words in the traditional vocabulary of cowboys that signify unowned or unbranded livestock.[9]

Rogers's inability to locate or interpret the brand is like that of other twentieth-century writers. On the nineteenth-century range, the brand enabled owners to distinguish their stock from other mobile, promiscuous herds. With the fencing and partitioning of range land and with the resulting separation of stock on individual parcels of ground, the brand became removed from its original purpose, as various owners' animals became literally detached from one another. The continued branding of livestock testified to the needs of an earlier time and to the ancient routine of the cattle regime, whose workers imprinted the brand as part of a vestigial act.[10] Rogers makes this connection between work and ritual clear when he turns the work of branding into a representation of the contemporary rodeo "game." He releases the "animal" from the chutes and lets it run into the "Corral"—not onto the open range, but into the fenced-in space of the athletic arena, surrounded by man-made barriers and, beyond that, by the audience of readers for whom he performs. Twentieth-century rodeos reenact aspects of the nineteenth-century cowboy's original labor. They transform historical acts into theatrical spectacles, just as Rogers transfers the brand from the range to the stage or corral, obfuscating its meaning, which becomes part of an impenetrable linguistic artifice. Seeming to abandon his quest for the meaning of brands, Rogers reasserts their significance, using only the typography of the printed page to persuade us that "EVERYTHING is right" with his text. Relying on the certitude that capital letters deceptively seem to convey, he says that the ambiguity of brands is characteristic or "NORMAL." But this ambiguity is ironically represented by the writer's own specificity and emphasis—by the capitalized and pronounced presentation of a word that is semantically fuzzy.

The brand exists in this world of fiction or artifice, and, as the twentieth-century western novel develops, the sign becomes linked with the creation and narration of a fictitious tale. Larry McMurtry's first novel, *Horseman, Pass By* (1961), unfolds through the eyes of the boy Lonnie, who recounts the story of his brother Hud to the reader. McMurtry establishes the literary significance of brands when Lonnie remembers that his grandfather and "other cowboys" once sat around campfires, "telling stories or drawing brands in the dirt" (5) after roundups on ranges out West. The speaker tells his story and the audience draws its brand on the ground and reifies or repeats the language in concrete form with this storytelling device, demonstrating the creative task of the cowboy or the means by which the listener transcribes and relates the events that occur. Lonnie listens to his grandfather's "stories of his days on the big ranches, or of cowboys like his dead foreman Jericho Green," and, taking in "every word" of his grandfather's verbal narration, Lonnie flips his "pocketknife into the soft dirt of Grandma's lilac beds" (4) as he sits on the ground. Here he becomes a medium through which language passes, as he later becomes the novel's narrator, repeating to the reader the story that he has learned by witnessing Hud's unfolding history. The mark is a condensed and allusive reproduction of the grandfather's original text and an appropriate vehicle later for Lonnie, who interprets the novel's action through the eyes of a child and who perceives its meaning with the blinkered vision of a confused and only partially omniscient narrator.

Lonnie's work suggests what nineteenth-century history had already shown— that the brand is an indelible text and at the same time a mutable substance, prone to obliteration or change. The nineteenth-century cattleman could not "erase" his brand on the open range in order to sell his stock to another man: instead, he put a vent brand on cow hide, canceling his mark by combining it with a later sign and allowing the succeeding owner to engrave his brand below or to the side of the symbolic void. But in asserting the hypothetical absence of negated cattle brands, the seller and buyer created not a void or an invisible text, but a pageant of additional marks that glorified brands as material constructs, and testified to the permanence and continuity of beef-borne hieroglyphs. Rustlers could illegally circumvent the conventions established by ranchers and cattlemen and superimpose details on existing brands or destroy them completely. Rustlers demonstrated—as did brand books—that although owners could invent systems to signify ownership, they could not prevent others from subverting those systems or from reconstructing and reinterpreting cattle brands. Brands would later express their semantic instability in Andy Adam's and Larry McMurtry's narrations, which use cattle signs as explicit storytelling devices for representing and transporting "fictions."

II

Without single, reliable readings of cattle brands to consider, one is left, then, with only various interpretations of signs. These interpretations typically fall into two groups: one established by cattlemen who create brands to identify their personal property, and one acknowledged by cowboys who imprint brands on livestock as part of their job. For cattlemen, brands illustrate wealth or signify ownership of material goods.[11] Like family crests, they appear on stationery letterheads, on buildings and on furniture in homes, as well as on livestock. The Transamerica Title Insurance Company provides a story of the branding process in a preface to the abstract of a ranch in Colorado, for instance, and indicates the extremes to which an equation between brands and the cattlemen's material goods may be taken.[12] In a picture on the upper portion of the cover page, a group of cowboys gallops over a hill and discovers a man who has changed the brands on some cattle. They brandish their revolvers but retreat into the background when their boss, a cattleman, appears on the scene. The cattleman picks up a burning tree limb, which the rustler has used to cancel the existing cattle brand, and confronts the rustler with this criminal evi-

Ranchers have always used brands to signify ownership. In addition to livestock, any other objects that constitute property can therefore wear a ranch owner's monogram. In this 1933 photograph, for example, the owners of a Kent, Texas, ranch stake out and emblazon their property: the brand of the X Ranch appears on a gate and on the roof of a building that serves as a combined ranch office, bunkhouse, kitchen, and dining room. (Photography Collection, Harry Ransom Humanities Research Center, University of Texas at Austin)

dence. But the rustler refuses either to defend himself or to admit to the cattleman that he has broken the law. Tossing his rope to the hired hands, the owner then orders the cowboys to hang (i.e., murder) the rustler. The text, entitled "Cattleman's Justice," omits a description of the murder and concludes with a blithe admonishment to the reader instead: "Before the days of effective courts in the West—when the cattle industry was getting started—cattlemen often had to prove that their best defense was an unrelenting offense. The protection of brands was necessary to stay in business, for the owner's brand was the only practical means of identifying his cattle from among the thousands of others that roamed at will across the open range." The *economic* significance of the brand is so important, therefore, that it overrides any *moral* objections. Hence the Transamerica Title Insurance Company can endorse murder (in theory), for the ideological connection between this passage and the text is acknowledged. Branding assigns or reassigns the possession of animal property, and land abstracts or insurance titles verify the ownership of land and record land titles as they pass, in a series of legal transactions, from party to party. Like the insurance company's document, the brand asserts the worth and interprets the status, ensures the possession and inhibits the movement, of chattel and tangible purchases.

In his own literature the cattleman-author, like the insurance company's fictional narrator, is a capitalist entrepreneur and the brand is part of an economic language of warranty that he uses to indemnify stock against loss and theft. For instance, having opened a cattle trail to Abilene, Kansas, in 1867, Joseph G. McCoy published *Historic Sketches of the Cattle Trade of the West and Southwest* (1874), which traces the language of the cattleman back to the hieroglyphs of ancient Egyptian society.[13] According to the biblical typology of McCoy's autobiographical text, the "Sacred Writ" in Egyptian society is now a model for brands, and the men who used it are prototypes, in the Old Testament, for McCoy and other western cattlemen. The author reminds the reader that the "wealth and possessions of the Patriarchs" consisted of stock: that Jacob bred the "speckled" cattle, that Noah became an "extensive live stock shipper," and that God preferred the offering of Abel to that of "the Granger Cain" (1–2).

McCoy creates a biblical myth in order to invent an illustrious genealogy for cattlemen and to sanction the job of ranching, which had fully come into existence only in the preceding ten years, since the end of the Civil War. Good works replace faith or an allegiance to the chosen people, however, as the author quickly moves from a discussion of his Christian ancestors to a list of contemporary cattlemen in the American marketplace. J. P. Farmer, for one, has begun "at the foot of the ladder and by industry, perseverance and determined labor, climbed up round by round to a substantial income and a competence that might with propriety be desired by any one" (343). Always "ahead of his appointments, never tardy" (16), L. B. Harris has risen above the cowboy on a corporate version of Jacob's ladder and prospered. James F. Ellison has remained "sober, honest, upright, and true-hearted" (17) and has capitalized on these qualities to become a rancher, not a biblical patriarch. In a sense, the author has revised Benjamin Franklin's *Auto-biography* or provided a similar, autobiographically based "how-to" text that informs would-be ranchers how to succeed in a new western industry. A Christian reading of the brand within a literary biblical framework is therefore replaced with a catalog of affluent businessmen who are virtuous only in a pragmatic sense, and with the creation of a text that sees the economic expansion of the West as its primary subject.

McCoy's quest for economic success is disguised as genuflecting religious sincerity. The cattleman's uneasy equation of Christian salvation with financial solvency is not disguised, however, but exposed and criticized by McCoy's contemporary nonranching counterparts. In *Roughing It* (1872), for example, Mark Twain portrays Brigham Young as a patriarch-rancher. The polygamous Mormon elder acquires a series of wives, but treats them like cattle and numbers them as a rancher would brand his possessions, in order to distinguish them from one another and from other inhabitants' property.[14] The women scatter themselves "far and wide among the mountains and valleys" (123) of the patriarch's land and multiply the fold by reproducing and thus swelling the ranks of his congregation and by extending his sway as a religious divine. "No. 6" and "No. 11"—and other numbered women—give birth, or calve out, on a regular basis, and, in a section of Chapter 15 entitled "Children Need Marking," the narrator suggests that Brigham Young should brand his children, or "two-year-olds" (122), in order to name and control them as well. Here Twain satirizes the cattleman's attempt to disguise his economic exploitation of the female "herd" as a godly enterprise. The cattleman's branding language has an ostensible religious foundation, for the Christian names of the women appear by their numbers in "the family Bible" he keeps (123), and the text in turn reveals the way in which the elder would have the reader interpret his relations with his mates and their numerous "calves." But ultimately the Bible enables the elder to exploit the harem, or "herd"—not only to enshrine women's names in the Book, but also to order his capital in a numerical sequence or to index his stock and take his inventory of it at leisure.

Twain's representation of the Mormon group anticipates fictional portraits of ranchers in twentieth-century American literature. In *To a God Unknown* (1933), for example, John Steinbeck's protagonist Joseph Wayne ranches on the California frontier. Like Brigham Young, he develops an obsession with the growth and extension of the animal herd and equates the magnification of his cattle operation with the reproduction of the human community surrounding him. He picks his wife as he would pick a breeding cow: "to be a good cow, perfect in the activity of cows—to be a good wife and very like a cow."[15] When Elizabeth finally gives birth to a son, Joseph goes to the barn to tell the "cattle" the news (93), and the stock, sensing fertility in the community, reproduce in the barn (95). Joseph articulates his son's presence by burning his own brand "into the skin of the stock" (96–97), and Elizabeth performs the female equivalent of branding, stitching with her needle to quilt designs on the sheets and embroidered covers of the bed in which she gives birth. In the material world, the cattleman and his wife reduce human language to a series of inhuman, nonverbal signs—to a list of economically significant brands— and, in the same sense, Joseph compares his son to a cow in his herd. " 'It's our stock,' he [says], 'just a little changed' " from the livestock outside (109).

Still later, in a political farce, Steinbeck caricatures the cattleman's appropriation of people by equating the owner's control of the brand not only with the dehumanization of the cattleman's family, but with the disempowerment of ranch hands who work for him. After the French people crown her father king, Clotilde Héristal decides to refurbish Versailles. She renames a portion of the palace "Le Petit Round-Up" and imagines that she will build a series of "small ranch houses, corrals, barns, [and] bunkhouses" on the land adjacent to the historical monument. Here "branding irons" will heat constantly in bonfires, for where else can "passionate and inarticulate men gather?" (49). In *The Short Reign of Pippin IV* (1957), silent and dispossessed cowboys have connections to ranchers that are like servant–master relationships in French feudal society. As the remainder of this section indicates, cowboys do articulate their relation to branding, but here the king and his daughter own the palace-cum-cattle ranch, the bunkhouses, and the brands, while "inarticulate" cowboys who cannot use brands freely are effectively silenced in Steinbeck's western parody.

If brand owners also own, silence, or dispossess cowboys, then cowboys subvert the brand owners' notions of ownership by using brands not to indicate their economic submission, but to suggest their religious elevation in heaven. On December 2, 1884, for instance, a reporter for the *Denver Tribune-Republican* recorded the following speech of a worker.

> "[C]annot brands be studied at church as well as on the range?" said a member of the cowboy fraternity to a *Tribune-Republican* reporter yesterday. "What matters it whether the gathering be one of quadrupeds or bipeds—of cows or human beings? Brands can be studied in both, for the mavericks that bear no marks are rare. In the human herd the red-hot iron has not burned into the skin a J B or a hash knife [brand], but nature wrote on every part of the face another mark. Would it be fair to say that in the human herd, the most numerous brand is that of the great proprietors—the firm of the world, the flesh and the devil? . . .
>
> "Nature is a keeper, a herdsman who always brands. But her skill is subtle. Upon the persons of men she does not always put the brand in comeliness and strength. Often in the bowed frame and melancholy eyes she writes 'this is my worthiest.' And upon the figures of women it is not always with forms and color, but with a beauty which is painted only by a pure mind and soul—on a plain face often—that the brand is read, 'This is my best.'" [16]

Real cowboys never spoke as the character in this passage is represented as speaking. Instead, the reporter has taken away the words of a real working cowboy and replaced them with the sentiments and vocabulary of an educated Victorian gentleman. In doing so, the writer has inadvertently emphasized the issues of language and power that control a discussion of cattle brands. The cattleman creates language and allows cowboys to become a medium for printing brands on stock that he owns. Workers do not own brands or the stock on which brands appear, nor do they determine the meaning and interpretation of signs as they move through herds on ranges and in pastures. As writers, cowboys are subject to the dictates of a rancher who controls the pen, or the brand, and who owns the page, or the stock, on which the words of the branding language appear. Cowboys are no more in control of the language they write than they are of the words that the newspaper reporter edits and cleans up when allegedly quoting the thoughts of a real working cowboy.

The cowboy quoted in the *Denver Tribune-Republican* equates the "propri-

As risk-taking entrepreneurs, ranchers were free to prosper or fail. But re-
gardless of how much or how little ranch owners profited, cowboys who
worked for them were almost guaranteed not to make money. In the late
nineteenth and early twentieth centuries, cowboys earned between $15 and
$35 each month and did not receive raises for helping employers succeed,
sometimes by obscene leaps and bounds. This turn-of-the-century photograph
captures the unromantic semisqualor of a small ranch operation out West.
(Barker Texas History Center, University of Texas at Austin)

etors'' of the brand with the world of the ''flesh,'' for, like a proprietor, the
cattleman uses the brand to sign the flesh or meat of the stock and to market the meat
in the economic world of supply and demand. The cowboy struggles with the owner
for control of the brand, and he succeeds in his own culture in replacing its commercial meaning with another, mythic reading. According to this cowboy, the brand is
deployed by God or by a force more potent than his earthly employer. The cattleman
assesses his holdings in order to determine what they will bring at market or auction,
and he brands healthy stock in order to possess it and sell it for profit when he takes it
to town.[17] Hence he discounts the weak, unattractive members of the congregation
or ''herd,'' for he judges them only by their outward appearance and decides that
they are too sick to labor or too unsightly to be sold off the ranch. But the last shall be
first, in the cowboy's sermon to the frontier reporter. The worker witnesses and
interprets God's branding of the lowly and meek, and defines His mark of approval
as a more glorious form of distinction than that which the rancher or ''devil''
inscribes on objects that he considers unworthy.

A 1914 photograph of the King Ranch's headquarters in Texas proves that if one cashed in one could really build laurels worth resting on.

The cowboy identifies with the congregation's oppressed and unwanted because he envisions himself as being oppressed by his ranching employer. He makes this point not only in the reporter's quotation, but in early poems that he composed on the range. Branding poems reveal a two-part process in which the cowboy subverts the cattleman's economic sign of possessive oppression, first transferring the brand from the rancher to God, and then submitting while God marks the cowboy with a sign of religious distinction. For instance, "A Cowboy's Prayer," an anonymously composed nineteenth-century oral poem, entreats God to rope cowboys "with the cords of love—/ Brand us with the iron of truth / And mark us with the cross of Calvary" (Fife and Fife 94). The worker becomes the animal or object on which the brand is placed. But paradoxically, instead of debasing and dehumanizing himself by becoming an animal, the cowboy acquires an elevated sense of religious worth by submitting to God, by wearing God's brand, and by joining other branded cowboys in God's chosen herd. "The Cowboy's Dream," another anonymously composed nineteenth-century oral poem and one of the best-known and most important songs in the cowboy's work culture, turns the acts of driving, rounding up, and branding cattle into metaphors for being saved and made saintly, being damned and made penitent. I reprint the poem, as well as others, in order to acquaint novice readers with songs that cowboys sang in bunkhouses at home on the ranch, around campfires, or on the range during cattle drives.

Payroll records for July 1, 1890, indicate that a cowboy named T. N. Harrell has contracted his services out to the XIT Ranch in Texas for $25 each month. Like the King Ranch, the XIT Ranch was one of the most prosperous and opulent ranches at the turn of the century. Its good fortune, however, did not rub off on T. N. Harrell and other cowboy employees, who continued to work for low wages. (Photography Collection, Harry Ransom Humanities Research Center, University of Texas at Austin)

Last night as I lay on the prairie,
And looked at the stars in the sky,
I wondered if ever a cowboy
Would drift to that sweet by-and-by.

Roll on, roll on;
Roll on, little dogies, roll on.
Roll on, roll on, roll on;
Roll on, little dogies, roll on.

The road to that bright happy region
Is a dim narrow trail, so they say;
But the bright one that leads to perdition
Is posted and blazed all the way.

Oh, bring back, bring back,
Bring back my night horse to me.
Oh, bring back, bring back,
Bring back my night horse to me.

They say there will be a great round-up.
And cowboys, like dogies, will stand,
To be mavericked by the Riders of Judgment
Who are posted and know every brand.

I know there's many a stray cowboy
Who'll be lost at the great final sale,
When he might have gone in green pastures
Had he known the dim narrow trail.

I wonder if ever a cowboy
Stood ready for that Judgment Day
And could say to the Boss of the Riders,
"I'm ready, come drive me away."

For they, like the cows that are locoed,
Stampede at the sight of a hand,
Are dragged with a rope to the round-up,
Or get marked with some crooked man's brand.

And I'm scared that I'll be a stray yearling—
A maverick, unbranded on high—
And get cut in the bunch with the "rusties"
When the Boss of the Riders goes by.

I often look upward and wonder
If the green fields will seem half so fair,
If any the wrong trail have taken
And will fail to be over there.

No maverick or slick will be tallied
In that great book of life in his home,
For he knows all the brands and the earmarks
That down through the ages have come.

But along with the strays and the sleepers,
The tailings must turn from the gate;
No road brand to give them admission,
But that awful sad cry, "Too late!"

For they tell of another big owner
Who's ne'er overstocked, so they say,
But who always makes room for the sinner
Who drifts from the strait narrow way.

They say he will never forget you,
That he knows every action and look;
So, for safety, you'd better get branded,
Have your name in his big Tally Book,

To be shipped to that bright mystic region,
Over there in the green pastures to lie,
And be led by the crystal still waters
To the home in the sweet by-and-by.
(Lomax and Lomax 45–47)

In "The Cowboy's Dream," the cowboy is encouraged to "get branded" by God and to go with the Lord to "the great final sale": after leading a moral life (after walking like cattle on trail drives down the "dim narrow trail"), the cowboy will reach greener "pastures" and find happiness in the afterlife as a member of God's chosen herd. On Judgment Day, at "the great final sale," there will be a roundup, and "cowboys, like dogies, will stand, / To be mavericked by the Riders of Judgment / Who are posted and know every brand." Like the cattleman, the worker will be economically successful now, for the brand will be his symbol of profit "at the great final sale." But more importantly, the auction will spiritually empower the man-as-livestock who wears the Lord's brand and who spends the afterlife on God's open range, unlike "mavericked," or unbranded, sinners.

Initially, branding poems were orally co-authored by workers who made the brand reflect the religious concerns of the cowboy's group culture. Although twentieth-century poems have been written by individual poets and have been published for a noncowboy audience in magazines, newspapers, and books, nineteenth-

Cowboys are united by tasks that they act out together as well as by group myths that explain the importance of communal work. Branding is one chore that fosters team dynamics and then spawns a myth that represents branders as members of God's chosen race. (Cunningham-Prettyman Collection, Western History Collections, University of Oklahoma Library)

century oral poetry grew out of songs that the cowboys sang to one another at night or to the cattle that they soothed during the day and at night to prevent stampedes. At the end of each day, workers gathered around campfires and composed songs that they would later perform by constructing a skeleton text and by fleshing it out with improvised lyrics and music. Songs, as Alan Lomax and Joshua Berrett suggest, sprang up naturally on these festive social and labor-intensive occasions. Some were original compositions, and others were based on songs heard elsewhere. But, in any case, "whatever the most gifted man could produce must bear the criticism of the entire camp, and agree with the ideas of a group of men. In this sense, therefore, any song that came from such a group would be the joint product of a number of them, telling perhaps the story of some stampede they had all fought to turn, some crime in which they had all shared equally, some comrade's tragic death which they had all witnessed" (Lomax and Lomax xxv).[18]

These poems exemplified the traits of an entire work culture: first, because the dynamics of the group made the process of collective composition possible, as Lomax and Berrett suggest; second, because oral poetry itself presented the worker with a convenient form of expression; and third, because the brands in these branding poems embodied the essence of the worker's philosophical thoughts. In 1905, for instance, the National Livestock Association published a nostalgic look at western culture and called it *Prose and Poetry of the Livestock Industry of the United States*. No poetry appeared in the text. The title, instead, reflected the "artistic" enterprise of the people who compiled the book: the attempt, through "poetry," to substitute a romantic reconstruction of the West for a factual documentation of frontier existence. The authors portrayed the cowboy as a laconic man who had developed "to a remarkable degree the faculty of expressing himself in the terse, crisp, clear-cut language of the range."[19] Actual poetry allowed the cowboy, in his group, to express his thoughts in the nondiscursive world of song or nonprose—in a poetic version of the only slightly less "terse" world to which the writers referred. Song compressed thoughts in verse, condensed ideas and framed them in metrical stanzas, and moved elliptically from line to line in the language of poetic allusion. The brand became a microcosmic illustration of the poetic world, for it condensed and reflected a reading of the culture in its brief and simple lines or re-presented the cowboy in its picturelike significations.

The brand embodied both the economic dependence of the working underclass and its hope for religious salvation. In the nineteenth century, for example, a cowboy might refer to himself as Square Two Jim and use the "Square Two" brand—or the name of the Square Two Ranch, from which the brand had been taken—to connect the workplace with the worker's identity.[20] But while the cowboy was dependent on the cattleman for his nickname, as well as for his material sustenance, he was able at the same time to exploit the potential for religious salvation inherent in the history of cattle brands. The "Three Christian Crosses," for instance, allegedly the first brand used in the Americas, introduced Cortez and his livestock on the continent and used the image of the Trinity both to mark the stock and to proclaim the annexation of the New World by the Spanish Catholic Church.[21] In the cowboy's poetry, these economic and religious functions of the brand come together. The brand defines the cowboy's work function, for it names the cowboy and the role that he plays in the economic process of branding, slaughtering, packaging, and marketing beef. But it also indicates his spiritual elevation by God, who marks the worker and who offers salvation or inclusion in the herd of heaven by branding and thus possessing the cowboy, and who distinguishes the cowboy from cattlemen or from other unmarked, unrepentant sinners in the process of doing so.

In appropriating the employer's brand, the cowboy seeks to displace his employer, but not to escape necessarily from the work that he performs on the range. Giving the brand to God, the cowboy links himself with other significant branders and glorifies his task by inventing a labor genealogy for himself and his cowboy compatriots. For instance, "Cowboy's Soliloquy," an anonymously composed nineteenth-century oral poem, compares the cowboy's work to that of the Old Testament prophets. Noting that "Abraham emigrated in search of a range" (Fife and Fife 14), it adds that each of the patriarchs "owned a big brand." It relates the work of the cowboy not only to that of the prophets, but, by extension, to that of their antecedent in Genesis. Like Adam, who names the animals in the Garden of Eden, the worker uses the language of branding to "name" the stock in the Edenic landscape of the American West. Like Adam, his language is inspired by nature or by the objects in a physical setting. Early branding irons, for example, were often constructed with the ores of the earth or built with the limbs of trees that grew out of the ground. The pictures used in brands also frequently reflected an image of wilderness life—mountains and rivers that lent their names to ranches on which cowboys worked and from which they derived their own nicknames.[22] For workers, then, the brand became a symbol for the simple language of Adam, before the Fall in the Garden of Eden. It maintained the basic connection between the "word" and the "thing," and illustrated its meaning by living and moving on the frontier's wandering and promiscuous cattle herds.[23]

Like the cattleman Joseph McCoy, in *Historic Sketches of the Cattle Trade of the West and Southwest,* the cowboy invented a religious genealogy for himself in order to enhance his standing in a mythic world. Unlike his relation to Old Testament prophets, however, his connection to Adam was and is often unstated. The Edenic myth links work to sin, for work is the punishment that Adam receives from God as a result of the Fall. In order to glorify his labor, the cowboy therefore cannot identify himself overtly with Adam, whose labor is a sign of his sinfulness. Instead, he compares his work to the labor of Isaac and Abraham, who seek in the aftermath of Adam's fall in the Garden to please God by working to cleanse themselves of original sin. Gail Gardner's "The Sierry Petes" (1917), one of the first written and individually authored poems to become well known outside the cowboy group, dramatizes the cowboy's obsession with his cyclical fall from grace and with his return to it as a result of branding or working. In the poem, Sandy Bob and Buster Jig brand livestock, but eventually come to dislike the smell of "burnin' hair" on the cattle. They go to town for a drink at the "Kaintucky Bar," but on the way home they meet the devil, who says that he has come to gather their souls. The men lasso the devil, then

> stretched him out an' they tailed him down,
> While the irons was a-gettin' hot,
> They cropped and swaller-forked his yeres,
> Then they branded him up a lot.
>
> (Ohrlin 71)

These lines illustrate the function and effect of labor in maintaining the range, for the cowboys can enjoy the protection of the Lord only when they brand in the workplace. When they leave their work and go to town, they move symbolically from the safety of the range to the fallen world and risk their standing, both as workers and as members of God's chosen group, by allowing their fate to rest in the devil's hands. They can regain their place in a privileged religious world only by working, defeating Satan, and branding him.

Branding is not only an aspect of the cowboys' work in this poem, but a part of the poet's own artistic process. In the 1920s, a publisher printed "The Sierry Petes" without citing Gardner as having written the poem. The author then published *Orejana Bull* (1935), a collection of poems that highlights this one, in part to indicate that he had written "The Sierry Petes" and to state that he had not approved of its earlier, unauthorized appearance in print. As Warren E. Miller points out in his 1985 introduction to this collection of poems, an "orejana is a calf old enough to quit its mother, a maverick," or an unbranded animal. "The Sierry Petes" is therefore an unbranded text, or a poem that has appeared in print without the poet's name attached to the work. Gardner makes the connection between composing and branding by using the name of an unbranded bull to advertise his publication, and Miller makes the connection again by stating that "The Sierry Petes" appeared in the 1920s in print without the benefit of the poet's "brand" to distinguish this work as his own (x).

Religious themes are so clearly inscribed in cowboy poems about brands that even noncowboy writers acknowledge these themes by analyzing the equations in poems between religious salvation and branding. John Herlihy's *Midnight Cowboy* (1965), for instance, envisions the brander as a New York prostitute and as a confused man with homosexual yearnings. Joe Buck trades on the image of the nineteenth-century cowboy frontiersman: he makes a living by marketing the machismo that his cowboy costume conveys and by using it to attract paying customers. Like Sandy Bob and Buster Jig—who go to town in "The Sierry Petes" and who give up their branding in order to have a good time—Joe Buck, the cowboy prostitute, goes to New York and engages in immoral sex when he should be repenting and preparing for religious salvation in heaven. Throughout the novel, he remembers a refrain from the cowboy poem "The Last Round-Up" (also known as "The Cowboy's Dream" and quoted earlier as an example of religious branding poems). The poem distinguishes between a single brand, on the one hand, which a cowboy wears throughout his entire life and which he shows to the Lord when he enters the kingdom of heaven, and a "road brand," on the other, which a cattleman puts on his cattle at the final moment before sending his multiply branded livestock to market.

The Lord will not acknowledge the sinner who repents with the sad awful cry: "Too late!" After leading a profligate life, one cannot repent at the last moment, brand oneself at the doorstep of heaven, and enter it like the rancher, who brands or cashes his stock right before sending livestock to market. Joe has committed a similar greedy and immoral act: he has sought to market a myth on the streets of New York and to prostitute the cowboy's tradition for cash. Having denied Christ (23, 95) and having traded the cowboy's heritage for the prospects of wealth in New York, he has lost his chance for religious salvation by discrediting the western heroes he imitates. *Midnight Cowboy* and "The Sierry Petes" describe the same conflict, for the authors of both texts, in spite of their cultural and historical dissimilarities, use brands to signify roles that cowboys play in the spiritual afterlife.

Reinventing the brand enables poets to refute Philip Rollins, who suggested in his influential study *The Cowboy* (1922) that frontiersmen were "religiously asleep" (84), or unaware of any connection between themselves and a construct of mythic proportions. Clearly the brand establishes a link between the poet and other branding frontiersmen, while relating them to a Christian sense of salvation.[24] The branding myth allows the cowboy to discard the economic interpretation of the cattleman's sign and to replace it with a reading that allows for God's inclusion of cowboys in— and exclusion of ranchers from—heaven. In "The Sierry Petes," Gail Gardner examines the fallen world—the city, or the urban frontier—and rejects it, returning his cowboys to branding pens that prevent men like *Midnight Cowboy*'s Joe Buck from wandering and succumbing to the temptations of the vice-ridden city.[25]

III

Although nineteenth-century cowboys could control brands in their poetry, they could not forestall the unfolding of historical events that sought to displace cowboys and their interpretation of branding. The inability of cowboys to secure their place on the range—or to base their spiritual status on branding—became a problem in the late nineteenth and early twentieth centuries and began to manifest itself in the aftermath of a historical movement to fence the frontier. The invention of barbed wire in 1874 enabled the cattleman to divide and destroy the range in the last decades of the nineteenth century and to sever the connection between the brand and its original function.[26] The cattleman accepted fencing because it allowed him to en- close the land and to prevent his rivals from using it to graze their migrating herds. It provided him with the means to claim and surround the water on government land and to defend it against men and women who came to the West to stake their homesteads and farms. In addition to feeding his livestock, the cattleman could conserve grass in supplementary pastures and put aside space that he would later need to breed heifers with quality bulls. Fencing increased the value of livestock: it encouraged the cattleman to invest in bulls that would maintain the purity and continuity of bloodlines, and it kept out "scrub"—or wandering and inferior—cattle that could breed with "blooded" stock and diminish their worth. With the advent of fencing, cowboys began to lose jobs. It was no longer important for them to watch cattle, because stock could now be controlled by man-made enclosures, and it was no longer necessary for cowboys to drive livestock to town, for cattlemen could

Barbed-wire fences domesticated the West in more ways than one. In an advertisement for the American Fencing Company, probably drawn in the late nineteenth century, a gentrified bull and a heifer go courting by the light of the silvery "moo." (American Steel and Wire Collection, Baker Library, Harvard Business School)

position herds in pastures near railway lines and ship meat to market by freight cars instead.

Cattle branding lost its purpose as well. Originally it enabled the rancher to wound, define, and distinguish his stock on the open frontier. But barbed wire later allowed him to separate and hold his cattle by wounding them in fenced-off enclosures. The theorist Umberto Eco has defined the tension between the signifier and the signified as the ''wound''—the place where content and expression wrestle with each other to produce a sign's meaning.[27] Eco's language has its material analogue in the ranching world, for branding not only creates a ''wound'' on the hide of an animal, but also leads to a ''wound'' or rupture of meaning—a further difference between the ways in which cowboys and ranchers read cattle brands. For ranchers, brands begin to lose their importance as indicators of possession once fences take over. Although branding still occurs and continues to play a role in the twentieth century's rounding up and ritual counting of cattle, it loses its status as the sole means for determining ownership of stock in the 1880s and afterward.[28] Since then, cowboy branders have played less crucial roles in distinguishing cattle, but they have compensated for their decreasing importance in history by vaunting their increasing importance as branders in poetry. Men who brand stock are honored and rewarded by God for their work, or allowed to ride on His heavenly range unencumbered by the fence's restriction, in cowboy poems that have been composed since the advent of fencing.

Lacking the materials to build their enclosures on prairies, landowners found substitutes for the rock and wooden rail fences of the nineteenth-century Midwest and New England. Honey locusts and thorn locusts, pomegranates, mesquite, and cactii were planted and later replaced by *bois d'arcs* or osage oranges and by Cherokee roses or briars[29]—thickets whose thorns could withstand harsh winters and summer droughts, and whose hedges could restrict the space and discourage the movement of cattle by wounding them, as barbed-wire fences would do later. Jacob Haish, an Illinois lumberman, bought and sold the seeds of the *bois d'arc* and developed an interest in barbed wire, producing five patents for his fences between

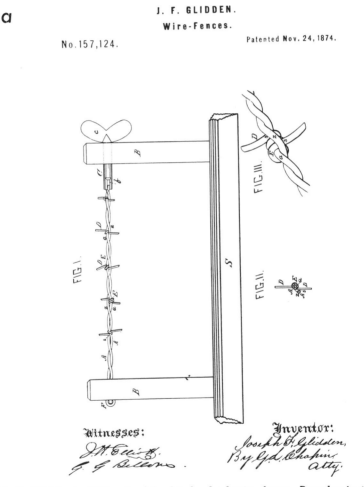

(a) J. F. Glidden's 1874 patent for his barbed-wire fence. Popular in the late nineteenth and early twentieth centuries, it competed mainly with Jacob Haish's "S" barb, sketched in its 1875 patent (b). Notice that the scientific line

January 20, 1874, and August 31, 1875.[30] He was bested in his efforts to monopolize the market, however, by J. F. Glidden, a farmer from De Kalb, Illinois, who received his first patent four months after Haish, but who joined I. L. Ellwood to form the Barb Fence Company shortly thereafter. Ellwood later became a shareholder in the firm of Washburn and Moen and, with Glidden, took credit for creating the fence and controlling the market in the following years.[31]

Farmers used fences to keep cattle out of their fields, but ranchers used fences—more frequently—to keep cattle *in* their new man-made enclosures.[32] In 1873, for instance, Henry Rose attached a series of wire points to a wooden board and brought it to the county fair in De Kalb. Demonstrating his invention to the audience, Rose placed the "prickered board" on the *head of a cow* in order to prove that the animal would retreat from a fence when it pressed against it, driving the points on the board into the skull of the advancing animal. After witnessing the performance, Ellwood,

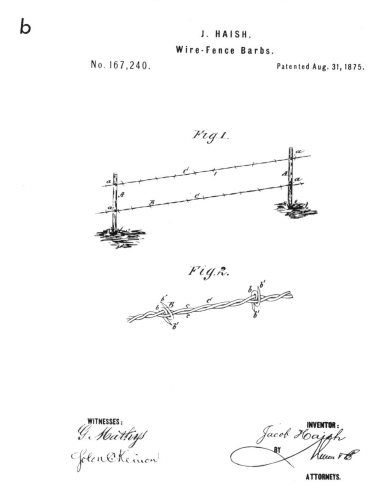

b

J. HAISH.

Wire-Fence Barbs.

No. 167,240.   Patented Aug. 31, 1875.

Fig.1.

Fig.2.

WITNESSES:

INVENTOR:

Jacob Haish

BY

ATTORNEYS.

drawings derealize and almost aestheticize pain, giving no sense of a fence's primary purpose: to wound and injure sentient objects that run into it. (American Steel and Wire Collection, Baker Library, Harvard Business

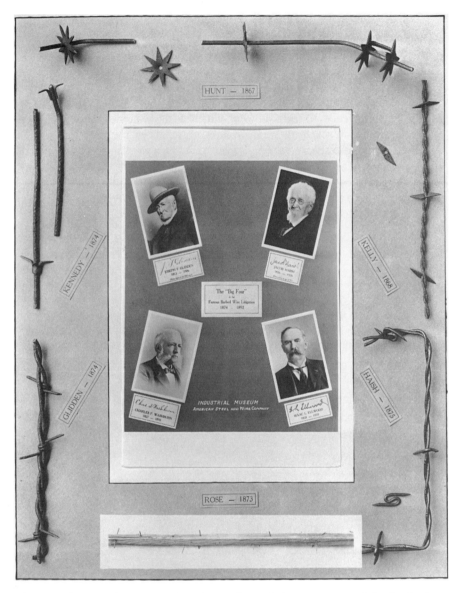

The "Big Four," who invented and popularized their versions of the barbed-wire fence in the 1860s and 1870s. Clockwise, from upper left: Joseph F. Glidden, Jacob Haish, Isaac L. Ellwood, and Charles F. Washburn, surrounded by samples produced by these men and others. The wheel barb at the top and other early barbs like it advertised their functions as crude, none too subtle sources of pain. (American Steel and Wire Collection, Baker Library, Harvard Business School)

Glidden, and Haish developed the barbed-wire fence by moving the barbs from the head of the cow to the *fence,* and convinced the cattleman that he could control the herd by wounding it within the confines of a prickly enclosure.[33]

In the following year, fence companies produced and distributed 10,000 pounds of barbed wire, and by 1880 their annual output had increased to 80.5 million pounds.[34] Thus in 1888, Theodore Roosevelt could publish *Ranch Life and the Hunting Trail* and refer to the past as a time when "cowboys and branding-irons [took] the place of fences" (1), for fences had spread through the West by then and confined livestock, as well as cowboys who worked with them. In the succeeding year, Mark Twain would publish *A Connecticut Yankee in King Arthur's Court* (1889), representing the protagonist as a rodeo cowboy who defeats Merlin the Magician with a revolver and lasso, but who then defeats himself by surrounding his army with circles of electric wires and fences (309). Twain's novel was prophetic, for the XIT Ranch in Texas perfected a fence in the early 1900s that even further constricted the movements of cowboys. Management now attached a telephone wire to the top of the fence and used it to relay the orders of cattlemen to cowboys in outlying fields. Later installing an electric fence, they equipped cowboys with portable telephones and told workers to report their positions and to receive their instructions by attaching the phones to the fence.[35] Electric wires shocked cattle and discouraged their movement more effectively than barbed-wire fences. But the wires also controlled workers by sending a current through the fence and by tracking cowboys on their daily rounds—thus equating cowboys with animals and restricting the movement of both within the boundaries of electrical barriers.

Simultaneously with the invention of the barbed-wire fence, orally co-composed and individually written cowboy poems became concerned with the ideological ramifications of fencing. The anthem that one associates with cowboys—"Don't fence me in!"—had its origins in the economic conditions that made entrapped cowboys expendable, with the development of fencing techniques. This anthem had its corollary expression in religious poems that cowboys composed. "Panhandle Cob," for example, deals with a cowboy who has "got no religion" (Lomax and Lomax 106), but who has nevertheless attained a martyr's status by branding stock and by saving a cattleman's daughter. The poem opens with a condemnation of the "derned wire fences" that run "from the strip of the Rio Grande" to the north (105) and with a stanza of praise for cowboys who "burn a brand" (106) on the cattlemen's stock. It then moves into a lengthy retelling of a cowboy's rescue of a cattleman's daughter while branding animals in a fenced-in corral (107). Panhandle Cob saves Sissy when she crawls through the fence and makes herself vulnerable to a steer, which then chases her with his menacing horns. Because the fence is inadequate as a means of looking after the cowboy's best interests, the brander throws himself between Sissy and the rampaging steer and saves her but fatally injures himself (109). His heroism is established in this poem about branding and fencing, and his courageous act is compared to a holy deed that leads to his martyrlike ascension to heaven: "He hadn't got no religion; but top o' the golden stairs / There'll be heap o' church members missin', but Cob you bet'll be there" (106).

Writers who were noncowboy outsiders made these religious and economic connections between branding and fencing as well. In 1897, for instance, Owen

Wister published *Lin McLean* and clarified the distinction between the brand and the barbed-wire fence—a distinction on which the cowboy had already commented in "Panhandle Cob." At one point, Wister's narrator says that "one man has been as good as another in three places—Paradise before the Fall; the Rocky Mountains before the [barbed] wire fence; and the Declaration of Independence" (119). The brand confers on the cowboy both a religious distinction in heaven and a recognition of his subordinate economic condition on earth. The narrator clarifies these two different points when he equates the cowboy with God's chosen race or with prelapsarian man and with members of the unfettered working class, who should be free to compete or to be "as good" and as successful as anyone else in the marketplace. The Declaration of Independence, which grew out of the American colonists' needs both to worship independently and to protest against Britain's taxation, here becomes a metaphor for the tension between cowboys and cattlemen, for it represents the religious *and* economic needs of cowboys on the fenced-in frontier.

More recently, *Leaving Cheyenne* (1963) has located this tension within the context of the twentieth-century American novel. Larry McMurtry's book indicates the way in which cattlemen appropriate, interpret, and devalue the brand, elevating the significance of the fence and diminishing the importance of the brand and the men who wield it out West. Here a Texas cattleman, Adam Fry, finds his stock in the pasture of Cletus Taylor, his neighbor, and sends his son Gideon and Johnny McCloud through the fence to retrieve them. After capturing and returning the cattle, the boys track a coyote back across the same property and then chase it until Taylor catches them. He claims that the coyote is his, and he orders the boys to release it; but Fry comes to their rescue and tells the neighbor that the coyote wears *his* brand—that he has notched its ear to distinguish it from the coyotes on Taylor's property. Gideon and Johnny believe this tall tale, and Taylor, who understands the joke, finally agrees to buy the coyote from Fry. Adam Fry then tells the boys to go home because they "got all them calves to brand" at his ranch (41).

As cowboy-figures and as servants of the cattleman Fry, Johnny and Gideon perform a task that begins with the herding and concludes with the branding of cattle. Like the cows that move tamely within a fenced-off enclosure, the workers themselves are domesticated and unable to recognize the original branding marks of the cattleman. Taylor and Fry trick them by taking the brand from the cowboys and investing it with a significance of their own making in order to punish the boys for jumping the fence and for leaving their branding while hunting game on a neighbor's land. The fence thus becomes a symbol for the confinement of cowboys and for the ability of the owner to control the workers who wander outside the boundaries that he has erected. The cattleman does not obey these boundaries himself, for Gideon says that Taylor is "sly"—"you couldn't hem him up for long" (41). But Gideon and Johnny have their own physical actions curtailed by men who wrest the brand from the boys and who then create a fictional context that anchors the boys to the men and places the cowboys, as branders, in the position of economic dependence. The boys may brand Fry's cattle within the boundaries of his fenced-in enclosure, but they lose their capacity to read and interpret the sign when they stray outside the boundaries that Fry has established.

Like the rustler, the cowboy acknowledges the ability of a brand's signs and meanings to change. The rustler alters a brand in order to rewrite the cattleman's language and to claim illegal ownership of the cattleman's stock. The cowboy reinterprets the sign in order to reexamine the ideological implications of branding: to shift the economic center of the workplace to the cowboy employee in his fiction and poetry. But the fence cannot be so easily compromised or made, like the brand, to adjust itself to the needs of the cowboy *or* rustler. It can be cut, as the brand can be changed, to facilitate the theft of livestock, but it can't be subtly or artistically fashioned into a version of its former self, as the brand can be redesigned or rewritten. The fence impedes the movement of objects, locates itself in a specific space, and resists attempts to transform it into a symbol of accommodation in art. It can be built or destroyed, but it can't be "remade" by the cowboy interpreter.

Horseman, Pass By illustrates both the characteristics of the unyielding barbed-wire fence and the interpretive pliability of the cattle brand. Grandad, a former cowboy and present-day cattleman, finds his place on the cowboy's unfenced heavenly range, not in the cattleman's fenced-off enclosures. Lonnie describes his grandfather as a cowboy who once branded another cattleman's herd (5), but compares him before his death to a man trapped "on the other side of a high barbed fence, with each wire a year of [his] life. . . . I couldn't go over it and I couldn't crawl through" it to save him (137). As a former cowboy, Grandad has an early identification with branding; as a cattleman, he has a later association with the barbed-wire fence, which refuses to relent or to let Lonnie go through it to save his grandfather from a tragic demise. The fence's impediment to the cowboy's survival contrasts with the brand's connection to the cowboy's religious salvation. The family attends his funeral, when Grandad actually dies, and the preacher defines the grandfather's death as a sign of displacement—a form of release from the fenced-in land or from the cattleman's world, and a means of moving to the heavenly world of unlimited movement that the nineteenth-century cowboy portrayed in his poems. Brother Barstow says that God has taken Grandad "to [an unfenced] range it is not ours to trod." The Lord has rewarded the cowboy who once tended a cattleman's herd and who will watch the Lord's herd now and forever, as part of his eternal "contract" with God (171).

Removing the fence from the landscape enables the worker not only to brand on the open frontier, but in his poems to write or sing about the branding that he performs. Henry Herbert Knibbs's "Riders of the Stars" (1916), like many other songs that were written after the West had been fenced, distinguishes between the artistic inspiration or freedom lent by the brand and the inhibition brought about by the fence. Ten thousand riders of the range go to heaven, and a spokesman for their group petitions the Lord to give them a job in "the unfenced blue" sky. The spokesman says that the cowboys want to brand the maverick "comets that's running wild" as they branded the stock "in the long ago," before society partitioned the land. They also want to sing about their branding task, but they can't make their songs "fit in up here" on the fenced-in heavenly range. The Lord grants their request at the end of the poem and lets them work and sing about brands that they place on the cattlelike "comets" (Fife and Fife 21).

"Riders of the Stars" glorifies branding as a physical chore and as a part of the cowboy's creative compositional process: signs are first placed on the sides of the stock and then used to inspire and articulate songs about work. But sometimes songs written by twentieth-century poets such as Knibbs obscure the religious importance of brands, set forth in nineteenth-century oral poems about Christian salvation, and substitute the "book" for the "brand" as a sign of a cowboy writer's identity. N. Howard Thorp compiled the first collection of cowboy oral poetry in 1908, setting a precedent both for other researchers, who could now publish traditional songs that the cowboy had sung, and for living cowboy poets, who could print their work at once or reach a larger audience by constructing a text and distributing a facsimile of it to noncowboy readers. As cowboys moved into the twentieth century, they began to abandon the disappearing cowboy group and to *write* their songs in isolation for the publishing industry and for a book-reading audience. As a result of this transition to writing, the brand is sometimes displaced by the "book" as a sign of distinction in a literate culture, for it emphasizes the "texts" that twentieth-century cowboys inscribe. In Bruce Kiskaddon's "Judgement Day" (1924), for example, the angels in heaven cut and group the cowboys as though they were cattle and prepare to brand them with a sign of religious salvation. The Lord has judged other mortals by a "book of rules" that He uses to distinguish the sinners and the saved, but He exchanges it now for a "range law book" that allows cowboys to be judged by a different standard than the Lord's other petitioners. (Brand inspectors often referred to range law books, which itemized a county's legally registered brands, while verifying brands during roundups out West.) Here the poet forestalls the act of branding and introduces a *book* with brands written in it showing that the cowboy has earned God's special treatment or favor. In "Judgement Day" the book has the same function that the book of Revelation has in the Bible—to separate the sinners from the saved on the day of the Lord's final judgment (66).

The publication of the cowboy's poetry leads to the availability of his ideas in the marketplace and to the appropriation of his culture by writers outside the group, who pick up on such symbols as the fence and the brand while confusing important distinctions between them. *The Sea of Grass* (1936), for instance, illustrates the way in which these ideological constructs may be taken from cowboys conditioned to passing their art orally from singer to audience, and instead fashioned by a literary noncowboy culture to suit the purposes of conventional novelists. Here Conrad Richter marginalizes the cowboy by moving a romantic heroine to the center of a debate about the respective merits of the brand and the barbed-wire fence. Lutie marries a Texan and feels trapped by the "barbed wire" on his ranch, which represents the domestic life that stultifies and confines her (11). On the lonely prairie she becomes bored with her life and takes a lover, leaving her husband for this other man and encouraging other ranchers' wives to think of her as having been marked with "a final ugly red brand" (91)—the scarlet letter of a frontier adulteress. Richter's story of a romantic triangle owes more to Nathaniel Hawthorne's canonical novel than to the cowboy's own marginal poetry, which *distinguishes* between the functions of the brand and the fence. The cowboy makes the brand into a sign of independence and freedom, but Richter alters the myth and equates both the fence and the brand with society's confinement and condemnation of Lutie.[36]

The shifting meanings and functions of branding are due, first, to the introduction of fencing and the subsequent displacement of branding. Fencing, in turn, leads to the unemployment of cowboys, to the unraveling of their closely knit group, and to the discontinued composition of their group's oral poetry. Initially composed by a collection of workers who translated their notions of branding into artistic renditions of religious salvation, songs are now individually written and published for readers who extend beyond the fringe of the cowboy's own circle. The appropriation of branding by ''writing'' cowboys and noncowboy outsiders leads to an attenuation of the original myth of religious salvation—the replacement of the brand with the ''book'' in poems that cowboy writers compose and the equation of the brand with the fence in texts that noncowboy outsiders create.[37]

At its best, the brand locates the cowboy in a material world and defines him as a worker who labors for a menial wage. It inspires the poetry and fiction that transform the cowboy into a mythic prelapsarian man who roams on a heavenly range. However, even in paradise he must grapple with ranchers who control his actions at home, with fences that usurp his function on the closing frontier, and with writers who compete to displace his traditional oral poetry. In addition, the cowboy fights with the rest of us for the right to represent his own culture. In fiction and film we portray him as a gunslinger like Billy the Kid, but instead of killing his target, the cowboy wounds it by imprinting livestock with the language of branding. He denies economic interpretations of the cattleman's brand and turns it into a grammar of religious salvation, developing a myth that can be examined and made to speak through the lips of the wounds that brands leave on the skin of the ranch owner's animals.

CHAPTER TWO

FRONTIER GENDER
Livestock Castration and Square Dancing

I

In August 1911, a woman was tried in a Colorado opera house for allegedly having stolen another ranch owner's stock.[1] Ora Haley had recently purchased a parcel of land that straddled the Colorado and Wyoming state borders. His ranch adjoined Ann Bassett's homestead, which lay to the south of his land. Haley stated that, in March 1911, two of his cowboys and a stock detective had discovered the carcass of one of his heifers in Bassett's supply room. Later they had found the animal's hide on her property and had noticed that someone had cut a piece of skin—with the brand—from the right flank of the animal. The missing brand prevented Haley from contending in court that the heifer had belonged to him or from proving that Bassett had rustled his stock. But Haley triumphed over this absence of evidence, claiming that his cowboys had not only branded his heifer, but spayed it by performing a unique surgical task that differed from the technique that Bassett and his other neighbors used to castrate their animals. His removal of the heifer's internal reproductive organs had left an external scar that one could read as a brand mark and interpret as a distinct sign of ownership.[2]

Typically, cowboys brand and castrate their employer's calves at the same time: in the spring and, with the late arrival of stock, in the fall.[3] So closely associated are the acts of branding and castrating cattle that one task sometimes stands in for the other one: in order to tally the number of bull calves that they wound and mark with a sign of possession, cowboys sometimes toss the castrated scrotums into a corner and count them at the end of each day, thereby confirming how many male calves they have simultaneously branded and castrated.[4] Both branding and castration wounds define property and, hence, leave scars that raise issues of ownership. The posses-

Branding and castration often take place at the same time, during spring and fall roundups of stock. In this 1890s photograph of a ranch in the Texas–Oklahoma Panhandle area, the calf on the left is branded while the one on the right is castrated. (A. A. Forbes Collection, Western History Collections, University of Oklahoma Library)

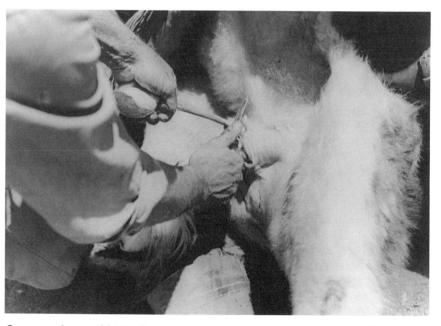

On a ranch near Marfa, Texas, a man uses a knife to remove a bull calf's testicles, circa 1939. (Photographed by Lee, for the Farm Security Administration. Denver Public Library, Western History Department)

sion of livestock is so clearly symbolized by the branding and castration wounds that scars left by those wounds sometimes become symbols for working out larger issues of ownership. Earlier, for instance, Haley had learned that his land could not support a sizable herd. Over the following years, he had therefore overrun his boundaries and grazed his livestock on Ann Bassett's property. At her trial, one of Haley's cowboys admitted that Haley had been searching for a way to run Ann Bassett out of the state and to step in and purchase her homestead, after which time he would convert it to range land and use it to feed his stock, which had already been illegally grazing in Ann Bassett's pastures.[5] By accusing Bassett of having stolen an animal that belonged to him, Haley could present himself as the victim in a struggle to control the rights to a spayed heifer, not as the aggressor in this feud over land. However, the spayed heifer's scar merely symbolized Ora Haley's ambition to pirate away Ann Bassett's property.

In addition to bringing up questions of ownership, castration wounds complicate conceptions of gender: they not only represent an animal's inability to breed with, impregnate, or give birth to livestock, but sometimes signify ways in which rival ranchers, such as Haley and Bassett, symbolically castrate each other. After Bassett received an acquittal in court, J. S. Hoy—another of Bassett's archrivals—wrote a book in which he contended that Bassett had, in fact, stolen Haley's heifer, slaughtered it, and hidden the carcass in her supply room. In a letter that she wrote to a friend, Bassett noted that Hoy's editor had promised not to send the book to press until ''he had worked it over and cut out the wicked personal venom that is so very obvious in Hoys [sic] writing.'' Bassett added that she might ''take up the subject of the *casteration* [sic] *of J. S. Hoy''*; she might respond to Hoy's accusations against her by writing her own book and by repeating some ''juicy scandal'' that she knew would harm him more than his allegations could injure her.[6] An economic dispute over a spayed heifer had become a fight about which disputing party could castrate the other. If the editor did not ''cut out'' certain language, then Bassett would write her own book and ''castrate'' J. S. Hoy personally.

Economic displacement took the form of sexual disempowerment not only in quarrels engaged in by men and women, but also in communities lived in by members of the same male sex. Hence cattlemen economically subordinated cowboys by making them, in effect, sexually nonfunctional. Historical accounts of the range industry indicate that cattlemen tended to hire only unmarried men.[7] The owners sent cowboys away on trail drives, cattle roundups, and extended explorations of range land, preferring to employ single men, who could leave the ranch without disrupting family relationships. On ranches, owners maintained single-sex bunkhouses and line camps for cowboys.[8] They made no provisions for married men, who left ranches, moved to town, and tried to commute to work, therein donating to cattlemen only part of their time. Married cowboys were both less dependable and more expensive to keep: in addition to dividing their loyalties between family and work, these men needed separate housing to shelter and higher wages to support wives and children. Cattlemen created cheap and reliable work forces, then, by symbolically castrating men who worked for them. Husbands could act regularly on their sexual impulses, claiming the conjugal privileges that marriage conferred on them. Bachelors, however, could not enjoy frequent access to women.

They lived in isolated locations, on ranches outside town, and met paramours or paid visits to prostitutes only when they cashed their checks once a month in saloons or entered cowtowns at the end of cross-country drives. On ranches, if they engaged in sexual activities that did not include women, they did not write about or acknowledge those practices. Instead, they remained temporarily celibate men who dammed their sex drives and unleashed them infrequently. Economic benefits accrued to cattlemen who allowed these men—and no others—to work on ranches out West. Castrating bull calves in order to turn them into fattened beef steers that sold for higher prices at market, ranchers also separated men from the opposite sex in order to maximize their employees' labor and loyalty and to minimize the amount of money that they paid cowboys at the end of each month.

In *Civilization and Its Discontents,* Sigmund Freud wrote that men in society are torn between wishing to work, on the one hand, and wanting to love, on the other (48). What Freud thought of as conflicting drives were also present in nineteenth-century America's cattle economy. Cowboys who wanted to work could not marry, although they might love somewhere, somehow, intermittently; those who wished to marry could not do so without risking their employment. They not only were required to isolate themselves from society and to abstain from expressing "love" for great lengths of time, but were paid to act out their isolation and abstinence by castrating stock.[9] Social isolation and castration were often equated with each other and thought of as the same state of being. In the vocabulary of the cowboy's work culture, the verb *to cut* meant both "to castrate" a bull or bull calf and "to separate" a cow from the herd.[10] During roundups on the open range, cowboys rode "carving," "chopping," or "cutting" horses, cutting one cow from the rest and separating it for the purpose of branding and castrating it.[11] Cutting a cow was a prelude to castrating it; "carving" reproductive organs out of its body was equivalent to "chopping" a cow out of a communal body or herd.

In a sense, cowboys were metaphorically castrated when they were cut off from society, isolated from women and families, and allowed to live only with other single men on ranches out West. Apparently they did not believe that cowboys found sexual outlets in this all-male group, for they never sang or wrote about homosexual or homoerotic relations in poetry or in prose accounts of their lives on the range. But they did occasionally cross-dress or address one another in language suggesting that cowboys could sometimes take on nonmale roles.[12] In all-male groups, they compensated for the absence of women by fulfilling functions that women were not present to enact for them, and men who performed "feminine" functions were not perceived as erotic, but seen as somehow less "masculine." Therefore, in addition to reining in their sexual appetites, cowboys adopted nicknames, disguises, and functions that denied their gendered identities. Chuckwagon cooks most often took on these nicknames, disguises, and functions, for kitchen chores linked them to traditional domestic female roles. In *The Story of the Cowboy* (1898), for instance, Emerson Hough noted that cowboys called the cook "old woman" or "lady" (138), and other writers made the same point as well.[13] Even men who worked at the chuckwagon only once had to accept the role of "old woman" or challenge that label and stake out different identities. Hence in *The Log of a Cowboy* (1903), Andy Adams writes that a ranch hand who once made bread for the men, before rolling and

*Although they were men, chuckwagon cooks were often thought of as taking
on women's work. Here, a black cook named Sooner dries dishes at the Flat
Top Ranch in Texas while wearing his androgynous apron-overalls-skirt.
(Photography Collection, Harry Ransom Humanities Research Center, University of Texas at Austin)*

cutting dough, "threw off his overshirt, unbuttoned his red undershirt and turned it
in until you could see the hair on his breast" (283), daring cowboys to deny that he
was, in fact, masculine.

Men with power were perceived as more masculine, and men without it were
reduced in stature, mocked, and typecast as silly women or gossiping girls. Cowboys and cooks were not locked into these respective male and female roles; instead,
they were apt to alternate roles as power switched back and forth between cowboys
and cooks. In *The Log of a Cowboy,* for instance, when the cook's bread turns out
successfully Adams writes that word of his culinary skills spread "faster than a

secret amongst women'' (283). In some sense, cooks were masters and cowboys were ''girls'' by comparison. Cooks were valued on drives that took cowboys out onto prairies and plains. Stranded in the middle of nowhere, cowboys were forced to rely for survival on cooks, who not only fed them, but also gave them medicine (perhaps only a bottle of brandy, if cowboys were snakebit). Thus trail-drive foremen and cooks were paid more than cowboys because they were invested with greater responsibilities and authority.

At the same time, cooks were usually older men who were no longer able to execute grueling chores such as breaking livestock, which younger, more athletic cowboys were paid to perform. They were also likely to be Native American, Hispanic, or black—able to labor, but stigmatized because of their color as outdoor domestic servants and menials.[14] Cowboys, in contrast, conceived of themselves as more masculine, wrestling with rough stock and acting out more ''macho'' assignments than cooks, who washed dishes, stood over boiling pots, and waited on cowboys at the end of each day.[15] One rarely documented example of homoerotic behavior indicates that chuckwagon cooks referred to special dinners that they prepared as ''wedding feasts,'' tempting cowboys to come eat her ''while she's hot and juicy'' and comparing the cowboys' consumption of the cook's ''female'' food to a groom's ravishment of his bride on their wedding night.[16]

This photograph, taken near Ute Creek, Colorado, in 1885/1886, shows a cook posing by a chuckwagon, with cowboys surrounding him. Most chuckwagons had compartments that held food, medicine, gear, and other provisions. Tables often folded out from the rear, providing flat surfaces on which cooks could prepare and serve meals. (Denver Public Library, Western History Department)

Men who worked for the Three Block Ranch in Texas at the turn of the century are seen in various stages of work and repose, equipping themselves to ride watch over livestock at night, sleeping, and preparing for bed. Cowboys were frequently posed or informally photographed at chuckwagon campsites. After working and dispersing themselves out on the range, ranch hands collected here at the end of each day, providing photographers with convenient opportunities for taking composite group portraits. (Barker Texas History Center, University of Texas at Austin)

A night scene of a chuckwagon campsite at the XIT Ranch in Texas, 1901. One's mental image of cowboys does not necessarily correspond with this picture of several grimy-faced men, lying prone in their long underwear, with their legs in the air. (Panhandle-Plains Historical Society, Canyon, Tex.)

The constant reversing and reassigning of sex roles—the depiction of cooks as "old women" and cowboys as men; of cooks as men and cowboys as "girls"—suggests that representations of western male gender were problematic and prone to revision, depending on who was defined as acting out what kind of role. If ranchers took part in suppressing the libidos of ranch hands, then those hands also voluntarily took part at times in disguising their gender. In *The Outlet* (1905), for instance, Andy Adams describes a mock circus that cowboys put on near a chuckwagon. As one cowboy introduced "the actors and actresses," a cowboy traipsed forth wearing "a skirt made out of a blanket" and won "the admiration of all as the only living lady lion-tamer" (236) that other spectating, cheering cowboys had witnessed. The circus was a metaphor for historically documented, carnivalesque forms of behavior—for episodes of cross-dressing and for verbally named acts of disguise that lead one to rethink one's notion of frontier male gender, as John Wayne embodies it. Not surprisingly, one western scholar has compared the movement of chuckwagons, during trail drives, to the traveling of circuses,[17] for what confronts one who studies the West is the way in which western movies sometimes misrepresent what was really a Felliniesque Mardi Gras.

On occasion, cowboys playfully dressed up as women. They were more apt, however, to assert certain notions of manhood, even during light-hearted times when they played pranks on chuckwagon cooks. In *The Cowman's Southwest, Being the Reminiscences of Oliver Nelson* (1953), the author recounts his adventures out West between 1878 and 1893, including his embarrassing stint as a cook at a cattle ranch. Here he remembers the comic confusion that ensued when a black cowboy played a joke on him, asking Nelson to fry up a bull's castrated testicles.

> One day Nigger Henry brought in half a peck of the clippings [testicles] from the bull pen, and poured them in my dishpan. I bawled him out, and dumped them in the creek. When the boys sat down to supper they said, "Henry, where's the 'oysters'?" "Mustah Olivah done trowed dem in de creek." I come near getting into trouble. I said, "Fellers, I never heard of eating such. I thought Henry was putting up a job on me. I'll cook anything you'll bring in to eat, only let me in on it." (110, 113)

In order to trumpet their masculinity, cowboys sometimes exploited a castration myth, contesting the premise that they were like members of the opposite sex or like castrated men with no gender at all. Paradoxically, they accomplished this feat by transforming the bull's castrated testicles into signs of their own male dominance. Typically, cowboys not only castrated bulls, but fried and ate the castrated testicles. In fact, "oysters" were the only food that cowboys—not cooks—prepared and consumed on the range.[18] Throwing a bull calf, holding it, and cutting its organs were rough-and-tumble segments of the cowboys' difficult and often dangerous work assignments out West. Because cooks did not share in the danger, they also did not share in the glory of eating the trophies that cowboys prized away from their animal antagonists. Hence the black cowboy Henry reveals the cook's unfamiliarity with roasting the organs by tossing them into Nelson's kitchen space and confounding him. It is an additional indication of the cook's femininity that he is flustered at the sight of organs that are signs of male sexuality's indisputable presence.

In western chronicles, castrated animal testicles were often seen both as food and as love medicine, conferring sexual potency on cowboys who consumed these prized aphrodisiacs.[19] Charles Goodnight, a nineteenth-century cattleman, noticed once on a trail drive that his bull's testicles tended to swing against its legs, causing its scrotum to swell and to develop an infection that, if not stopped, could spread through its body and ultimately threaten the animal's life. In an effort to preserve the testicles so that the bull could later be used to breed heifers, Goodnight pushed the organs up against the animal's belly, cut off its scrotum, and, "with some unraveled manila rope and a knife point to punch holes, . . . sewed the wound up by whipping the edges together like the cook snubbing up a hole in a flour sack."[20] Oliver Nelson later elaborated on the notion that the scrotum held food or testicles, noting that cowboys referred to these organs as "oysters." We continue to call them "prairie," "mountain," or "Rocky Mountain oysters,"[21] acknowledging their power by associating them with oysters, which allegedly boost a man's potency. Eating testicles or "oysters," in the cowboy's work culture, did not necessarily lead to his conquest of the opposite sex, but it did contribute to his reinforced sense of virility.[22] It enabled the cowboy to illustrate his hardihood, and his status as killer and victor, by consuming the vestige of other physically strong male opponents, which he had wrestled with, overpowered, and conquered.[23] Ingesting the spoils of triumph, the cowboy then took on new male strength and heightened his potency, appropriating those very organs that defined male gender and generated biological sex drives in bulls.

Hence the castration myth did not represent cowboys as castrated eunuchs or as women and girls. It celebrated cowboys as uncastrated men who subdued weaker, castrated animals, eating bull testicles and sometimes even other parts of beef carcasses. Bruce Siberts, for instance, began *Nothing but Prairie and Sky* (1954) with a campfire tale told by a chuckwagon cook. The cook recounted the death of Harriet, a four-hundred-pound prostitute who was unable to be buried in a coffin because of her size and who was therefore taken by the undertaker to his friend at a meat-packing plant. The butcher trimmed down Harriet and stuffed her into two two-hundred-pound kegs that he kept on hand to package beef. Then he accidentally sent them off to a ship, where sailors mistakenly ate a prostitute's corpse instead of the beef that the butcher had promised them (2–3). Siberts said that the chuckwagon cook liked to talk "about sex" and to repeat this story in order to explain to men that eating so much "beef" could whet their sexual appetites (182). "We had the general idea that our sex hunger was caused by such a heavy meat diet, but I never heard of anyone going vegetarian because of this" (161). In fact, he noted that cowboys credited eating beef with magically fueling their sex drives and pointed, as their example, to Harriet, who was both meat and prostitute.[24]

Without wives to serve as sexual outlets, cowboys had only occasional opportunities to gratify their desires by resorting to prostitutes or by choosing to prey (as people in cowtowns sometimes suggested) on members of the "weaker" sex who were decent but vulnerable.[25] Even though cowboys were metaphorically castrated and forced to abstain from sexual intercourse for long stretches of time, they were still a recurring threat, appearing in cowtowns on payday and consorting with women, having reined in their libidos for weeks and months at a time and now having a chance to unharness them. Cowboys could never be completely "castrated" or set apart from the rest of society. Baxter Black's poem "The Oyster" makes light of this fact and privileges both the cowboy and noncowboy sides of this argument. Written in the 1980s and distanced from the origins of cowboy life by more than a century, Black's text still depicts cowboys as ladies' men who eat "oysters"; he presents respectable women who live in noncowboy society as sexually preyed on by cowboys but, at times, capable of resisting their overtures.[26] In the poem, a cowboy takes his date to a restaurant whose menu lists "oysters" as one of its delicacies. Mistaking the euphemistically described testicles as real oysters, the woman engages the cowboy in a debate about how to gather, cook, and consume them, leading him unwittingly into a conversation with sexual overtones.

> The sign upon the cafe wall said OYSTERS: fifty cents.
> *"How quaint,"* the blue eyed sweetheart said, with some bewildermence,
> *"I didn't know they served such fare out here upon the plain?"*
> "Oh, sure," her cowboy date replied, "We're really quite urbane."
>
> *"I would guess they're Chesapeake or Blue Point, don't you think?"*
> "No m'am, they're mostly Hereford cross . . . and usually they're pink.
> But I've been cold, so cold myself, what you say could be true
> And if a man looked close enough, their points could sure be blue!"
>
> She said, *"I gather them myself out on the bay alone.*
> *I pluck them from the murky depths and smash them with a stone!"*
> The cowboy winced imagining a calf with her beneath
> "Me, I use a pocket knife and yank 'em with my teeth."
>
> *"Oh my,"* she said, *"You animal! How crude and unrefined!*
> *Your masculine assertiveness sends shivers up my spine!*
> *But I prefer a butcher knife too dull to really cut.*
> *I wedge it in on either side and crack it like a nut!*
>
> *I pry them out. If they resist, sometimes I use the pliers*
> *Or even Grandpa's pruning shears if that's what it requires!"*
> The hair stood on the cowboy's neck. His stomach did a whirl.
> He'd never heard such grisly talk, especially from a girl!
>
> *"I like them fresh,"* the sweetheart said and laid her menu down
> Then ordered oysters for them both when the waiter came around.
> The cowboy smiled gamely, though her words stuck in his craw
> But he finally fainted dead away when she said, *"I'll have mine raw!"*
> (*Croutons on a Cow Pie* 28)

The cowboy repeatedly attempts to assert himself sexually, but the woman staves off each advance that he makes. When she says that she would *"smash* [the oysters] *with a stone,"* the cowboy winces because he puts himself in the calf's place and identifies with the castrated victim: the woman's cracking the *"nut"* is the intended pun that drives this point home. As Oliver Nelson's book did, Black's poem portrays the cowboy as adhering to the time-honored notion that castrating cattle illustrates the cowboy's own hardihood. Hence his description of the castration act briefly impresses the woman with the cowboy's theoretical dominance: *"You animal! How crude and unrefined!/Your masculine assertiveness sends shivers up my spine!"* She sallies forth, however, metaphorically castrating her date by unknowingly describing the castration act and by making her escort faint dead away. Losing consciousness and command of his body is the cowboy's final sign of submission in a struggle that is variously represented as a seduction and disarming of each sex by the other.

In addition to exposing the cowboy's fear of castration, contemporary poems such as "The Oyster" reveal women's fears of being sexually overpowered by cowboys who castrate. Other recent events that have occurred in the West suggest that the cowboy's overpowering of women is simply a metaphor for his overthrow of all of noncowboy society. Castrating cattle gives men not only strength that they use to seduce decent women, but also power to "feminize" noncowboy society, weakening it and somehow making it vulnerable. In recent years, for example, the cattle industry has sought to improve the weight gain and carcass quality of stock that it sells to noncowboy beef-eating consumers, first by castrating the bull's organs and then by infusing its body with estrogenic and nonestrogenic chemical compounds.[27] These compounds are packaged as pellets that are implanted in the bull's ear[28] and designed to stimulate the pituitary gland, which produces somatotropin, the bull's natural growth hormone. The compounds enhance protein deposition, promote skeletal growth, and improve the quality of the animal's carcass by reducing its fat and increasing its leanness.

Consumer advocates fear that the results of this process will be passed on to them—that shoppers who buy beef will unsuspectingly eat meat with estrogen residue, slowly building up great amounts of it and finally manifesting side effects because of it, including the inhibition of "puberty in little boys" and the early breast development of "six year old girls."[29] If cowboys are empowered because of livestock castration, then noncowboy society is emasculated, abruptly feminized, or victimized because of it. *Victimized* is the right word to use, in that cowboys who castrate calves and then implant the pellets are portrayed as the equivalents of gunslinging killers. Cowboys are said to implant chemicals with pellet "guns" and to keep pellets in revolving gun "cartridges." Anchor, a company that supplies implanting equipment, describes its version as a "Magnum CP-20" or pellet gun. In livestock journals, it advertises that its weapon has a "pistol grip and low resistance trigger," which facilitates the deployment of pellets while maximizing "operator accuracy."[30] The cowboy not only castrates, but risks killing his victim, miming the threat that he poses to noncowboy society by brandishing a castrating "gun."[31]

Cowboys castrate a bull calf, eating its testicles and passing on the rest of its carcass to consumers in beef-eating noncowboy society. While consumers wonder whether the beef they eat has been tainted or rendered unclean, cowboys continue to savor the castrated organs that most noncowboys don't see and won't eat—remnants that seem to be more unclean than the meat that they purchase in stores. Even in the nineteenth century, a rancher was loathe to let a cowboy kill stock and eat beef that had come from his ranch. The XIT Ranch in Texas, for instance, once issued commandments stating what activities cowboys were not permitted to engage in at work. Rule 8 stated that the "killing of beef by any person on the ranch, except by the person in charge of the pasture, or under his instruction, is strictly forbidden," for killing stock reduced the size of the herd and diminished the profits that the rancher would reap when he sent the livestock to market. Testicles were removed before the steer went to auction, and, hence, they were given to those men who wanted them and who, in taking them, fulfilled the final clause of Rule 8—that no part of a cow could be eaten unless it could be "distributed and consumed without loss."[32]

Ranchers discouraged cowboys from manifesting aspects of maleness, isolating cowboys from women and preventing them from acting on the heterosexual impulses that one assumes existed, at least among some of them. Cowboys disguised other aspects of maleness, adopting names, roles, and costumes that did not tend to acknowledge homosexual and homoerotic behavior as forms of alternative, acceptable, conduct, but did serve to disguise men as women. Opposed to images of cowboys as eunuchs or women (mental pictures that surely strike us as odd) were equally radical portraits of cowboys as sexually engorged men who were anatomically larger than life. At the XIT Ranch in Texas and elsewhere, cowboys took the testicles that they cut off and ate and, while disseminating a castration myth, transformed the acts of castration and consumption into signs of their increased sexual stamina. As they took the cattleman's brand and translated his economic language of dominance into a myth of cowboy salvation and primacy, so the men now turned their isolation from—and their occasional equation with—women into an equally significant fiction of potency, mythologizing their self-representations of manhood.

II

Ironically, cowtowns, which depended for economic survival on sex acts taking place among animals—bulls breeding with and impregnating herds, which then reproduced and provided ranchers with new stock to send off to markets and auctions in cowtowns—nevertheless turned a collective blind eye to the fact that animal sex, reproduction, and pregnancy played roles in economically sustaining the human world. Influenced by Victorian notions of genteel decorum, the townspeople did all that they could to depict bulls as castrated entities. Brand books and newspapers, using pictures of cattle to illustrate the description and location of brands on a cattleman's livestock, refused to show organs on bulls or even udders on cows: they printed pictures of only nongendered stock, believing that depictions of an animal's external organs would somehow constitute a breach of decorum.[33] Citizens in Abilene, Kansas, even forced the proprietor of the Bull's Head Saloon to change the publicity for his establishment in 1869 and to alter his portrait of a "thoroughly masculine bull." At that time, Abilene was the northern terminus of the Chisholm Trail, and as such it expected to profit by the trade that developed as a result of the continued breeding and expansion of herds. Certain citizens, however, felt that the saloon's advertisement was an "insult to women" and a titillating means of inciting society's youth. They not only petitioned the owner to paint over the organs, but persuaded representatives of the Bull Durham Tobacco Company to change its logo by using a "fence plank to hide the testicles of their trademark printed on all packages of cigarette 'makings.'"[34]

Cowboys were perceived as threats to cowtowns such as Abilene. Castrating

α

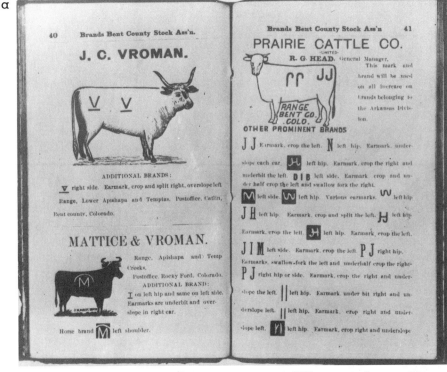

A nineteenth-century sense of propriety prevented Westerners from noting that livestock (and humans) had sex organs and gendered identities. (a) Colorado's Brands Bent County Stock Association (1885) and (b) Texas's Panhandle

bulls, overseeing the impregnation of cows, and attending at the breech birth of calves desensitized cowboys to graphic acts that horrified some of their noncowboy counterparts. Hence when ranch hands entered cowtowns on payday, they acted out their shed inhibitions and alleged barnyard mentalities, not only consorting with women, but sometimes making light of the "worshiped" female sex by scatalogically parading mock women in front of people, shocking onlookers and breaking safeguarded taboos. When he wrote *We Pointed Them North* (1939), E. C. Abbott acknowledged that he and other cowboys had put on displays of this sort in the late nineteenth century. In Miles City, Montana, for instance, they got drunk and ran down streets with women's stockings draped over their arms, scarves and jewelry wrapped around the brims of their hats, and petticoats drawn up over their pants (111–13). In a sense, they mocked the cowtown's attempt to hide and protect decent women from ranch hands by knocking women off their pedestals, bringing them out in the open, exposing and sometimes "undressing" them, and leading through town a procession that was both a licentious parade and an effigy.[35]

Cowboys were rarely given formal permission to meet "decent" women and mix with them. Often these encounters took place after the spring and fall roundups, when towns and ranches held dances to celebrate the rounding up, branding, and castration of cattle herds.[36] But instead of allowing unharnessed cowboys to mingle

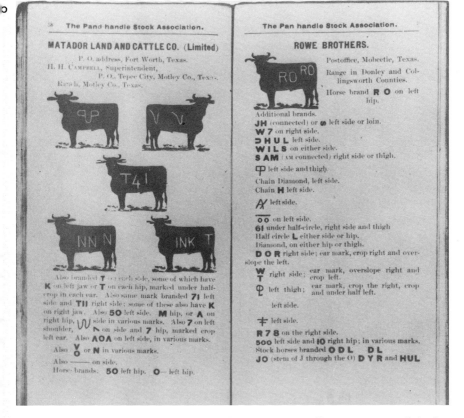

Stock Association (*1886*) *brand books show anatomically incorrect stock lacking penises and scrotums or udders. (Panhandle-Plains Historical Society, Canyon, Tex.)*

with women at will, dances supervised conduct between men and women and acted out moral constraints that kept loose cowboys from engaging in socially unacceptable forms of seduction and courtship.

Square dances were microcosms of cowtowns and, hence, means of reflecting by acting out cowtown "morality." In the nineteenth century, square dances competed in popularity with circle dances, longways dances such as the Virginia Reel, and round or couple dances such as the polka and waltz.[37] In *Cowboy Dances* (1948), Lloyd Shaw suggests that square dances evolved from Kentucky running sets, which migrated to the southern Appalachian Mountains from England, and from New England quadrilles, which passed over from England and France (27, 29). Like quadrilles, square dances were performed by four couples; as in running sets, the four couples moved according to the dictates of "callers" who choreographed the four couples' steps. Typically, dances were programmed to alternate between two square "sets" and one round or couple dance (70). As the waltz and polka fell out of favor, new versions of the couple dance, such as the one-step and fox-trot, came into fashion and replaced square dances as new crazes became popular (104).

*A square dance held after a roundup on the Mayfield Ranch, near Asper-
mont, Texas, circa 1927. A chuckwagon, a cook, and cowboys appear in the
background. (Photography Collection, Harry Ransom Humanities Research
Center, University of Texas at Austin)*

In their prime, however, square dances gave people a chance to gather in groups,
to reassemble microcosmic societies, and to reflect values acted on by macrocosmic
societies in daily life. Callers, singing or shouting out directives to dancers, drew on
language that listed rites and customs of social life. People formed squares by
joining in "couples" of two and then "groups" of four. Facing inward toward one
another, they turned their backs on the audience, creating little townships or neighborhoods. In the course of dancing, couples paid "calls" on one another, and when
they circled around, stepped toward, or paused by one another, they dramatized
what the caller called "visiting" (131, 138). When dancers returned to their places,
the caller said that they went "home" (136), and when they finished dancing, they
performed a step called the "balance home." Facing one another, they took four

*At the SMS Flat Top Ranch in Texas, circa 1930, dancers perform on a wagon
sheet while a guitarist and fiddler look on. (Photography Collection, Harry
Ransom Humanities Research Center, University of Texas at Austin)*

A diagram of a typical square, distinguishing the four ladies in relation to the first gentleman. (From Lloyd Shaw, Cowboy Dances. *Courtesy Enid Cocke, Lloyd Shaw Foundation, Inc., Manhattan, Kans.)*

steps backward and forward, and then met and turned (131, 136). Social equilibrium was established by balancing home: during dances, squares might collapse as each couple, together or separately, left home, paid visits, and exchanged rooted positions for free-floating movements. But returning home reconfirmed that social groups and homes could be reassembled intact, and that dancers would acknowledge their partners or mates as bound in some kind of union at the end of each dance.

Certain square dances seem to repudiate enactments of restricted social intercourse—depictions of controlled visits, stable homes, and monogamous male and female relationships. But dances that show a woman's leaving home to engage in promiscuous or adulterous behavior always end with examples of that woman's punishment. In "Adam and Eve," for example, a woman leaves her partner and goes to the couple on her right, swinging first the man, and then the woman; she proceeds to the next couple and continues to "swing" until she has engaged with all the other square dancers (228–29). As "Eve," she disobeys her "Adam," or mate, and exchanges her place in the Garden of Eden or sanctified home for an unrespectable role in the sinful outside environment. In "Old Arkansaw," the same basic movements lead to Eve's crashing Fall. After swinging the man on her right, she takes his "wife" and swings her as well. But in doing so she provokes the group's laughter. Shaw writes that the woman and her female partner incorrectly swing with each other because "neither lady knows which [one] will take the man's" lead (231). The women shake off their male partners' control, giving the rest of the square the right to laugh at, embarrass, and punish them. Female dancing is performed "for the sake of its comedy" (231), according to Shaw, and for the chance that it gives men to exercise dominance. For example, "Cheat and Swing" equates

Two women dance with each other during "Adam and Eve." (Lloyd Shaw, Cowboy Dances. Courtesy Enid Cocke, Lloyd Shaw Foundation, Inc., Manhattan, Kans.)

In "Cheat and Swing," a man cheats and swings with a homewrecker while his abandoned partner looks on. (Lloyd Shaw, Cowboy Dances. Courtesy Enid Cocke, Lloyd Shaw Foundation, Inc., Manhattan, Kans.)

swinging with cheating romantically. When an unattended loose woman comes to swing at his home, the man has the right either to swing with her or to send her home chastised and ungratified (233).

Men as well as women are punished in dances for flaunting morality, tradition, or etiquette. In "Bow and Kneel to That Lady," the caller tells the man to move to the home on his right, to bow and kneel to the woman who lives there, to swing and watch her "smile," and to swing and watch her "grin" again (234). Descended from French and English quadrilles, square dances preserve the flavor of medieval French and English romances and their notions of chivalry. Here the knight pursues a married and, hence, unattainable woman, kneeling with his "left hand on [his] heart" (235) and posing as a love-stricken suitor. Other dances, like "Honor That Lady," instruct men to act out their parts with "mock chivalry" (237), using comic gestures to manifest adultery as not only morally wrong, but ludicrous.

Dances lay bare taboos that people in daily life attempt to conceal. Hence callers prefer to force single-visit dances on men and women who have never performed them before: newcomers need to know what moral codes the rest of the social group values, so they submit to initiation rites that ridicule and punish them for transgressing those codes. Under these circumstances, unsuspecting men who "Honor That Lady" are "surprised and embarrassed" as newcomers "at having to bow again and again" and at having to court a woman outside the "home" while the rest of the group laughs at them. The men's "discomfiture" (237) assures other dancers that the men will not leave home and court other women again without thinking twice.

In spite of its socialness, square dancing seems somehow unintimate and even asexual, making any demonstration of desire seem inappropriate and therefore discomfiting. Unlike one-on-one dances, which permit men and women to pair off and

"Don't You Touch Her" suggests that there is nothing personal, intimate, or erotic about scenes of this sort. (Lloyd Shaw, Cowboy Dances. Courtesy Enid Cocke, Lloyd Shaw Foundation, Inc., Manhattan, Kans.)

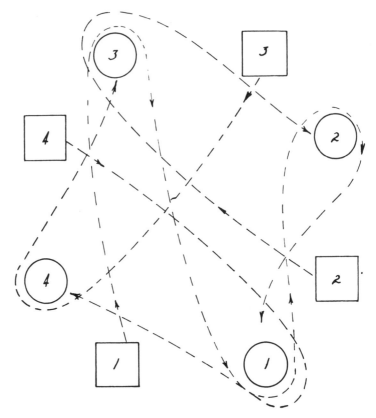

A diagram charting the movements of dancers in "Don't You Touch Her" indicates just how complex circumnavigation and noncontact can be. (Lloyd Shaw, Cowboy Dances. Courtesy Enid Cocke, Lloyd Shaw Foundation, Inc., Manhattan, Kans.)

cling to each other—to move slowly and romantically—square dances deny lingering contact and privacy, forcing partners to disperse themselves and to spread their energy among three other couples, all of whom skip around, establishing no more than temporary physical contact with others. "Don't You Touch Her," for instance, is like all other square dances in that it rules out expression and rewards men and women for resisting it. As they navigate quickly around other pairs in the square, the people "often almost touch finger tips, but are careful" not to do so until the end of the dance, when they grab the hands of their partners, "joyously" celebrating their "relief" at having safely returned "home" (246).

In the nineteenth century, square dances prevented contacts between men and women not only by ordering them not to touch or caress, but by turning certain men into women and by forcing these men to dance with other men instead of with women. Because men outnumbered women out West[38] and because cowboys enjoyed fewer social privileges than did wealthy, influential, and "respectable" cattlemen, cowboys often made up for the absence of women by wearing handkerchiefs (called "heifer brands") on their arms, posing as women with other cowboys in couples, and joining with other couples in square dances.[39] Cowboys were trans-

Because men outnumbered women out West, cowboys sometimes paired off with each other at "stag" dances. Scenes like this one, circa 1920, now seem shocking or camp. They were quite common, however, and were not thought of as manifestations of homosexual or homoerotic behavior. (Panhandle-Plains Historical Society, Canyon, Tex.)

A "stag" dance at a ranch, featuring men and boys of all ages. (Erwin E. Smith Collection of the Library of Congress on deposit at the Amon Carter Museum, Fort Worth, Tex.)

formed into nonmen, partly because they were economically and socially powerless. Commonly, bosses and ranch foremen made cowboys wear "heifer" (i.e., female) brands and ruffled skirts, which they borrowed from women, and made them act out in gendered disguises what they experienced, on ranches, as a denied access to power: cowboys took orders from men stationed above them and did as ranchers and foremen requested, both in square dances and at home on the ranch.[40] Voluntary cross-dressing, which occurred infrequently on ranges and ranches, became involuntary, mandated actions that more powerful men imposed on cowboys at regular intervals—at dances held after spring and fall roundups. Ranch hands could be expected not to threaten society—not to rabble-rouse in public or to compete for the one woman who existed for every four cowboys—if they were checked, held in place, and allowed to go through their paces only as nonmen in square dances.

Square dances sometimes referred to all men, not only cowboys, as castrated stock. In "The Old 'Square Dance' of the Western Range," for example, the dancers are described as a "herd," the women as "heifers," and the men as "steers," or castrated bulls: "All big steers do th' 'buck and wing,' / Young steers 'double shuffle.'"[41] The word *steer* often appears in calls for nineteenth-century dances like this one, suggesting that even though men took dance leads, escorting women through sets that callers announced, they still were not rendered as sexually aggressive, but as eunuchs whose unthreatening pursuit of the opposite sex took the form of politely expressed Victorian metaphors.

However, cowboys are more likely than other men to be excluded from dances and, in some cases, to be metaphorically castrated in fiction written by members of noncowboy society. When Colonel Lee Ripple dies in Zane Grey's *Knights of the Range* (1936), for example, his daughter, Holly, inherits his property, leaving her convent in New Orleans and coming out West to run Ripple's ranch. Knowing nothing about how to herd cattle, she hires a foreman named Renn and falls in love with him after he stops rustlers from making off with her animals. Her ranch hands are heartbroken: all these "knights of the range" seem to have crushes on Holly and hope to compete with Renn for some sign of affection by holding a barn dance and outdancing their rival in order to show Holly that her cowboys are more impressive than Renn. With "the music and the beating of time with hands and feet" calling him, Jackson flings himself into the "violent motion" of dancing; Mason follows, "bent upon out-doing" his cowboy competitor. Unfortunately, the dance exhausts Jackson; its "speed and fury" with centrifugal force spin out Mason, who falls on the floor (161) while Holly ignores both cowboys and dances with Renn.[42] Leaving the convent, she enters a world marked by sexual conquests, flirtations, and rivalries. Having scared off rustlers, Renn now holds other suitors at bay, not only dancing with Holly and romantically winning out over Jackson and Mason, but also using his office as foreman to illustrate his superiority over cowboys who work for him. His enhanced stature and heightened sense of virility both serve to intimidate the underlings Jackson and Mason, who slink off defeated and frustrated.

When the ranch hands return the next day to break a horse in the barnyard, Holly stays in the ranch house and looks out a window, watching them (187). The horse-taming episode comments on the dance scene that Grey puts before it. Having sought to displace Renn, Jackson and Mason now try to subdue and metaphorically castrate a stud horse: both attempts fail, for even though Jackson triumphs and stays on the horse, he cannot convince Holly to marry him. He will be the horse's master or its equal, but he will never be hers. His place is outdoors in the barn; her place is inside and upstairs, on the other side of a window, or invisible wall, through which she looks down on him.

Three years after Grey published *Knights of the Range,* Nathanael West wrote *The Day of the Locust* (1939) and continued the saga of cowboys, representing them as romantically dislodged and, in this novel, as almost literally castrated. Moving from the nineteenth to the twentieth century, and from the plains to the Pacific Coast, West focuses on Earle Shoop, a cowboy who has left Arizona and come to Hollywood, only to act bit parts in westerns and to fall in love with a would-be starlet named Faye. When his friend Miguel dances with Faye, Earle—unable to participate—looks helplessly on. Then he jumps up and does his own hoedown, whooping and clicking his heels in the air. But West writes that the cowboy cannot become "part of their dance," for its rhythm is "like a smooth glass wall," with Earle on one side and Faye and Miguel on the other (75). Both Grey and West use images of the "smooth glass wall" or window to indicate distance between women and cowboys who love them, and both writers follow up dance scenes with representations of castration that demonstrate the cowboys' sexual ineffectiveness. Earle later meets Faye and again tries to dance with her, but the midget Abe thwarts Earle by inserting himself between the cowboy and Faye.[43] In this scene, only the midget is more physically handicapped than cowboys like Earle. Abe repairs the difference, however, by almost literally castrating Earle—digging "upward with both hands," grabbing Earle in the groin, and causing him to scream and "sink to the floor" (129–30).

In their poems, cowboys sometimes portray themselves in the same way that noncowboy writers like Grey and West do—as nonpollinating wallflowers prevented from dancing and sexually coupling with women. For instance, Badger Clark's "The Bunk-House Orchestra" (1915) repeats scenes of castration first witnessed in late-nineteenth- and early-twentieth-century prose and poetry. Here ranch hands are portrayed as living in all-male bunkhouses—nonhomes for nonmen who can't mate, marry, and set up coed houses with hearths (48) that keep the home fires burning and that symbolize the satisfaction of blissful, conjugal relationships. When they go to town dances, they don't find women to mate with, but stay on the sidelines or play in the orchestra. One site (bunkhouses) stands in for the other one (orchestras): the first is on ranches outside town; the second, on the edge of the square dance's social group. According to Clark, men must "die or marry" (50)—remain unpartnered, unmarried men or find spouses and breed like bulls, acting out functions that "steers" (48), or metaphorically castrated cowboys, in this poem, are unable to. In another turn-of-the-century text, "A Dance at the Ranch," a cowboy hopes to find a woman to couple with, even though he fears touching her body and feeling her hair fall like "silken castigating whips" on his flesh when she lashes out, rejecting and cutting him (Lomax 117).

Instead of going to dances that society sponsored and setting himself up to be rejected by a woman who might not choose him over other male competitors, all of whom fought for the right to dance with her, a cowboy might go to a saloon and dance with a prostitute, then sneak off to a back room behind the saloon and sleep with her.[44] Unlike square dances, these dances were clearly preludes to inter-course—foreplay or occasions to work out financial terms of illicit transactions that took place afterward. Historical accounts of western saloon and brothel life often pay heed to the clothes that cowboys wore during dances with prostitutes, often because their equipment and clothes called attention to their "cowboyness" and quintessential maleness.[45] Cowtowns, for example, almost never let cowboys wear spurs during square dances: spurs projected from boots, tripping other dancers and endangering them.[46] However, these phallic extensions of "cowboyness" stayed on in brothels and made noise as ranch hands jumped up and down with loose women, jangling their spurs and visibly and audibly calling attention to tools that distin-guished them from men who worked in other professions. A perceived empower-ment in the workplace could also be seen as enhanced stature in sexual environ-ments, for as cowboys could use spurs to dominate horses and make horses herd cattle, so dancers could wear spurs to signify their conquests of women.[47] Hence brothels were sometimes called "ranches" or "hog ranches"[48] and envisioned as cowboylike settings where men could round up and harvest loose women, not stock.

In the West, human sexuality often represented itself animalistically. Castrating cattle, putting signs on buildings like the Bull's Head Saloon, stamping animal logos on packages of Bull Durham cigarettes, defining brothels as "ranches" and mem-bers of dance "herds" as bulls, steers, and heifers—these strange acts seem discreet but, at the same time, graphic indications that gendered identities and forms of sexual intercourse, or the respective fears of expressing and enacting them, con-cerned cowboys and noncowboys alike. What seem to be indirect metaphorical ways of representing and displacing gender and intercourse (by alluding to livestock on ranches, in advertisements in cowtowns, and in recreational pastimes like square dances and brothel visits) show themselves to be clearly noted and consciously acted out substitutes—signs for expressing out West what could not be stated explicitly, but what did, in fact, dominate many forms of discourse in various configurations of frontier society.

III

Early cowboys illustrated notions of manhood in nineteenth-century oral poems that, in many ways, were like oral texts that dance callers sang when citing men as castrated "steers."[49] Calls not only verbalized, but choreographed dancers to em-body abstract concepts of gender and assumptions about courtship that held sway in frontier society.[50] Cowboy oral and written poems, such as "The Bunk-House Orchestra" and "A Dance at the Ranch," performed the same functions, sometimes representing cowboys as castrated "steers," but also depicting these men as em-powered—not diminished—because of their separation from women during mixed cowboy and noncowboy gatherings.

"The Harrington Barn Dance," an anonymously composed nineteenth-century oral poem, portrays cowboys as set apart from society. Mat Miller plays "the fiddle," and Tom Kenyon calls the dance "sets"; but, like the ranch hands in "The Bunk-House Orchestra," neither man leaves the band or finds a female partner to frolic with (Lomax and Lomax 244–45). This segregation is phrased as a form of empowerment in "The Cowboy's Christmas Dance," an early-twentieth-century poem written by Bruce Kiskaddon. What is emphasized here is not the cowboy's sexlessness or his perceived femininity, conveyed by cross-dressing signs such as "heifer brands." Instead, muscularity (equated with masculinity) plays a role in deciding which cowboys go to the Christmas dance. Strong men who chop ice and feed stock are then permitted to leave the ranch, after doing chores, and to go to town, where they celebrate (Kiskaddon 34). At the Harrington barn dance, cowboys perform feats that are seen to be more important than dancing with women: they build the barn and drag the piano into it, creating an environment conducive to dancing and providing an instrument that makes music possible (Lomax and Lomax 244). Cowboy poets often acknowledge the historical fact that ranch hands did not always dance with women, but they sometimes refuse to state that not dancing makes cowboys less masculine. Men who do not dance are seen as indispensable parties who make the dance happen—not as participants, but as hardy attendants and musclemen.

These poems do not equate social isolation with metaphorical castration. They argue that tough guys don't dance. Cowboys demarcate privileged positions and set themselves off from the dance; if they do dance, they dance alone because partners of the "weaker" sex do not have the stamina to keep up with them. In "The Cowboy's Dance Song," an early-twentieth-century poem written by James Barton Adams, a cowboy breaks with the "aristocratic ranks" of society and shakes his "shanks" independently (Cannon 30). In order to escape the "huggamania pleasures of a high-toned dance," he wriggles out of the clutches of the "heifer" who hugs him, tells the band to speed up its tempo, and jumps about all by himself. The rafters and floor sag as he acts out his balletlike Bunyanesque pirouettes, causing the woman who pursues him to fall, admit defeat, and stagger to a seat on the sidelines. Scholarship indicates that cowboys at "stag parties" sometimes danced alone, as the ranch hand does here, "solo dancing," athletically competing for recognition of prowess, and working for the kind of attention that they were not apt to receive at mixed social gatherings.[51]

In certain poems, cowboys hook up with women, but when they do so (at dances or elsewhere) they represent themselves as controlling the unions between men and women: the men, not the women, choose partners to join with, forcing women to accept their decisiveness. Cowboys who court women conquer them, acting as competitively and aggressively as they do when they cast off women in other poems. In "The Peeler's Lament," an anonymously composed nineteenth-century oral poem, the cowboy compares subduing a woman to lassoing a calf with a rope and choking it (Lomax and Lomax 189). In *The Log of a Cowboy,* Andy Adams tries to account for this metaphor, arguing that ranch hands had not developed their sense of "the poetical . . . to an appreciative degree" and that they therefore sang about human subjects in poems as though they were "horses and cattle" (82): like all artists, cowboys sang only about what they knew, drawing on images in their environment when they composed cowboy poetry. Hence they moved in their poems from unfamiliar realms of courtship and romance to more familiar settings of ranches and range life, translating their infrequent encounters with women into recognizable portraits of western labor experiences. If one accepts Adams's hypothesis, then such poems as "The Peeler's Lament" somehow transform themselves into heartfelt, albeit awkwardly rendered, expressions of tenderness.

So frequently do cowboys equate rough stock with women that occasionally one cannot ascertain which is which. For example, in "The Cowboy's Life," attributed to the early-twentieth-century poet James Barton Adams, the speaker says that

> . . . his jolly songs
> Speed him along,
> As he thinks of the little gal
> With golden hair
> Who is waiting there
> At the bars of the home corral.
>   (Lomax and Lomax 281)

Throughout the poem, it remains unclear whether a horse with a light-colored mane or a woman with blond hair waits for him. Will he ride a horse when he comes home or make love with a woman and ride her to climax? Such necessary questions are answered in other poems. "Bucking Bronco" (ca. 1878), for instance, makes no bones about it and shows breaking livestock to be more than a metaphor for quaint bestiality.

> My love is a rider, wild broncos he breaks,
> Though he's promised to quit it, just for my sake
> He ties up one foot, the saddle puts on,
> With a swing and a jump he is mounted and gone.
>
> The first time I met him, 't was early one spring,
> Riding a bronco, a high-headed thing.
> He tipped me a wink as he gayly did go,
> For he wished me to look at his bucking bronco.
>
> The next time I saw him, 't was late in the fall,
> Swinging the girls at Tomlinson's ball:
> He laughed and he talked as we danced to and fro,—
> Promised never to ride on another bronco.
>
> He made me some presents, among them a ring;
> The return that I made him was a far better thing;
> 'T was a young maiden's heart, I'd have you all know
> He'd won it by riding his bucking bronco.
>
> Now, all you young maidens, where'er you reside,
> Beware of the cowboy who swings the rawhide,
> He'll court you and pet you and leave you and go
> In the spring up the trail on his bucking bronco.
>   (Thorp 14–15)

Although N. Howard Thorp confessed that he had expurgated the poem before publishing it in 1908 (14), he still did not manage to rid it of its ribald suggestiveness. In this poem, the female narrator meets a cowboy while he is riding a "bronco" and later sees him swinging "girls at Tomlinson's ball." His dancing with women is just like his breaking of livestock; his breaking of stock is just like his quick, acrobatic love-making with women, for in each instance he "ties up one foot, the saddle puts on, / With a swing and a jump he is mounted and gone" (15). Thorp attributes the poem to Belle Starr,[52] a woman, but includes it in a collection of cowboy songs. In fact, few nineteenth-century women composed cowboy poems or, if they did, their works were deemed not to be good enough to merit inclusion in anthologies assembled by early-twentieth-century folklorists such as John Lomax and N. Howard Thorp. If Thorp is correct in attributing "Bucking Bronco" to Starr, he is therefore likely to have printed it only because it reinforced, rather than contradicted, poems that depicted cowboys as robust conquerors, sexually expending themselves in ways that could best be expressed by bronc-riding metaphors. As the last section of this chapter indicates, women almost never portrayed themselves as enjoying these kinds of rambunctious relationships (making Thorp's claims of authorship suspect at best). This poem seems in sync with other songs in the cowboy tradition, however, in that it imagistically mirrors and tonally echoes them.

In cowboy poems dancing, flirting, or sleeping with women is one thing; marrying them is something else, not a prospect that cowboys relish with glee, as a verse from an anonymously composed nineteenth-century oral poem, "The Range Riders," indicates. The poet says that you "cowboys" can

> . . . roam this world over, and do just as you will,
> Hug and kiss pretty girls and be your own still.
> But when you get married, boys, you are done with this life,
> You have sold your sweet comfort for to gain you a wife.
> (Lomax and Lomax 186)

Tonal shifts take place when cowboys switch from boasting about sexual conquests to lamenting permanent unions with women. Both marrying women and not being able to marry them are causes for Hamlet-like brooding. The ominous forewarning in "The Range Riders" reminds ranch hands that marriage represents loss of freedom and servitude. Other poems state that not being married means not being able to exercise freedom—not being able to choose whom to marry, but being rejected by women who choose to wed more desirable noncowboy suitors. For instance, in "The Trail to Mexico," another nineteenth-century oral poem, a cowboy is hired to drive a cattleman's livestock to Mexico. In his absence, his girlfriend leaves him and marries a businessman. The poem moves back and forth, narrating two stories, both of which portray the cowboy as expendable. The rancher, not the cowboy, profits when the cowboy drives the rancher's livestock to market; the businessman also benefits, stepping in, courting, and finally wedding the woman, now that the cowboy has left and taken the livestock to Mexico. The cowboy's subordinate economic status in the first story plays a role in the second one, influencing the woman to marry the businessman, who can offer her a "richer life" than the cowboy can (Lomax and Lomax 55).

The cowboy can marry a woman only by becoming like the businessman-cattleman. In "The Cowboy's Valentine," for example, the ranch hand claims a woman by branding her:

Yo' savvy who I'm runnin' so,
Yo' savvy who I be;
Now, can't yo' take that brand—yo' know,—
The ♥ M-I-N-E.

(Lomax 76)

The cowboy is a cattleman now, in that he owns the brand and everything (including the woman) that wears the brand, as the possessive adjective (''M-I-N-E'') signifies. Possession is nine-tenths of the love, so to speak, for men who own cattle are in better positions to court women and to use their wealth to provide their wives with financial security. At the same time, wives become chattel—something else that men dominate. In such love poems, cowboys stop reading brands as signs of Christian salvation and, like cattlemen, start reading them as mere signs of ownership. In ''The Cowboy and the Maid,'' for instance, the narrator plans to give up cowboy life and buy his own property, making the transition from cowboy to cattleman. After staking out land and purchasing cattle, he looks for a woman to top off his shopping spree. The woman he marries must ''ornament'' his cattle ranch, wearing his ''brand'' and comporting herself as though she were not only his wife, but his most valued possession (Lomax 63). It is easy to become swept up by the logic of metaphor and to think of brands as quaint wedding rings that men give to women, for in cowboy love poems the branding metaphor operates so frequently that it manages to escape its physical referent and to associate itself only with abstract conventions of poetry. Charmed by the marriage trope, readers tend to forget that it refers back to the very real acts of burning and inscribing skin, making men masters of women's flesh. Poems in which cowboys marry and poems in which cowboys sexually conquer women without wedding them therefore exhibit the same strategies: marriage poems such as ''The Cowboy's Valentine'' and ''The Cowboy and the Maid'' show cowboys subordinating and branding wives; conquest poems such as ''The Peeler's Lament'' show cowboys roping, choking, and subduing them. Both kind of poems privilege male notions of female submission and servitude.

Cowboy poems have a history of representing relationships between men and women as struggles between rivals, each of whom uses a metaphor taken from cowboy life to act out his or her dominance. Men brand, rope, and choke women; women metaphorically castrate men by denying them access to some form of their work culture. In ''The Married Man'' (1915), for instance, Badger Clark's cowboy sets up house, stops reciting ''restless'' songs of the ''heart,'' and starts listening to ''slow little'' songs that his wife sings instead (81). In ''The Bunk-House Orchestra,'' Clark defines unmarried men as castrated ''steers.'' Here, he indicates otherwise. ''The Married Man'' portrays the cowboy as artistically castrated. Forced to cease singing, he no longer glorifies male independence and restlessness—trademarks of roaming cowboys on horseback. He stops singing, as nineteenth-century cowboys who participated in an oral culture were wont to do, and sits back and listens to songs that his wife, a ''tired woman,'' sings about weary domestic life (81).

In prose, as well as in poetry, cowboys are sometimes inclined to view marriage as some kind of artistic castration. *We Pointed Them North*, for example, recounts E. C. Abbott's life as a cowboy and ends with a description of his marriage to the daughter of Granville Stuart, the well-known cattleman: "And that in a way writes the end to the story of my life on the open range, because from now on I wasn't a cowpuncher any more. I took a homestead, kept milk cows and raised a garden" (207). Marriage represents, if not artistic castration, then closure: it cuts off narration and ends the text, leaving the speechless Abbott with nothing left to write about. As "The Married Man" forces the cowboy to relinquish artistic control and to let his wife take up singing, so in this book Abbott turns his text over to Helena Huntington Smith. In the late nineteenth and early twentieth centuries, formally uneducated and semiliterate cowboys were sometimes deemed unable to express themselves with the clarity and propriety of experienced professional writers, who often took over and edited cowboy manuscripts—censoring, shaping, and even rewriting them.[53] Smith, for example, admits in her introduction that she took written fragments and verbal anecdotes that Abbott had offered her, excising salty remarks that the author had made, arranging what was left of the text in rough chronological order, and emphasizing dramatic passages that she thought would appeal to a noncowboy readership. After he married, Abbott recovered his "cowboy" voice to the extent that he was able to look back and write about his past retrospectively. But as with being married, being matched with an editor meant that Abbott could not continue or control his text after uniting himself with a noncowboy editor.

The cowboy's self-representations were often as complexly rendered as noncowboy society's figurations of cowboys in the late nineteenth and early twentieth centuries. Cowboys responded to the square dance's use of "heifer-branded" cowboys as "women," on the one hand, and to its images of cowboys as castrated "steers," on the other, by presenting themselves in various ways in their literature. At different points in their prose and poetry, cowboys suggested that men who did not dance were stronger, more muscular, and therefore more masculine than noncowboy square dancers. Cowboys who chose to dance or to "couple" with women outside the dance (in any sense of that word) did so by physically overpowering and conquering women by means of their perceived strength and stamina. Their seemingly unromantic—even antagonistic—attitudes toward the opposite sex were often motivated by their fears of being rejected by the women they flirted with and, at the same time, of being "castrated" by the women they married or cut off from cowboy life and forced to give up privileges and freedoms conferred on them by bachelorhood. Cowboys therefore responded to women by metaphorically branding, roping, and choking them; they depicted love–hate relationships in poetry, romantically courting and physically torturing women whom they both desired and feared.

IV

A perceived diminishing or disguising of the male sex took place when cowboys entered noncowboy societies: in mixed cowboy and noncowboy gatherings such as square dances, diminishment was acted out as livestock castration and disguises were adopted during cross-dressing rituals. When women who lived in noncowboy societies entered all-male cowboy groups, they also found that their gender disadvantaged them.

Even today, the fact that women seldom write cowboy poems indicates that they continue to encounter obstacles in nearly all-male cowboy groups. Outnumbered by men in cowboy workplaces, women also find that their voices are drowned out by men who write cowboy poetry, a genre that for more than a hundred years has been considered a form of all-male discourse. In "Bellerin' and Bawlin'" (1985), for instance, Linda Ash wonders why she has agreed to help cowboys round up stock at a cattle ranch. Unlike cowboys who perform important surgical tasks like castrating cattle, Ash only nurses, mopping up blood and smearing salve on dehorned and castrated cattle in order to prevent their wounds from developing infectious diseases. In addition to being pushed away from the operating table and physically marginalized, Ash feels aurally assaulted by bleating, castrated calves and by men who laugh and "cuss and swear," working to exclude her while engaging in exclamatory male discourses that muffle her (Cannon 116).

Outnumbered, women sometimes defer to men, hoping that not threatening men will enable women to receive men's protection and tolerance.[54] The author of one of the most widely read and critically acclaimed accounts of a western woman's experience, for example, defers to men by using this strategy. In her memoirs, Agnes Morely Cleaveland refers to her success in life as proof that women can prosper out West. At the same time, she demurs in her title and states that her life is *No Life for a Lady* (1941). In textual asides, she repeatedly reminds readers that a woman is "unable successfully to cope" (37) with demands made on her in the process of running a cattle ranch. "What does Susan B. Anthony know about the cow business?" (97) her brother jokes, mocking his mother's protofeminist efforts to manage a ranch without a husband's help. Cleaveland gives her jeering brother something to crow about, admitting that her "physical limitations" (127) prevent her from aiding her mother effectively. When "it came to the actual applying of a hot iron to sentient flesh, I couldn't do it" (110), she concedes, indicating that branding is no task for young girls whose nerves are too fine-strung and delicate. Unequipped to do ranch work, women are also unable to write about ranch life convincingly. Cleaveland heaps scorn on a lady novelist who commits the cardinal sin of confusing a steer with a "robust young bull" (273); then in the next chapter, Cleaveland gazes critically at her own allegedly feeble fiction. Unlike books written by the now well-known author Eugene Manlove Rhodes, Cleaveland's short stories are "mere yarns," not "literature." After reading Rhodes's work, she gives up writing, feeling that her stories "could never hope to compete" with his masterfully rendered, more authentic depictions of cowboy life (286).

Instead of competing with male writers, some women reconnoiter literary landscapes that cowboys and cattlemen seldom investigate. Looking at the West as alien outsiders, these women write about fragile lives that hang in the balance, poised on precarious margins and borders. In *The Land of Little Rain* (1903), for example, Mary Austin examines a fence on a cattle range: "along its fifteen miles of posts one could be sure of finding a bird or two in every strip of shadow: sometimes the sparrow and the hawk, with wings trailed and beaks parted, drooping in the white truce of noon" (15–16). Instead of noticing what lives *on* the border, one tends to look only at what exists on each *side* of the border that a barbed-wire fence demarcates—at land and the cattle that graze on it, parceled in fenced-off enclosures. The barbed-wire fence, which plays such a large role in the world of cowboys and cattlemen, instead of wounding livestock, here shelters lesser-known animals. Austin selects and poetically commemorates creatures whose tenuous existences are testified to by the fact that they live, according to delicate truces, on strips or in shadow worlds. Elsewhere in her text, a water hole sustains not only cattle, but mice, grasshoppers, lizards, and other "small" desert insects and animals (38). Only once does Austin mention vaqueros or cowboys (36), reminding us instead that cowboys, cattle, and cattlemen all too often claim our attention and cause us to overlook smaller environments, filled with organisms struggling against man-made and climatic conditions that mathematically decrease their odds of surviving in hostile and hot arid deserts. Ranchers transform the land into a "recruiting ground" for their "bellowing" cattle herds (126–27), while Austin turns the cattle kingdom into smaller principalities, each of which harbors its own distinct populace.

Elinore Pruitt Stewart intensifies this kind of female vision, inserting herself in her narrative and replacing Austin's omniscient third-person voice with Stewart's firsthand female perspective on western life. *Letters of a Woman Homesteader* (1914) chronicles Stewart's life after her husband dies, leaving her widowed and forced to support her daughter, Jerrine, by taking in laundry. Later, Stewart and her daughter leave Denver and move to Wyoming to keep house for an unmarried rancher. Exchanging the bucket and scrub brush of an urban female domestic for the liberating compass and pack horse of a roaming frontier homesteader, Stewart begins writing about her outdoor excursions—her encounters with sheepherders (8, 42), her experience at a roundup with cowboys (164–74), and her overland journeys to newfound friends in distant parts of Wyoming. With a pioneer's spirit, Stewart resurrects herself, describing how ranching fosters independence and nurtures her repaired sense of self-worth. Unlike cowboys, Stewart never feels "homesick" (170), glad to be working outdoors, free of domestic chores. She compares cowboys to truculent, "sleepy-headed" (174) boys who have just gotten up from their naps, rubbed their eyes with their fists, and stumbled out into the living room in their pajamas, looking for mother-love. Stewart treats them like children who need supervised guidance, bringing them into her house to wait on her table (58) while she goes outdoors to tend her garden, milk cows, and plow fields. Instead of relying on cowboys or even on the rancher who hires her, she ends the book having proved that women homesteaders can learn self-sufficiency: "I have tried every kind of work this ranch affords, and I can do any of it. Of course I *am* extra strong, but those who try know that strength and knowledge come with doing. I just love to experiment, to work, and to prove out things, so that ranch life and 'roughing it' just suit me" (282).

Stewart's first appearance out West, in the guise of a hard-working maidservant, seemed to belie the fact that she would one day conquer the ranching world, casting her apron off, rolling her sleeves up, and setting out to work side by side with cowboys and cattlemen. In the late nineteenth and early twentieth centuries, some women entered all-male work groups already dressed as men, tricked out in costumes that made their transitions into western life easier. Mrs. E. J. Guerin, for instance, wrote that she assumed the name Mountain Charley, cross-dressed, and worked as a cattle rancher, railroad brakeman, and miner.[55] Unlike Stewart's book,

α

*Women adapted to western life differently, sometimes distinguishing them-
selves from men in the workplace and sometimes blending in with all-male
groups. (a) A woman ropes stock on a Colorado ranch in 1903, riding sidesaddle and wearing a dress. (b) One of the few known photographs of Martha*

Mountain Charley (1861) reads more like a dime novel than a factual historical
narrative: avoiding flat and natural notes, it hits every sharp key, running up and
down the scale of sentimentality, melodrama, and luridness, performing a literary
arpeggio in sensational forte. Her husband's murder provides Guerin with a pretext
for cross-dressing. Disguised as a gunslinger, Guerin sets out to track down the man
who killed her husband (18), but then seems to lose sight of her purpose and starts
wearing men's clothes simply because her "new [male] character" gives her "freedom" to come and go as she pleases (22). Abandoning the goal of finding her
husband's unavenged killer, she takes assignments working with men, all of whom
mistake her for one of their own. Deciding to pan for gold, for instance, she travels
with sixty men to California and secretly writes about her trip in her diary. On June
3, 1855, she notes that the water is "fine . . . antelopes plenty" (38); on June 22,
she marvels that the "high, rockey and clayey hills" that she passes through rise up
like "grotesque cities" (42); and on July 3, she exclaims: "Cold, with west wind
which feels as if it came from snow. Scenery here magnificent beyond all conception" (44). Paradoxically, becoming part of a *male* world helps Guerin find her
female voice and identity. No longer striking the false notes of the dime novel's
music, she writes realistically, describing the landscape authentically, as only a
firsthand observer would be able to. Only as a "man" can she pan for gold and have
access to scenic landscapes that all-male mining groups wander through. But, at the

Jane Canary (1850?–1903), alias Calamity Jane, now famous partly because of her habit of wearing men's clothes. (Panhandle-Plains Historical Society, Canyon, Tex.)

same time, being disguised as a man makes her more aware of her tenuous place in an all-male group and more attuned to her otherness. Two years later, she returns to California with fifteen men, driving a cattle herd (54). Now more sympathetically attuned to women who struggle to survive in hostile environments, she writes about coming across the emaciated remains of a woman and the carcass of a cow that the woman had apparently tried to drive through the desert (50–51). Finding a woman who has died attempting to do what Guerin does inspires Guerin to pause and to commemorate women whose presences out West, like her own disguised features, go unnoticed—expressed only by this female skeleton and the absence it signifies.

If cowboys cross-dress as women when they enter noncowboy society, then women like Guerin disguise themselves as men when they leave noncowboy society, assimilating or searching for places in all-male cowboy groups. Guerin, on the one hand, sees cross-dressing both as a handicap and as a source of empowerment. Some male writers, on the other hand, view a woman's cross-dressing only as a feeble antidote for curing (by disguising) symptoms of womanhood. Emerson Hough's *North of 36* (1923), for example, makes light of Taisie Lockhart's cross-dressing. In order to prove herself as an equal to cowboys, Taisie stops riding sidesaddle, puts on pants, and goes on a cattle drive. Hough, alas, exposes Taisie's femaleness and feebleness: Taisie's hat flies off, her clothes get caught in the crotch of her saddlehorn, and everyone quickly discerns that this is no working cowboy. Helpless, she relies on the foreman to manage the cattle herd, hoping (in between stampedes, lightning storms on the prairie, and quick-draws with rustlers) that the cute Texas Ranger, whom she has her eye on, will marry her. Reading *North of 36* is like watching a Shakespearean comedy. A boyish-looking man turns out to be a cross-dressing woman, whose presence on stage sets in motion awkward romantic predicaments and sexual double entendres. Taisie's disguising herself as a man is a clearly doomed strategy. As an undisguised woman, she would never have to say: "I am a woman." As a camouflaged woman, however, she risks being discovered and having to say: *"I am not a man,"* perhaps the worst thing in this novel that one can say about women. Her futile attempts to imitate men make Taisie Lockhart seem all the more pathetic and ludicrous.

In novels written by men, women who assume cowboy functions almost always risk discovery and ridicule. *Even Cowgirls Get the Blues* (1976), by Tom Robbins, seems to deny—even though the novel finally exposes—this tendency. Lesbian cowgirls work at the Rubber Rose Ranch, in their off-hours engaging in group sex and bonding in other (often comic) expressions of sisterhood. Feminism and lesbianism, however, are nothing more than garden paths that misguided cowgirls on horseback walk, trot, and canter down, as they search in the 1970s for women's support groups to help them cope with "male hegemony" and other equally tongue-tripping rhetorical tag phrases. According to Bonanza Jellybean, the women's ringleader, true cowgirls are not really lesbians: they sleep with each other only because "every eligible male's been scared away" from the Rubber Rose Ranch (180). Same-sex relations are like a baby's first steps. Like learning to crawl before walking, "women have got to love women before they can start loving men again" (279). Lesbian sex is therefore nonthreatening; it simply leads up to the heterosexual "real" thing and, as foreplay to that act, seems somewhat erotic. Hence Robbins never misses a chance to describe women performing cunnilingus under cherry trees, exchanging soulful French kisses on horseback, and coming at the same time in bunkbeds that sway back and forth, squeaking and groaning orgasmically. As author, narrator, and character (his alter ego, Doctor Robbins, appears in the novel and comments on its action extensively), Robbins directs his triple gaze at cowgirls on the Rubber Rose Ranch. As a character, (Doctor) Robbins finally has intercourse with one of these women; as an omniscient narrator (he can see them, but they can't see him), Tom Robbins almost masturbates as he spectates, voyeuristically watching cowgirls express themselves sexually and making lascivious comments about these acts in asides to assumed male readers, who look over the narrator's shoulder and who turn the novel into an exercise of reading-as-gang-bang. The laughter generated by Robbins's rollicking and, in many ways, big-hearted comedy drowns out the fact that cowgirls are not the source of jokes, but the butt of them. Taking *North of 36* many steps farther, *Even Cowgirls Get the Blues* exposes, ridicules, and almost rapes women, defining "lesbian" cowgirls not as wanna-be men, but as women who need men and who get what they need without knowing it, unsuspiciously stripping for Peeping Tom Robbins.[56]

His novel seems like a male heterosexual's lesbian fantasy—a funny, well-written *Hustler* centerfold—compared with a real-life account of frontier life as described by Judy Grahn, a lesbian essayist. Unlike Bonanza Jellybean, her fictional nemesis, Grahn is a committed lesbian and a none-too-thrilled observer of male western rituals such as rodeo.[57] In "Boys at the Rodeo" (1981), she explains how she and her lesbian friends once sneaked into a rodeo when its ticket taker mistook them for "boys" wearing pants, T-shirts, and hair cropped close to their scalps. Once inside the boy's club, Grahn notices that the club honors bronc riders, bull doggers, and calf ropers for practicing "horse*man*ship," but overlooks women who ride in only one event, the "girl's" barrel race (130–31). The only way to get men's attention is by competing for "queen" in a contest that makes women put on brightly colored polyester pantsuits, fit rhinestone tiaras around the brims of their hats, wear white gloves, and ride around waving to sticky-fingered, cotton-candy eating spectators in grandstands (132). Grahn walks away from this nightmare, only to enter into another scene that brings home the first one's reality. Watching a cowboy rope his girlfriend, throw her, and hog-tie her, reenacting what relations between the sexes out West really constitute, Grahn almost crosses herself, as though warding off evil, and vows: "oh how much I do not want to be her; I do not want to be the conquest of the West" (135). A hundred-year-old tradition embodies itself in the mud, right at Grahn's feet. Nineteenth-century cowboy poems such as "The Peeler's Lament," which show cowboys roping and choking women into submission; twentieth-century novels written by noncowboy authors, which show men subordinating and disparaging women in the process of committing other but equally disturbing atrocities; and all other historical or fictional acts that take place during this hundred-year history crystallize in the image of one woman, bound by a rope and forced to lie on the ground, prone on her stomach.

During this hundred-year history, men and women represented but at the same time confused gender, alternately revealing, concealing, and metaphorically castrating themselves and each other while role-playing, acting out functions conferred on them by heterosexuality, homosexuality, cross-dressing, and castration. On the one hand, cowboys saw themselves as castrated: their living in physically isolated all-male groups that cut them off from women, forced them to abstain from engaging in intercourse, and kept them from marrying and setting up homes in noncowboy society seemed to express itself in the language of square dancing, which defined men as "steers" who could not set up "homes." On the other hand, cowboys perceived themselves as virile men who castrated bulls and ate castrated testicles. Consuming these organs, increasing their physical strength, and enhancing their sexual potency, cowboys then conquered women, either by dancing with and athletically besting them or by metaphorically roping, choking, and subduing members of the opposite sex in their poetry.

Self-representations were nothing more than self-contradictions. In historical accounts of range life, as well as in poetry, cowboys not only portrayed themselves as lasso-roping lotharios and, at the same time, as castrated eunuchs, but also defined themselves as men and, at the same time, as women. Chuckwagon cooks were "old ladies" as well as male authority figures whose providing of food and keeping of medicine enabled them to wield more power and command higher wages than ranch hands. Cowboy "girls," on the contrary, rounded up, branded, and castrated rough stock, acting out grueling "macho" assignments that cooks or "old ladies" were too old, weak, and feeble to execute.

Men competed with women, as well as with other men, for the right to claim dominance. In the world of labor, Ora Haley, J. S. Hoy, and Ann Bassett fought over cattle, illustrating each sex's effort to castrate the rival sex. In the world of leisurely pastimes, not labor, each sex also tried to deny, conceal, or otherwise suppress the presence of the other. Men at square dances involuntarily isolated themselves, neutered themselves, or cross-dressed as women, while women at rodeos competed in marginal events such as the girl's barrel race, submitted to being roped and choked on the fairgrounds, or involuntarily (unwittingly) disguised themselves as "boys," as they did when Judy Grahn and her butch-looking friends went to a rodeo. Whether they unknowingly confounded the perception of gender in the world of leisurely pastimes or voluntarily cross-dressed in the world of labor, as Mountain Charley did when she went on a cattle drive, women—like cowboys— either obfuscated their gendered identities or protested, but submitted to having their identities diminished or castrated. Hence the significance of what Ann Bassett did in 1911, when she took the witness stand in court and defended her right to ranch livestock—a right that had suddenly been called into question by the unexplained presence, in her supply room, of a symbolic spayed heifer.

CHAPTER THREE

DUAL/DUELING IDENTITIES
Rustlers and Cowboy Detectives

I

On its way to Count Dracula's castle, Jonathan Harker's train stops at a station. While looking at the Transylvanian peasants on the train station's platform, Harker sees the Slovaks and describes them as a group of "harmless" barbarians, wearing boots and "cow-boy" hats on their heads (Stoker 3). Later he learns that the "harmless" cowboys work for the count and that they have shipped him in his coffin to England (45–46, 55), where Dracula plans to infect new victims and establish a new kingdom of slaves.

Bram Stoker's novel includes this reworking of the cowboy castration myth. Initially that myth enabled the cowboy to explain his isolation from women as a manifestation of his sexual empowerment. But as the castration myth moves from the poetry and prose of the cowboy to the text of the square dance, it evolves into a dramatization of the worker as a predatory castrator, to be displaced and castrated by others. As it travels from popular American dance into transatlantic Victorian fiction, the myth again exposes the cowboy as a dangerous sexual threat and links him with representations of evil, supernatural lust. *Dracula* (1897) continues to trace a conflict that first appears in western recreational pastimes, for, like the people who seek to exclude the cowboy from society's square dance, Jonathan Harker tries to prevent the count from leaving his legion of cowboys, from crossing the borders of England, and from seducing and killing its women.

Phenomenological studies of the cowboy in his literature, in society's traditional dances, and here, in the Victorian novel, suggest that the count, like the cowboy, translates the ritual consumption of the body into a sign for the sexual act. The cowboy eats the bull's testicles not only to sate his physical hunger, but to sustain his sex drive; the count stalks his female prey both to drink her blood—or to satisfy his physical cravings—and to do so by committing an act that indirectly constitutes rape. The count invests his cowboys with the capacity to seduce and consume their own victims, and he displays a sign of this capacity on the workers' external bodies. For instance, Jonathan Harker assumes that one of the Slovaks suffers from "goitre" (8), but the swelling on the cowboy's neck indicates that the count has bitten and empowered him, allowing the cowboy-cum-vampire to prey on women, like his master Count Dracula.

Dracula's leaving the cowboy group, or the neighborhood that harbors the Slovaks, and entering England enable Stoker not only to comment on Victorian sexual taboos and hysterics, but also to focus on xenophobic reactions that the appearance of "foreign" outsiders elicit. In moving from Transylvania to England, the count threatens to pollute a domestic, politically democratic, and racially homogeneous island with a member of a sexually promiscuous, traditionally autocratic, and discernibly foreign family of vampires. Like the cowboys, the "gipsies" (43) who camp outside the castle share Count Dracula's compulsion to "drift." Traveling in caravans from campsite to campsite, and skirting the borders of civilization, the Transylvanian gypsies objectify Count Dracula's invisible movement and his status as a drifting social outsider. His trait of evaporating from sight and reintroducing himself in a new place, and his tendency—in his coffin—to carry his dirt or ground with him suggest that the Count can invade another culture while keeping with him and preserving a piece of his origins.

The cowboy shares this drifting tendency and liminal status with the count and his gypsies.[1] Unlike blacks on plantations, Indians on reservations, and other politically disenfranchised or culturally marginal groups, the cowboy tended in the nineteenth century not to be bound by a specific American place, but to filter through the space of an open frontier. After grazing wandering herds on the range, the cowboy drove them to market, where he auctioned off the cattleman's stock. As he rode up the Texas Road or the Shawnee Trail through Oklahoma and into Missouri, up the Jones and Plummer Trail from Kansas to Nebraska and Wyoming, up the California Trail through Arizona, up the Oregon Trail through Idaho, and up the Goodnight-Loving Trail to New Mexico and Colorado, the cowboy enacted his itinerant, physical function by constantly crisscrossing the landscape.[2]

Frequently the cattleman fired his cowboys when they had completed their drive, for having auctioned off the cattle at a terminus point or having sold and shipped the stock to a meat-packing plant, he had no more use for expendable seasonal workers. An unemployed cowboy often drifted through the winter and returned to a ranch in the spring. In the summer and fall he continued to brand, castrate, and tend new stock on the range. But in the winter he wandered alone, riding from town to town in search of entertaining distractions, from ranch to ranch in need of employment and shelter, or from herd to herd in pursuit of livestock to rustle and eat. Stopping temporarily in cowtowns during the course of a trail drive and drinking or disturbing the peace, appearing in public on payday with prostitutes and with menacing loaded revolvers in hand, or stealing unbranded cattle while drifting from pasture to pasture, the cowboy convinced the cowtowns' citizens and their outlying cattlemen neighbors that drifting employed and unemployed nomadic frontiersmen were potential criminal threats. Like vagabonds, they destabilized settlements and stole from wealthy, landowning former employers in their depravity, desperation, or hunger.

Western communities defined cowboys as social and economic disturbances, and even as sexual deviants, by comparing them to vampirelike entities. On July 20, 1881, for instance, the Philadelphia *Times* reported that a man had encountered Billy the Kid on the New Mexico plains, where he lived with loose women in an adobe castlelike fortification. The man told the Philadelphia reporter that the cowboy's lips were "thin and his upper lip . . . short; two sharp, fierce-looking teeth, much longer than any others in his head, grew out from under that upper lip" and seemed to symbolize Billy the Kid's potential for savagery.[3] Like Count Dracula, the cowboy drifted into and preyed on society: he appeared as a deviant, surrounded by women who were sexually enslaved to their master, and as a misfit who economically and socially preyed on civilization by robbing and killing its citizens.

Bram Stoker associated cowboys with vampires sixteen years after this article appeared in the *Times*.[4] Later writers, however, have challenged the notion that drifting cowboys are social, economic, or sexual predators by suggesting that they are actually responsible for *protecting* western cities and towns from the threat of blood-sucking parasites. In 1947, for example, the United States Department of Agriculture first employed a mounted patrol to guard the Texas border in order to prevent Mexican herds infected with cattle tick fever from illegally wandering onto American soil.[5] In 1988, it expanded the program to include sixty-two more of these "animal health technicians" or guards, who were compared to cowboys in the job-

Dance, insect, dance! In Texas in 1988, tick riders Alonzo Zambrano (left) and Tony Romo search for their prey. The photograph suggests that the men have reached for their guns after spotting an insect that was trying to sneak over the Mexico–United States border without being caught. (Philadelphia Inquirer. *Photograph by Michael Wirtz*)

advertising brochures that the program put out.[6] The brochures stated that a technician "must be experienced in work in the cattle industry, capable of riding on
horseback in rough country for long periods, [and] able to trail, rope and handle wild
livestock." He must investigate cut fences on the United States–Mexico border,
"detect" the incriminating "cattle tracks" of illegally trespassing stock, and expose
himself to attacks when apprehending cattle smugglers at border crossings and
junctions.[7] In the last forty years, the Department of Agriculture has hired fence
menders, horseback riders, and cattle inspectors to contain the blood-sucking cattle
tick and the cattle that carry the "vampire's" virus, for only men endowed with the
skills of the cowboy can pursue and capture stock in open, rugged terrain. In a
sedentary urban society, only cowboy detectives can wander freely along the Rio
Grande, chase cattle, and live in outdoor tents that they move in gypsylike fashion
from one camp to the next.

This chapter's remaining sections expand on and explain these two extreme
forms of behavior while tracing the evolution and development of the wandering
cowboy "criminal" and the drifting livestock "detective." They argue that the
cowboy's itinerant life on the fringe of domestic society partially accounted for his
uncertain status and that this uncertain status led to contrasting representations of
cowboys, both in society and within their own group. Drifting cattle rustlers and
vagrants often left the group, were apprehended by lawmen, and were transported to
prison, where they were physically confined and forced to stop migrating illegally.
Other wandering cowboys, however, were solicited by society and *encouraged* to
drift while working for its legal organizations as livestock detectives, as Pinkerton
agents, or as "animal health technicians" in bureaucratic government agencies. The
unmonitored cowboy passed through and destabilized a traditionally domestic society and provoked its schizophrenic response to him—its isolation or incarceration of
the cattle thief and its assimilation or employment of the cowboy livestock detective.

The incarceration of cowboys in prison and their employment by stock associations led cowboys to develop their own schizophrenic response to society. Although
they worked for socially organized agencies that paid them to apprehend rustlers,
detectives sometimes returned to the cowboy group that had once united detectives
with cattle thieves. And although men convicted of rustling maintained ties to
cowboy culture in prison, they exchanged roles as cowboys for jobs as reformed,
wage-earning workers on leaving their cells, hesitating—as did cowboy detectives—in choosing between assimilation into and exile from mainstream society.

II

The cowboys' unemployment rate increased at the end of the nineteenth century
because the cattlemen's need for employees abated with the decrease in the size of
their herds and because their methods of controlling and transporting herds improved
rapidly with the passage of time. Livestock that had already been famished and
weakened by the summer drought of 1886 were then starved, suffocated, or frozen to
death by the winter blizzards of 1886/1887 and killed by barbed-wire fences that
prevented the cattle from escaping the snow drifts that accumulated on the fenced-in

frontier. In the 1890s, economically depressed cattlemen cut expenses by building more fenced-off enclosures, by shipping their stock to market over railway lines that crisscrossed the West, and by firing cowboys who had guarded the cattlemen's livestock on unenclosed pastures and who had then driven livestock to market. Now unable to find positions in ranching, and unwilling to settle down in town as merchants or businessmen, cowboys sometimes resorted to cutting the fences and to rustling the stock of their former employers. Stealing, rebranding, and selling the cattle that they stole allowed cowboys to support themselves by using skills that they had acquired as workers on the unfenced frontier. Often, however, they were caught by the cattlemen's livestock detectives, tried by the courts for their crimes, convicted by juries, and condemned to serve time in prison.

Noting the former occupations of convicts in rosters, western prisons suggested a correlation between the decline of the cattle industry and the development of a depressed cowboy class, which attempted to survive by turning to cattle theft in the 1880s and 1890s.[8] In 1892, for example, the Wyoming prison in Laramie held six men who referred to themselves loosely as "cowboys." It held eight of these men in 1893, fourteen in 1894, sixteen in 1895, and twenty-six in 1896. The cowboys' rising unemployment rate in the 1890s coincided with a steady annual growth in the number of convicted frontiersmen, who lacked the job security of their former employers. The same Wyoming prison, for instance, housed no cattlemen or employers in 1894, one in 1895, and only three in 1896.[9] Burdened by debt in the 1880s and 1890s, ranchers often kept themselves from becoming insolvent by cutting their payrolls or by dismissing their cowboys in order to compensate for natural seasonal slumps or economic depressions. Fired hands often remained in the West, as New Mexico's prison records suggest, and illegally supported themselves by stealing and reselling the cattlemen's livestock. Cowboys appeared more frequently in New Mexico's prison system than any other professional group, with the exception of miners.[10] Few of them passed through the system in the 1880s and 1890s, but nineteen cowboys had served time in the penal institution by 1902 and fourteen had served for having rustled livestock from ranchers and cattlemen.[11]

The warden's reports for the Nevada State Prison confirm the cowboys' escalating unemployment rate by documenting a similar dramatic increase in its number of convicts. The reports list no cowboy workers in the years between 1865 and 1878,[12] but they mention one "vaquero" who, in 1879, committed "grand larceny"[13]—a frequent euphemism for cattle theft. In 1881, four more "vaqueros" entered the prison, having also been cited for theft,[14] and in 1882, a "cowboy" appeared on the roster: under the column "Trade or Occupation," it listed him as a man imprisoned for "housebreaking."[15] By 1886, cowboys and vaqueros represented 11 of the Nevada State Prison's 132 convicts.[16] They also constituted a significant percentage of the Montana State Prison's population, according to the Prison Description Sheets of the State Convict Register. These records show that no cowboys entered the prison in the 1870s, when the cattle industry expanded and prospered. But one to four cowboys reported to prison each year during the following decade, and even more men did so in the years after that. The records list seven cowboys in 1892, eleven in 1893, and, in 1894, twenty-six men who describe themselves as "cowboys," "herders," "horsemen," "horsebreakers," and "horsetrainers."[17]

Western culture depicted the cowboy as a drifting social outsider and transient economic threat even before the decline of the frontier's livestock economy. But it consciously decided to punish that threat when the industry began to collapse in the late 1880s and the 1890s. Wandering now led to the worker's confinement or to legal attempts to restrict the worker's own movement: to prosecute unemployed vagrants, to incarcerate nomadic cattle thieves, and to penalize "housebreakers" or roaming social intruders. Incarceration encouraged the ideological split among cowboys that followed: prison labor programs allowed convicts to make works illustrating their past ties to a drifting, loosely knit group of frontiersmen. But, at the same time, the programs *prevented* convicts from drifting and discouraged rustlers from returning to cowboy life after they had finished serving their terms by enlisting inmates in programs that allowed them to develop new job skills and to sell handcrafted goods for legitimate wages when they left their prison cells and reentered society. Reformed ex-convicts could support themselves not by turning to rustling again, but by distancing themselves from the cowboy group and by thriving as artists, craftsmen, and tradesmen in town.

Eighteenth-century American prison systems defined convict labor as a form of physical punishment, torture, or pain.[18] But nineteenth-century penal institutions treated mandatory work as an aspect of convicts' reform.[19] American prisons now used labor not only to penalize convicts or to punish their bodies and make them consent to tiresome disciplinary tasks that a prison imposed, but to teach and reward convicts by providing them with useful, marketable, job-training skills and to benefit the community at the same time by letting convicts practice those skills in supervised community settings. Menial prison chores gave way to schemes for social and economic improvement: the development of the public works and ways system, which ordered convicts to commute from their prison cells to the outside world and to labor in chain gangs on the public's buildings, roads, and canals; the creation of work apprenticeships, which allowed inmates to leave their cells and to learn professional skills while living with tradespeople, who housed the inmates and reimbursed the prison for their labor and time; and the invention of the contract system, which permitted the tradesperson to commission work from imprisoned convicts, who remained continually inside their cells.[20]

Cowboy convicts worked primarily inside the prison, both for the prison and for the tradesmen who commissioned their labor. Frequently the cowboys created objects that they had made, used, or worn on the range and that they now produced in their cells for a society of noncowboy consumers. In Washington, Kansas, and Montana prisons, for example, cowboys wove horsehair bridles, halters, and ropes. In Arizona, Texas, and Nevada prisons, they fashioned bits, saddles, and saddletrees out of iron, leather, and wood. In the Utah State Prison, they worked in shops devoted entirely to the production of saddle cinches and horse switches.[21] And in the Colorado State Prison, they turned metal into spurs and engraved the spurs with distinctive designs.

Western prisons allowed the cowboy convict to perfect his artisan skills and to sell his handcrafted goods to a society that had imprisoned him for having victimized it earlier. Permitting the worker to sell his labor in prison and to profit indirectly from the crime that he had committed, the prison also repunished the worker by reminding him of his previous crime as a cowboy and of his status as a convict in prison. Just as wandering had resulted in the convict's incarceration and labor, so labor now led to the production of artifacts that "punished" the cowboy's earlier wandering movements. The goods that he manufactured inside his cell not only alluded to the previous life that the convict had led as a cowboy, but also objectified the present status that he had as an inmate. Halters, bits, bridles, and cinches restrained—by inflicting pain on—the bodies of imprisoned animal objects. Ropes and spurs, on the contrary, *provoked* the animals' movements on specific occasions dictated by the animals' riders and masters.

The prison often overtly compared the instruments that controlled an animal's movement to the discipline that the prison imposed on a wandering cowboy, who was punished, confined, and forced—like a "horse"—to submit to the prison's command. Creating these instruments therefore enabled the cowboy to dramatize his status as a vagrant, drifter, or migrating rustler, and to reenact the penalties for wandering in a stabilized domestic society. An artifact from the Yuma, Arizona, prison, for instance, documents the penal system's dramatization of labor. Convicts were housed outside Yuma, at the turn of the century, in cells that were hollowed out of sandstone cliffs near the Colorado River. Each eight- by eight-foot compartment held six men, who were locked in the summer inside these small, hot, unventilated cell blocks for great lengths of time. One day an overseer caught a cowboy who had escaped from his cell and who had previously attempted to elude detection and wander away. Because the prison had no stockade or solitary-confinement cell, the overseer punished the cowboy by attaching a chain to a cottonwood tree, placing one of the cowboy's legs inside a ring-bolt at the end of the chain, and giving the cowboy a disciplinary task to perform. For the rest of that day, the convict filed an iron ring-bit for a horse and reenacted the punishment that he himself had received. For having halted the convict's own movement and having used a ring-bolt to do so, the overseer now ordered the cowboy to produce an animal bolt or a ring-bit, which "bit" the animal's mouth and prevented its movement, just as the ring-bolt had bitten the ankle and restricted the motion of the incarcerated creator himself.[22]

Sometimes a creation told not only the story of the convict's confinement, but also his hopes for release from his cell. For example, the Dalton brothers lived in a Kansas prison at the turn of the century and manufactured horsehair bridles and ropes, which they sold in order to pay for a lawyer who would reargue their case in a court room. The prison paid the Dalton brothers only six cents an hour to collect over thirty thousand tail hairs from the horses stabled in prison, to braid these hairs together—inch by inch, over months filled with painstaking labor—and to stain the bridles with decorative vegetable dyes, whose colors included muted white and black and vivid blue and red hues. The gear demonstrated or "narrated" the way in which the brothers had chosen to serve out their terms or to fill the free time that they had in their cells. But the story that the gear told was subverted by a subtext or rosette on one bridle, engraved with the picture of a winged bird in flight. It dramatized the Dalton brothers' attempt to escape by selling their bridles and by paying a lawyer to argue and overturn their convictions.[23]

A cowboy's prison text frequently narrated this theme of escape, wandering freedom, or flight. As did the Dalton brothers, an inmate who probably lived in the

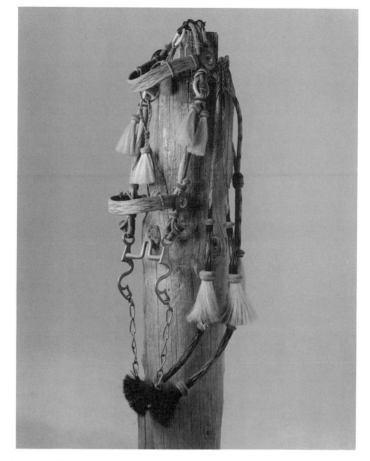

A horsehair bridle made by the Dalton brothers, who were incarcerated in a Kansas prison in the late nineteenth century. Note the intricate patterns stained and woven into the braids. (Bridle owned by Howard Miller, Tucson, Ariz. Photograph by Naurice Koonce, Manley-Prim Photography, Inc.)

Walla Walla, Washington, prison at the turn of the century contested his immobilization by weaving, staining, and engraving into a bridle a text that indicated the cowboy's allegiance to Theodore Roosevelt's Rough Riders. In 1898 the cowboy had gone with the Rough Riders to fight against the Spanish in Cuba.[24] Later, in prison, he made much of that moment by creating a "Rough Riders" bridle. Two American flags, facing left and right, appear on the nose strap of the bridle and display banners of brilliant microscopic white stars, which have been woven into the hair and thrown into relief by the stained, rectangular blue background. Fourteen red and white stripes ripple gently across each unfurling flag and point to the embroidered word ROUGH, on the left, and to the word RIDER, on the right. The forehead and side straps repeat these color motifs and sprinkle the bridle with visual variations on the American flag. The conchos, like the bridle rosette made by the Daltons, reserve a place for the artist's weaving or engraving of language into the text. The left concho, for instance, presents the letter *T* on its surface; the right one, the letter *R*. Initialing and dedicating the bridle to Roosevelt enables the convict to reestablish his link to the cowboy group of Rough Riders whom Roosevelt led, while serving his sentence as an inmate in prison. The elaborate bridle acknowledges the cowboy's current status as inmate, for it represents what only a convict with an unlimited amount of unoccupied time could produce at a leisurely pace in his prison cell. But the object also reminds us of the bridle maker's more illustrious past, for while coming to life in the confined surroundings of a closely guarded prison environment, the bridle nevertheless refers back to and glorifies the earlier nomadic life of the cowboy frontiersman. It salutes the career of a wandering rough "rider" who traveled with Roosevelt's troops and challenged the notion that he was no more than a convict by claiming that he was a patriot who had been involved in one of America's military and political victories.[25]

In assembling the bridle, the Dalton brothers created a text that narrated their hopes for an early prison release. On one rosette, they engraved an image of a winged bird in flight. (Bridle owned by Howard Miller, Tucson, Ariz. Photograph by Naurice Koonce, Manley-Prim Photography, Inc.)

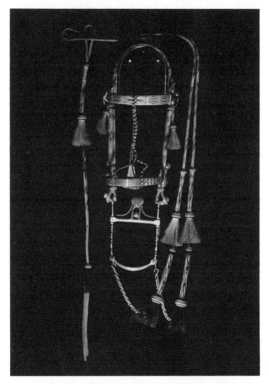

The "ROUGH RIDER" bridle, woven and constructed at the turn of the century by a cowboy inmate at a Walla Walla, Washington, prison. (Bridle owned by Linda Kohn, High Noon, Los Angeles, Calif. Photograph by Victoria Mihich)

A close-up of the nose strap of the "ROUGH RIDER" bridle, featuring American flags facing to the left and the right. The convict used vegetable dyes to stain each waving red and white stripe and each microscopic white star. (Bridle owned by Linda Kohn, High Noon, Los Angeles, Calif. Photograph by Victoria Mihich)

A side view of the nose strap, showing the word ROUGH on the left. The word is stained brown, with two rows of orange dashes running across it. The zigzag designs are red, yellow, brown, black, green, and orange. (Bridle owned by Linda Kohn, High Noon, Los Angeles, Calif. Photograph by Victoria Mihich)

A side view of the nose strap, revealing the word RIDER woven in brown and orange dyes on the right. (Bridle owned by Linda Kohn, High Noon, Los Angeles, Calif. Photograph by Victoria Mihich)

Like these bridles, the spurs that were made in prisons were more than cowboy equipment or tools: they were inscribed texts and artistic creations that convicts used to tell their own stories. Photographs of twentieth-century spurs that were made in the Colorado State Prison reveal the amount of attention that cowboys paid to the small details on the heel-band of the spur, the U-shaped piece of metal that fits around the boot's bottom; to the careful decorative touches that were put on the spur's "button," the protruding circular knob that caps the end of the band; to the delicate designs that were engraved on the shank, the connecting iron arch that forms a bridge between the extending spur and the band; and to the perfect geometric shape that characterized the rowel, the rotating device that includes the spikes and individual prongs of the spur.[26] These spurs and others like them indicate the amount of energy, dedication, and skill with which cowboys invested their labor as a result of their incarceration in prison. Nineteenth- and twentieth-century spurs, for instance, have between five and twenty prongs, each requiring hours of painstaking labor to make. The shanks and heel-bands have simple geometric designs or clever combinations of symbols engraved or embossed on them. Two sets of spurs, now housed in the ProRodeo Hall of Fame and Museum of the American Cowboy in Colorado Springs, Colorado, are products of the Colorado State Prison system and examples of the prison artists' great range.[27] The first set (ca. 1900) shows that each spur has ten prongs and a series of hearts, spades, diamonds, and clubs circling the band and shank of the instrument. The second set (ca. 1910) indicates that each spur has fourteen prongs, a shank with diamond-shaped designs on its sides, and a heel-band with horseshoes resting alternately on their sides and in the upright position.

Spurs are work gear as well as integral parts of a cowboy's identity. Here, ranch hands in Colorado in 1903 gather in front of a wagon and show off their spurs. (Denver Public Library, Western History Department)

These spurs, made in the Colorado State Prison around 1900, are now housed in the museum warehouse at the ProRodeo Hall of Fame in Colorado Springs. The heel-bands have diamonds, spades, hearts, and clubs engraved on their sides. (ProRodeo Hall of Fame and Museum of the American Cowboy, Colorado Springs, Colo. Photograph by Gordon Anderson)

These spurs, fashioned in the Colorado State Prison around 1910 and stored in the museum warehouse, have heel-bands that sport horseshoes resting on their sides and in the upright position. Diamond-shaped images fan across the shank of each spur, becoming smaller in size as they move from the heel-band out to the rowel. (ProRodeo Hall of Fame and Museum of the American Cowboy, Colorado Springs, Colo. Photograph by Gordon Anderson)

The texts that artists wove or stained into bridles and halters in Washington and Kansas state prisons—the fictional representations of a future release—have been erased, in a sense, and replaced on the spurs with the prison's own record or "text" of confinement. The Colorado State Prison's spurs, for example, were often signed inside the shank with the prison number of the convict who had made them, and the Texas State Prison's spurs were initialed and stamped "TSP,"[28] so that outside consumers who liked the spurs that they had purchased would know enough to return to the Texas State Prison if they wanted to commission another pair from its convicts. The institutions substituted a prison initial or number for the convict's own name—for the artist's identification and signature—and indirectly suggested that an automaton or anonymous man had unfeelingly manufactured these objects of labor in a prison system that merely kept him "employed." Erasing the artist's name from the products he crafted and thereby denying him the freedom to solicit or advertise

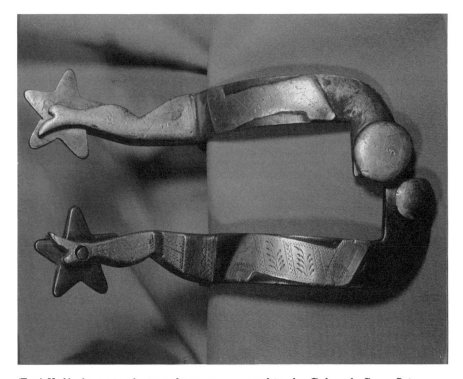

(Top) Half of a pair of spurs that were created in the Colorado State Prison around 1919. When the original owner lost the other half of the pair around 1927, he commissioned a blacksmith in Saguache, Colorado, to make another one (bottom). Note that each shank is shaped like a dancing girl's leg, beginning with the gartered thigh that kicks out from the heel-band and going down the knee and the calf of the shank to the high-heeled shoe on the rowel. This was and still is a common motif that can be found on custom-made spurs. (Spurs owned by Jim and Peg Curtis, Jr., Saguache, Colo. Photograph from the author's collection)

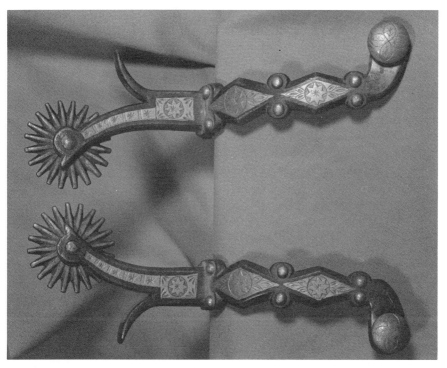

(a) Spurs made by a cowboy inmate in the Colorado State Prison in the early 1900s. (b) Another pair made around 1923. (Spurs owned by Jim and Peg Curtis, Jr., Saguache, Colo. Photographs from the author's collection)

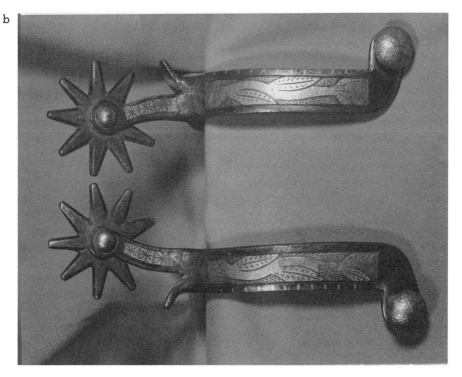

his work projected the notion that spurs were not art made by skilled humans who expended their talent, but utilitarian footwear that any convict could make by doing the kind of anonymous busywork that prisons initiated in order to keep convicts occupied. Unlike art objects, which are subjectively prized for their beauty and objectively appraised for their financial worth, prison spurs were marketed merely as disposable goods that consumers could buy, wear out, and replace simply by returning to the prison and purchasing new ones.[29]

Today it is difficult to find antique spurs or to trace their origins back to western state prisons, which covered up their records of spur making. A recently uncovered photograph from the Colorado State Prison shows spurs displayed and sold in its curio shop at least until 1940, if not afterward.[30] But in the absence of written or illustrated documents to prove their existence, the spurs themselves provide the sole record of spur making. The Colorado prison, for example, not only omitted the spur maker's name, but often neglected to print the prison's initials on the inside shank of the instrument. It revised its written reports to make sure that no record of the artist's work remained on its rosters as well. Colorado's nineteenth- and twentieth-century prison records, for instance, list prison brick making, stonecutting, and lime burning in their descriptions of labor.[31] They privilege these tasks and other traditional jobs on prison farms and in gardens, machine shops, and kitchens, while ignoring the cowboy's production and removing a record of it from their official reports.

Prisons seldom recognized the production of spurs and never acknowledged the extent of their value. Hence when contemporary allusions to prison spur making appear in American culture, they stigmatize spurs as mere objects of labor and as symbols of a convict's misdeeds. The film *Stir Crazy* (1981), for example, shows convicts turning spurs into pairs of concealed weapons and using them to break out of a fictitious institution that was filmed on location at the Texas State Prison. But while prison spurs were originally conceived of as weapons to inflict wounds on animals, and while they were later thought of as weapons to be brandished by convicts who were escaping from prison in *Stir Crazy,* they were also valued by their creators as intricately made, handcrafted art objects. By establishing economic conditions that made spurs into artworks that were expensive to buy and hard to market simply as cost-effective, utilitarian horse-riding gear, prisons indirectly contributed to the value of spurs and to the spur maker's definition of himself as an artist.

In the 1920s, a Colorado State Prison convict earned between ten and twenty-five cents for each day of work,[32] receiving his earnings from the state's general funds in a lump sum when he left his cell and returned to society to labor as a respectable tradesman.[33] Although his prison capital could sustain the worker for a short time, it could not establish him in an independent trade. Spurs could be made and sold cheaply in prison, for prison officials gave the worker a nominal wage and therefore figured only a small overhead cost into the price that the customer paid. The convict could profit even from the amount that he received for his work, for he had no clothing or food to purchase, no rent to pay, no shop of his own to maintain, and no operating costs to consider. But when he left prison and attempted to practice his trade in outside society, he charged higher sums to compensate himself for his overhead and to reward himself for the labor and time that had gone into the production of his handcrafted goods. An individual artisan could not compete with the low prices of efficient large companies. He had to market his products not as

A person might place a special order for a pair of custom-made spurs or simply walk into the prison and purchase whatever its store had in stock. In this 1940 photograph of the curio shop at the Colorado State Prison, convict-made spurs hang from shelves on the right. (Local History Center, Cañon City, Colo.)

cheap "tools," but as expensive man-made objects of "art" that had been crafted with an attention to detail, so that no two pairs of spurs were alike. The individuality of each set of spurs and the amount of human labor that went into their production distinguished the objects from impersonal, plain, and more practical goods that were turned out by assembly lines or automated machines. And the prison helped to make the ex-convict's art possible: allowing the cowboy to spend his prison time honing the skills that would later allow him to practice a trade in society, it gave him the raw goods and the market with which to experiment.

Prisons ignored the artistic value of the spurs that they had helped to inspire. They sometimes acknowledged the paintings and murals—or more traditional and recognizable art objects—of other convicts instead. Will James, one of America's most popular western artists and novelists, worked in Nevada in the late nineteenth and early twentieth centuries. In 1915, he pleaded guilty to the charge of grand larceny, or cattle theft, and served a one-year sentence in the Nevada State Prison. There he developed his artistic talent, observing animals in the landscape through a window in his prison cell and using a pencil to sketch them on paper. He initially worked outdoors on the woodpile, but later he avoided hard labor by showing his pictures and sketches to prison officials and convincing them to nurture his talent—to conserve his strength by letting him serve in the prison cafeteria, instead of toiling

Height	1 m	74.6	Head length	18.9	L Foot	26.8	Color L. Eye	brown		Age 22	Born in 18
Stretch	1 m	81.0	Head width	15.9	L Mid F	12.0		Class		Apparent Age	
Trunk'		93.3	Cheek width	14.3	L Lit F	8.9		Areola		Nativity	Montana
Curv			R Ear length	6.2	L Cubit	48.5		Peripn		Occupation	rider
Eng. Height		5-8¾	Remarks relative to Measurements					Pecul			

	Forehead	Inc		Nose	Profile	Bridge		R Ear	Border	Hair **dk ch**	Beard **ch blk**
		Height				Base			Lobe	Complexion **m dark**	
		Width				DIMENSIONS Height Projection Breadth			Teeth **poor**	Weight **135**	
		Pecul				Pecul				Build **slender**	

NEVADA STATE POLICE
CARSON CITY, NEVADA

Examined......5-4-15
By......Sergt. Stone

Mug shots and prints of Will James, convicted of cattle rustling in 1915 and sent to the Nevada State Prison. (Nevada State Library and Archives, Carson City, Nev.)

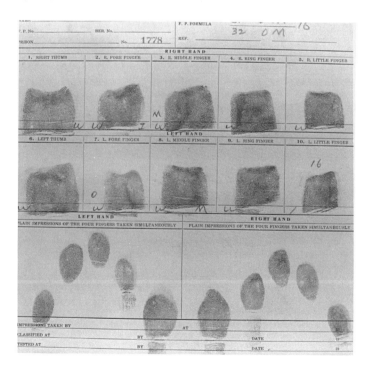

outside.[34] On August 19, 1915, James wrote a letter to the Nevada Board of Pardons and Parole in which he asked them to suspend his sentence for rustling. Once again, he used his art to justify his request for exemption from working and serving in prison.

Gentlemen

I herewith submit for your consideration an application for my release and parole.

I was sentenced April 28, 1915, from Ely, [Nevada] to from 12 to 15 months on a plea of guilty to Grand Larceny. I was in jail 7 months and have thus served altogether 11¹/₂ months.

I am a young man 23 years of age and this is the first trouble of any nature I was ever in.

I have a natural talent for drawing and during my imprisonement [*sic*] have done considerable of this work. It is my ambition to go East and study Art and I feel that if given an opportunity to develop this talent my future will be assured. As a sample of my work I am submitting for your inspection, a few samples drawn by myself.

During my imprisonement [*sic*] I have had ample time for serious thought and while this experience is unfortunate and to be deeply regretted it has not by any means embittered or discouraged me and if given an opportunity I feel I can go out of here and live and [*sic*] upright and honorable life and be of some use, not only to myself but to my fellow man.

I assure you Gentlemen that if my plea is given favorable action I will endeavor to live in such a way that you will never have cause to regret you kindness.

Respectfully Submitted
Will R. James
Nevada State Prison[35]

The board refused James's request, but approved his appeal in the following year and, on April 11, 1916, issued the convict a pardon.

With his letter to the board, James included a drawing entitled "THE TURNING POINT" (1915), which illustrated his intention to lead an "upright and honorable life." The drawing's subtitle—"HAVE HAD AMPLE TIME FOR SERIOUS THOUGHT AND IT IS MY AMBITION TO FOLLOW UP ON MY ART"—repeats a part of the convict's plea in the fifth paragraph of his letter and reflects the convict's decision to refashion himself into a respectable citizen-artist. The upper-left corner of the piece is entitled "PAST." It shows James rustling a cow, or committing the crime that led to his incarceration in the Nevada State Prison. The crime inspires the self-portrait entitled "PRESENT" on the lower-left part of the page. Now the formerly active, wandering cattle thief is immobilized by his restrictions in prison, lost in "serious thought," as he states in his letter and in his subtitle's plea. In the upper-right corner, "FUTURE" indicates the artist's desire to remake himself into a trustworthy citizen by transforming himself into a wage-earning artist who no longer rustles cattle on horseback, but draws portraits of nonthreatening cowboys on horseback instead. Both prison and prison art have made the artist's transition from the cowboy group into society possible. Wandering, or illegally trespassing on the cattleman's property, has led to the rustler's incarceration, and incarceration has subsequently led to the cowboy's attempt to free himself by creating an artwork. Representing the rustler's transformation in the "PRESENT" while presaging the artist's function in the "FUTURE"

Will James's letter to the Nevada Board of Pardons and Parole, written on

enables the cowboy to persuade the board that he can support himself as an artist, in a respectable trade, and that he can "be of some use, not only to [himself] but to [his] fellow man" also.

In eventually suspending James's sentence, the board acknowledged the artist's potential to benefit society by refining his talent. Although prison systems were unable to see the same artistic promise in other convicts' bridles and spurs, these works, as with James's three-part self-portrait, were conceived of and executed in prison and were concerned with the same issues of subjugation and triumph. As does "THE TURNING POINT," the bridle- and spur makers' products told the story of their submission to prison systems or social authority. They also indicated—because of their commercial, aesthetic, or practical value—the economic self-sufficiency, artistic talent, or social productivity of their creators. In this sense, they enabled their creators to benefit from or to triumph over their subjugation in prison. Prisons also established work programs that unconsciously turned the cowboys' labor into unacknowledged, but intensely dramatic, theatrical tasks. And in exchange for per-

while this experience is unfortunate and to be deeply regretted it has not by any means embittered or discouraged one and if given an opportunity I feel I can go out of here and live and upright and honorable life and be of some use, not only to myself but to my fellow man

I assure you Gentlemen that if my plea is given favorable action I will endeavor to live in such a way that you will never have cause to regret your kindness

Respectfully Submitted

Will R. James
Nevada State Prison

August 19, 1915. (Nevada State Library and Archives, Carson City, Nev.)

forming these tasks, prisons suggested that working cowboy convict "performers" could win their release while acquiring the skills that would permit them to work in society later as respectable artisans.

As recently as 1971, for instance, the Wild Free-Roaming Horse and Burro Act inspired one such program and required the United States Bureau of Land Management to protect endangered species while allowing them to graze on publicly owned government land. Since then, the bureau's vigilant protection and breeding of live-stock has led to the land's gradual overpopulation and to the bureau's decision, in 1973, to ship a portion of the expanding herds to prisons out West. There, inmates break horses and burros and distribute domesticated livestock to people in the private sector who want to own "pets."[36] The Colorado State Prison participates in this program and describes it as an effort to reduce the "idleness" of its convicts while teaching them "vocational" skills that will be useful when they return to society.[37] On one level, then, the program illustrates the traditional purpose of punishment and reform in American prisons: first it allows the worker to break stock or assume the

"THE TURNING POINT," a three-part self-portrait that chronologically charts James's life as rustler, inmate, and artist. The subtitle repeats a promise that appears in James's letter to the parole board at the Nevada State Prison. (Special Collections, University of Nevada-Reno Library, Reno, Nev.)

cowboy's traditional role, and then it permits the cowboy convict to leave his cell and return to society, where he markets these new legitimate job skills to ranching outfits and farms. To this extent, the program historically reenacts the cowboy's labor and attempts to transform the contemporary prison "cowboy"—through labor—into a conventional wage-earning worker.

The breaking of stock or the reenactment of cowboy work dramatizes the prison's rehabilitation of convicts by equating the domestication of animals with the reform of human workers. This dramatization begins with the simultaneous articulation and disguise of an animal's punishment—its removal from a nature preserve, its transportation to prison, its subsequent loss of freedom, and its final submission to the physically painful process of being "broken" by riders who tame and subdue it. As the convict's own seizure, incarceration, and punishment are euphemistically referred to as acts of "rehabilitation" and social "reform," so the horse's conquest is called a domestic "adoption" by writers of the Colorado State Prison's publicity pamphlets; its breaking, an act of "gentling" the animal's spirit in order to bend it to the will of society.[38] The functions of domesticated animals and incarcerated cowboys intersect, first, because prisons confine both wandering convicts and "wild, free-roaming" horses; second, because the possibility for physical harm exists both for convicts who break horses and for horses that are "broken" by inmates; third, because prison language describes the physical harm of both inmates and animals as euphemistically envisioned acts of "reform" or "adoption"; and fourth, because the breaking process ultimately enables transformed workers and animals to leave prisons and reposition themselves in society after their reform, rehabilitation, or "gentling."

Horse-breaking programs transform prison work into rodeos, and inmates enter them, risking injury in order to win early releases from prison. Like cowboy paintings, bridles, and spurs, rodeos are forms of prison art: theatrical spectacles whose subtexts illustrate that a convict's social reform or legal reprieve, like Will James's early prison release, depends on the practice of some kind of cowboy art—in this case, dramatic art. The labor occurs both on the outdoor theatrical stage, where it plays in the burro- or horse-taming corral, and in the prison system inside, where it develops into a more traditional and recognizable art form. Several convicts, for example, have made a mural on a courtyard wall in the Colorado State Prison, where horse breaking and burro taming take place. On one side of the wall, the mural charts "the history of Colorado" and displays a herd of "cattle with the cowboys, [who] have either local brands or the initials of corrections officers" on them. The convicts have translated their subjugation into an explicit art object, for they have articulated the connection in the mural between wild livestock and cowboys, both of which are defined by the owner's cattle brand, and they have equated the brand or the cattleman's sign of possession with the correctional officer's control of his convicts. Like all cowboy prison art, the mural speaks not only of the convict's subjugation, but of the cowboy's release and the social or economic rewards that depend on his future "improvement." One of the artists recently told a newspaper reporter, for instance, that the mural would ensure his success in society by demonstrating his artistic talent and by helping him to get into "commercial art with the greeting card" companies when he finished serving his sentence.[39]

Prison rodeos dramatize the cowboy's labor more publicly than these paintings or murals. The Texas State Prison turns "the spectacle of the match between man and beast into a form of art," for example, by staging an annual rodeo and by permitting its "Rodeo Convict Cowboys" to emulate the men who dared to "conquer and tame" western stock in the early days.[40] It expands on the premise of the Colorado horse-adoption program by letting as many as fifty workers ride livestock and compete in public as athletic performers.[41] The contestants reenact society's punishment of convicted cowboys in the Hard Money Event, which forces them to wear red shirts that anger a Brahma bull thrown in with them for "fun." Men who were both amateur and professional rodeo cowboys in the outside world are now expected to dodge a maddened bull to avoid being gored to death. In addition, they are encouraged to take from between the bull's horns a parcel of money that is placed in a "Bull Durham tobacco sack, just like the *cowboys* carried their cigarette tobacco in back in the 1800s" (emphasis added).[42] *Stir Crazy,* starring Gene Wilder and Richard Pryor, and filmed on location at the Texas State Prison, shows that rodeos also reward convicts for participating in these punishing rites of cowboy endurance. The film's warden bets that Wilder's character can win the Hard Money Event held during the state prison's annual rodeo: if he does so, the warden promises to reward him by suspending his sentence or by bringing him up for an early parole.

Stir Crazy traces the convict's submission to prison authority and his return to domestic society through participation in the cowboy's work process. It also demonstrates the prison's attempt to define the rehabilitation process as theatrical art. Animal taming or horse adoption leads to the rodeo's representation of labor as a theatrical spectacle and to the depiction of that rodeo as a filmed, fictitious entertainment in *Stir Crazy*. Programs written for the rodeo's audience also equate the convict's performance with the cowboy's work function in the Texas State Prison. They remind the audience that "convict cowboys" in no way diminish "the quality of entertainment" that the spectators witness, but that amateurs instead guarantee them "a good share of spills and thrills" for their money.[43] Amateur cowboys enhance the quality of entertainment by adding an extra element of danger to each prison performance and by permitting audiences to experience the heightened excitement of an already dangerous work ritual. The rodeo encourages spectators to picture real work as mere entertainment or sport, and to see real workers as mere ciphers or fictitious constructs. Rodeo programs portray convicts as members of a foreign culture who have adopted a fictitious second identity and language in prison. They devote a section of their description to this "other" prison culture by noting the inmates' "Prison Jargon" on a page of each program and by translating that jargon, second language, or "identification code"[44] into the standard written English of the rodeo's audience. The convict's enciphered self-representation is expressed in a series of code words that nonconvicts—who speak "real" language and who inhabit the "real" world—cannot understand, and the code words enable convicts to communicate prison traditions and concepts to one another inside their cells. Although the convict's terms do not refer to the cowboy's own traditions and concepts, they encode and mystify the life of the isolated, imprisoned convict as one mystifies and romanticizes cowboys, who are also part of a disappearing or an invisible work group. A spectator goes to a rodeo in order to witness a fiction, to watch a dramatic reenactment of the labor that the nineteenth-century cowboy performed. And the audience goes to a *prison* rodeo not only to learn about a disappearing work culture, but to gather information about the prison system itself and to participate in a world that normally remains hidden and detached from society. These rodeos feed the public's curiosity by equating convicts and cowboys—two kinds of invisible social outsiders—and by allowing the public to view the labor-art that convict cowboys enact.

Art involves this mystification of the cowboy convict's work process. Nineteenth-century prisons attempted to demystify the convict's art by defining his bits, spurs, and bridles as mere products of labor and by describing this labor as a form of punishment, busywork, or social reform to which the inmate submitted during his sentence. Twentieth-century prisons, however, turn work or ranch labor into artistic or dramatic performances. While nineteenth-century penal institutions denied the artisan's identity by marking his spurs with the anonymity of initials and numbers, by concealing his presence in prison, and by erasing signs of his labor from official prison reports, contemporary prisons acknowledge the inmate's exceptional skills and herald the convict as a "cowboy" if he participates in any rodeo or western work-related event. This new infatuation with and advertisement of the cowboy develops because of the cowboy's disappearance at the end of the nineteenth century. Prisons initially worked to contain the vagrant cowboy and to conceal him from society's sight. But the cowboy's historical dislocation within the economically unstable cattle industry—and his disappearance in prison—resulted in an absence that society, after a great length of time, wished to refill. After a hundred years, society nostalgically yearned for the reappearance of cowboys and for the glamorization of convict "cowboy" performers, forgetting that the cowboy's earlier role as a vagrant or cattle thief had once motivated its decision to deny and make invisible the cowboy's work culture. The resurrection of this culture in the twentieth century and its connection with the convict's acted-out social "reform" is ironic in light of that culture's suppression in prisons in the late nineteenth century.

III

Cattle thieves and livestock detectives were originally members of the same cowboy work culture. When the culture disbanded because of the cattle industry's economic decline, the men who had all once been characterized as outsiders were now seen *either* as outsiders who rustled society's chattel *or* as socially assimilated insiders who denied the cowboy group by apprehending these rustlers, or illegally operating outsiders. The rustler represented the cowboy's inability to conform to and abide by society's laws, while the detective confirmed the cowboy's potential to rise within society's ranks and to hold a position of prestige and stature. Instead of clearly defining the opposite ends of this behavioral spectrum, however, the convict and the detective confused the difference between criminal and ethical conduct: the released convict attempted to rehabilitate himself and to reposition himself in society, while the detective tried to leave it at times or to qualify his identification with institutions of legal privilege and power.

The convict belonged completely neither to the society that he had victimized nor to the cowboy group that he had abandoned. In the same sense, the detective maintained only superficial ties to the cowboy group that he had left and betrayed and to the social institutions or stock associations that began in Texas (1868), Wyoming (1871), Montana (1873), and later in other western territories and states. These associations blacklisted unethical cattle thieves by publishing lists of rustlers' illegal brands, by persuading stock inspectors to stop the sale and transportation of unlawfully rebranded animals, and by hiring detectives to capture men who stole, sold, and transported rebranded stock.[45] But while working in conjunction with society's propertied class, detectives maintained their independence from it as well.

Unlike marshals and policemen, who worked for frontier cities and states, stock detectives worked for autonomous and locally run agencies, associations, and interest groups. For example, Texas Rangers policed the communities to which they belonged, but freelance detectives shifted their allegiance from client to client, independently contracting their services out to different parties with each new assignment.

Having lived in the cowboy group gave livestock detectives an advantage in apprehending cattle thieves. A stock association preferred to do business with men who knew the land and the horseback trails that facilitated a rustler's escape, and who understood the patterns of migrating cattle herds and the telltale signs of a rustler's rebranding. Unlike a city lawman or sheriff, a detective who had once participated in the cowboy's work culture would not arouse its suspicion or call its attention to his presence if he donned the clothes and adopted the manners and customs of a cowboy once more. A stock detective could apprehend cattle thieves by pretending to be one himself—by consenting to reoutfit himself in the uniform of his former profession and by attempting to reinvent himself in the cowboy group while he spied—in disguise—on thieves who lived among the cowboy group's members.

The detective literally distanced himself from the society that employed him by returning to the thief's world in the costume of a cowboy frontiersman. In addition, he ideologically aligned himself with the thief by using violent or illegal procedures to accomplish his goals and by breaking laws to apprehend law-breaking rustlers. In doing so, he demonstrated the double standard of "justice" in which cattlemen and livestock associations, as well as cowboys, believed. During the Civil War Texas cattlemen, for instance, abandoned their herds and went off to fight for the Confederacy. Interloping cattle thieves came into the South, rustled newly born and unbranded calves that absent ranchers had been forced to neglect, and used the mavericked stock to start new herds of their own. After the war, these illegitimate cattlemen hypocritically prosecuted rustlers for committing the same acts that had made them wealthy during the war between North and South. Both cowboy bandits and cattlemen built their herds by rebranding cattle or by stealing unbranded stock. However, with larger property holdings on hand and with a greater self-interest at stake, cattlemen could afford to organize themselves into quasi-political groups or into stock associations that defended their herds against new generations of lower-class, displaced, and unorganized outlaws. The associations hired livestock detectives to make their illegal operations seem "legal" and gave detectives the illegal right to use violence and force when no other way could be found to discourage a cattle thief. A double standard distinguished between a cowboy's *illegal* theft of a cattleman's herd and a cattleman's *legal* theft of another man's stock, as well as his right to employ livestock detectives who used force to punish cowboys for "rustling."[46]

If ranchers were sometimes no more than rustlers on a much larger scale, then livestock detectives, who worked for these ranchers, were often no better than murderers, as the transcripts of Tom Horn's murder trial indicate. A former Pinkerton detective and cowboy, Horn worked for the Wyoming Stock Growers Association in 1901. On July 18, he allegedly shot and killed the fourteen-year-old son of a sheepherder while solving a case for Wyoming's association of cattlemen. The adolescent's death was formally investigated by the state of Wyoming, which put Horn on trial for murder in 1902. According to court transcripts, the prosecuting attorney accused the cowboy detective of having committed a capital crime. On October 11, 1902, attorney Walter Stoll questioned Horn about his detective work and his connection to other men who had been murdered by unknown assailants.

Q. You said your business was that of a stock detective. I will ask you to state whether or not, your business as a stock detective as you use that term did not include more than we understand by that term, merely a stock detective?

A. It does. My understanding of the word stock detective, my position includes more.

Q. It included so much did it not that your method detecting the stealing of stock resulted in no necessity for the trials by jury, witnesses in court, attorney's fees or anything of that kind?

A. Ordinarily not.

Q. In your letter of January 1, 1902, to Joe LeFors, in which you say "I do not care how big or how bad his men are, I can handle them, they can scarcely be any worse than the Brown's gang, and I stopped the cow stealing there in one summer," does that refer to legitimate work of detecting thieves or does it refer to the well-known fact that there were two men killed down in Brown's hole while you were there and in this way cow stealing was stopped?

At this point, the defense attorney objected to the implication that Tom Horn had murdered anyone. Attorney Stoll withdrew the question and asked Horn instead if he would define his detection as "simply legitimate work."

A. You asked me in the first place, if my work was more than that of the ordinary stock detective's work, I said that it was the reason I said it was, was this— ordinarily a man out handling stock in all manner of shape and form in connection with their detective work, the ordinary detectives as I understand them are men who go around and put up jobs on this man and that man and some other man, and that is something I have never done. I have got out where the stealing was going on and remained continuously in the country where it is a matter of stealing calves, I associate myself so directly with the neighborhood that stealing cannot go on without my being present; if they steal I will catch them in the act of stealing on account of being there consequently if a man is caught stealing he gets out of it the best way he can.[47]

Later, during cross-examination, the prosecuting attorney and defendant again debated the definition of a livestock detective.

A. . . . When I would find a man stealing my calf, I mean the people I represented, I would simply take the calf and such things as that stopped stealing.

Q. Go and take the calf and not have the party arrested, not have the party tried?

A. No sir.

Q. And not submit the matter to the judgment of the courts at all, is that right?

A. No sir, I had more faith in getting the calf than in Courts. [Laughter]

Q. And because of that fact, your business has been the carrying on the detection of the cattle stealing in that way and not by any process of law?

A. My business from that time on has been to prevent stealing cattle, not the matter of *detecting* people stealing cattle.[48] (emphasis added)

Stoll defined a cowboy "detective" as a murderer who disobeyed the law instead of enforcing it. Horn, in his effort to escape a murder conviction, sought to distance himself from this accusation, but the jury found him guilty of murder in the first degree and ordered him hanged on November 20, 1903.

The ambiguity about what constituted legitimate detective work was compounded by the uncertainty about who qualified as a livestock detective. The anonymously written biography of General David J. Cook, entitled *Hands Up! or, Twenty Years of Detective Life in the Mountains and on the Plains* (1882), recounts the career of the man who created Denver's Rocky Mountain Detective Association. On one occasion, Cook deputized fifteen actual "cowboys" as detectives and used them to locate and recapture a prison escapee (83). But on other occasions, he used non-cowboys disguised as frontiersmen to apprehend convicts and bandits. In one instance, the author writes that the officers deceived a suspect by donning the clothes of a "cowboy" detective: they wore "large sombrero hats, tucked their breeches into their boot-tops, and carried whips in their hands, which they twirled around and cracked as cow-boys do" (143). The distinctions between "illegitimate" cattle thieves and "legitimate" cattlemen rustlers—and between "legally" ordained livestock detectives and "illegally" operating vigilante patrols—had their analogues in the "acting out" of conflicting roles and in the random "costuming" and disguising of men who were or were not cowboys, on the right or the wrong side of the law, depending on the situation and the solution it called for. As the transcripts of Tom Horn's trial indicate, it was difficult to tell whether a detective was acting inside or outside the law. And as General Cook's biography suggests, the converse was true: it was equally hard to know whether a cattle thief was rustling a cattleman's stock or whether he was a detective who had simply posed as a thief in order to apprehend a bandit and send him to prison.

Karl Marx's brother-in-law, Edward Aveling, spoke to one such costumed frontiersman when he went out West to research his book *The Working-Class Movement in America* (1891). At a "dime museum" in Cincinnati, Ohio, Aveling encountered living cowboy models, who were posed on platforms, "clad in their picturesque garb, and looking terribly bored" (156). In a surreal scene, one model (John Sullivan, alias Broncho John) stepped down from his platform and gave a speech in which he denounced "capitalists in general . . . and ranch-owners in particular" (157). The questionable data that the dubious "cowboy" then cited in support of his argument became the basis of the Marxist author's complaint against cattlemen who exploited cowboys for profit. Almost as disturbing as the cowboy work culture's apparent disappearance at the turn of the century, and its distillation into an animated wax museum's costumed imitation of "real" life, was Aveling's acceptance of a midwestern model for a real ranch hand and of an actor's canned speech for a cowboy's firsthand understanding of his economic constraints.

When the cowboy group began to disband or disintegrate at its core, it had nothing left to show the outside world but its external costume or shell. Costumed cowboys maintained an image that deceived equally a researcher at a dime museum in Cincinnati and a cattle thief who fell for the livestock detective's disguise. Detectives worked not only for cattlemen's associations, but also for the Pinkerton Detective Agency, which hired men to sleuth for it while pretending to belong to a group of rustlers and bandits. Charlie Siringo, one of the agency's most famous "costumed" detectives, worked as a cowboy from the late 1860s until the mid-1880s. He published *A Texas Cowboy, or Fifteen Years on the Hurricane Deck of a Spanish Pony* (1885) before hiring himself out to the agency in 1886 and, after quitting the firm in 1908, published *Pinkerton's Cowboy Detective* in order to expose the corruption that he had encountered within the company's ranks. Threat-

Charlie Siringo, cowboy detective, looking like a cross between a matador and a mustachioed gentleman. (Reprinted with permission from Pinkerton Security and Investigation Services; Pinkerton's, Inc., Van Nuys, Calif. 91406)

The cover of the first edition of *A Texas Cowboy*, published in 1885 by Charlie Siringo. (*Barker Texas History Center, University of Texas at Austin*)

ening to take Siringo to court, the company managed to make him delete potentially libelous claims, to substitute fictitious names for the agency and its employees, and to retitle the book *A Cowboy Detective* (1912). Three years later, Siringo published *Two Evil Isms* (1915) and now openly criticized the company's bribery of important court witnesses, its illegal search and seizure of suspects, its harassment of labor unions, and its unethical entrapment of union leaders and socialists. Siringo contended here, and in *Riata and Spurs* (1927), that the agency allowed cowboy detectives to eradicate crime by implementing illegal procedural methods and by adopting more anarchic operating tactics than even anarchists used in defending themselves against cowboy detectives.

Usually Siringo went undercover to apprehend thieves in the cowboy group. To infiltrate that group, gather evidence against its members, and later testify against them in court, he adopted the dress and work habits of the cowboy's profession, as *Two Evil Isms* goes to great lengths to confirm. In one chapter, Siringo says that he disguised himself as a cowboy and used his expertise with a "lasso" to secure a job on a ranch, to win "the friendship of [its] foreman and . . . cowboys," and to indict guilty cowboys for stealing from their wealthy employer (20). Later he claims to have ridden "broncos" on a ranch and to have posed as a horse breaker while attempting to capture an outlaw (27). On the Texas–Mexico border, he says, he disguised himself as a horse trader—equipped with a "cowboy saddle and spurs"— in order to expose a band of robbers who worked for a railroad nearby (63). Later, in *Riata and Spurs,* he writes that he dressed variously as a "cowboy outlaw" (127), as an expert gunman (144), as a cattle brander (222), and as a whiskey-selling frontiers-man, who paddled up Alaskan rivers in a canoe under the pretext of selling alcohol to Eskimos while trailing a man who had stolen "ten thousand dollars' worth of gold" from a businessman (184–85).

Wearing cowboy disguises enabled Siringo not only to capture these men, but to "belong" to them temporarily by identifying with the cowboy group's customs. However, his identification with the cowboy group and his simultaneous debt to the agency that employed him to *spy* on that group accounted for Siringo's vacillating shifts in allegiance and for the schizophrenic tone and perspective that he took in his books about cowboy life and livestock detection. Criticizing Pinkerton's, Siringo nevertheless shows a grudging respect for it and a fascination with the theatrical roles that it allowed him to play. In *Riata and Spurs,* for example, he explains his desire to become a private detective not by suggesting that he respected the law, but by stating that as a child he had gone to a phrenologist, who had foretold his talent for livestock detection (123). In retrospect, Siringo's entire career seems to revolve around a recurring fascination with show business: if his love of theatrical roles and disguises was first predicted at a phrenology sideshow, then his writings were later motivated by a similar attraction to the bright lights of literary fame and success. Throughout his career, the author contradicted himself by suggesting that he had written about his cowboy-detective life simply in order to set the facts straight or really in order to make "money—and lots of it" (*A Texas Cowboy* 3). In his books, he schizophrenically praised and berated both groups, listing cowboys both as friends and as men whom he was paid to betray, citing Pinkerton's both as a reputable employer and as a corrupt and despicable agency.

Siringo's conflicting loyalties translate into self-contradicting perspectives that finally cancel each other out and account for the absence of a convincing authorial voice in each book that he wrote. Siringo warns in *Two Evil Isms,* for example, that he refrains "from giving the details of [his] work" because "the object of this volume is only to show up evils which have crept into this beloved, free and easy America" (13). But in refusing to analyze his work or his feelings about it, he prevents the reader from putting the text in perspective: in denouncing or praising the detective work that he did, Siringo would have forced himself to state categorically how he felt about his employment. In exposing a wealthy Denver widow, for instance, Siringo says that he extracted a "confession," which she had long nursed "in her bosom," by making friends with her, by receiving an invitation to visit her home, and by pretending to admire a photograph in her parlor on the day of his visit: "The result was we were soon seated flat on the carpet floor like two school children, with a large pile of photographs in her lap. Of course *she* had to show me pictures of her old eastern home and of herself when she was budding into womanhood. In the course of an hour I had the desired confession, which possibly meant the loss of a fortune to herself'' (69). The author opens this scene with a discussion of a secret confession, and he ends it with the "desired confession" in hand. In *Riata and Spurs* (188, 207), here in *Two Evil Isms,* and in almost every other account of his detective career, the code word *confession* or *confidence* signals the author's narration of a significant case and structures a text that depends for its momentum on an anecdotal list of the cowboy detective's adventures. But Siringo seldom confides in the reader as his suspects "confess" to him, for, while constructing the narrative's skeleton, Siringo withholds a key to his characters' psychology and a record of his own mental impressions. He never reveals the widow's story or his method of extracting her "secret," his reaction to her poignant account of her happier youth or his feelings about having deceived her.

The absence of a convincing, consistent authorial viewpoint characterizes not only his detective books, but also his accounts of his cowboy career. In 1919, for example, Siringo published *A Lone Star Cowboy* and *The Song Companion of a Lone Star Cowboy,* the second of which glossed his cowboy career by reproducing the songs that he sang in the first one. However, the songbook's opening poem— "The Lone Star"—has little to do with the cowboy group, and, written by Mrs. Lee C. Harby, it has nothing to do with male composition or oral recitation in the nineteenth-century cowboy's tradition (3–4). This "shoddy collection" of poetry, as the scholar J. Frank Dobie has termed it,[49] attempts to tie Siringo to the cowboy's tradition, but the standard "Home on the Range" (32–33) tells us nothing at all about Siringo's own role in the West. The preface to *The Song Companion* suggests that these poems "have caused the blood to stampede with joy through the veins of thousands of cowboys" (1). But even the preface's manufactured enthusiasm works only to expose Siringo's clichéd attempt to create a vocal "cowboy" persona for himself in the text. The absence of a fully developed authorial voice in the detective's account of his casework and the presence of an insincere voice in the cowboy's edition of verse are due to Siringo's two roles as detective and cowboy, and to the sense of falseness that comes through when he portrays himself as one man or the other, not both.

Both prison convicts and livestock detectives belonged to the cowboy group. But they exchanged their memberships in this marginal community of men for even lonelier lives and professions—solitary confinement in prison cells or freedom in independently and anarchically structured groups that patrolled the frontier. Distanced now from the cowboy group and from its cultural forms of expression, oppressed by their prison surroundings or paralyzed by their conflicting loyalties to their peers and to their new livestock-detective careers, cowboys found it difficult to verbalize or act out their uncertain functions and their feelings about this uncertainty. The criminal's acting out of the *cowboy's* role in a prison work program or rodeo and the cowboy's acting out of the *criminal's* role in texts such as those by Siringo dramatize the conflation of roles that took place when the distinctions among the three categories of cowboys, detectives, and convicts dissolved. The conflation of roles and dissolution of categories are witnessed by the use of costuming to facilitate the exchanging of roles and by the adoption of an uncertain authorial voice to characterize an author's shifting allegiance to and identification with cowboys, detectives, and convicts. Self-descriptive inscriptions and identifications on bridles and spurs that convicts produced also carried with them an uncertain force. These art objects testified to a prison artist's attachment to cowboy life and to social programs dedicated to an inmate's reform. But initials and numbers could replace an artist's name and make his feelings about *convict labor* hard to decipher, just as Charlie Siringo's ambivalent books and Tom Horn's prevaricating court testimony make their conflicting opinions about *livestock detection* difficult for the reader to synthesize.

Both detectives and convicts used some form of language to question their uncertain status. Convicts were concealed from society's sight, descriptions of their art were erased from reports, and stories in their art were embedded in engravings and weavings that seemed not to narrate the stories of these men's dreams of escape from imprisonment. But detectives were assimilated into the mainstream and were therefore apt to express themselves socially. They wrote books or used words in public court transcripts that conformed to standard notions of discourse and that enabled noncowboy writers and readers to comprehend cowboy-detective work. They assimilated into society not only by writing books or by communicating in forms of discourse that were seen as comprehensible and acceptable, but by paving the way for noncowboy writers to write about cowboy detectives in mainstream American fictions that built on foundations laid by such men as Siringo.

IV

Mark Twain would anticipate the appearance of the cowboy detective in mainstream American fiction by comparing a real "cowboy" politician with his fictitious detective, Tom Sawyer. On August 11, 1906, Twain defined President Theodore Roosevelt as the Tom Sawyer of the twentieth century when he wrote that Roosevelt "would go to Halifax for half a chance to show off, and he would go to hell for a whole one."[50] Twain exemplified Tom's need for social autonomy and his simultaneous craving for public approval by turning Tom into an amateur detective. Investigating Injun Joe in *The Adventures of Tom Sawyer* (1876), rescuing Jim in *Adventures of Huckleberry Finn* (1885), and solving a murder in *Tom Sawyer, Detective* (1896) enable Tom to escape from his family, to resolve a case, and to go back to Hannibal, where the people reward his efforts and predict his future success by suggesting that he will grow up to be "President" (*Tom Sawyer* 151). Going with the Rough Riders to Cuba and working on his ranch in the Badlands gave Roosevelt the same chance both to separate himself from the East Coast political establishment and to publicize his military exploits, or to promote his connection with the rugged frontier. Twain's scathing portrait of the president in "The Hunting of the Cow" illustrates the author's conviction that Roosevelt's tendency to indulge in these "cowboys and Indians" escapades bore more than a little resemblance to Tom's love for playacting, applause, and public approval.[51]

The tentative configurations that begin to develop in Twain's discussion of detective and cowboy figures come into focus more clearly in *Ranching with Roosevelt* (1926). In his autobiography, Lincoln Lang attributes his involvement in frontier politics to the motivation that he received from the future American president. Roosevelt's appointment to the Dakotas' stock-inspection association helps to reform the "shifting and generally unpopular stock inspector" (221), who neglects to report the stolen and illegally branded stock of the Badlands' cattlemen. His installation also inspires Lang's father to run for and win the office of county commissioner (265). Lang himself wins the office of county assessor and prosecutes eastern Montana ranchers who have avoided taxation by hiding their herds from the Montana government and grazing them on the plains of the Dakotas instead. As assessor, he attempts to foil this scheme and to prevent owners from grazing their cattle in the Dakotas until they agree to pay an acceptable tax. Having listened to his father and to Theodore Roosevelt talk about a cattleman's political duty, and having learned about his responsibility to the community from these models of civic-mindedness, Lang becomes the cattle association's equivalent of a stock detective, tracking down unwelcome trespassing herds and presenting Montana cattlemen with impromptu returns for past taxes (267–69).

If Roosevelt inspired detective associations that developed and succeeded out West, he also furnished western writers with a positive prototype for the cowboy detective in literature. In the 1870s, Owen Wister met Roosevelt at Harvard, formed a friendship with him, later compared notes with him about each other's visits out West, and consulted him about the stories that grew out of Wister's frontier excursions.[52] Dedicated to Roosevelt, Wister's *The Virginian* (1902) became a national best-seller and set the standard for subsequent romantic depictions of cowboys. It turned the titular character into a cowboy detective, who rises through the ranks of the laboring underclass to become a respected member of western society's law-enforcement patrol. The "drifting" Virginian (33) first appears in the book as a cowboy, but through hard labor he wins a promotion to the position of assistant foreman at the Sunk Creek Ranch, owned by Judge Henry (95). As bridles and spurs express the convict's exchange of a drifting life for confinement in prison—as they objectify his tendency to wander, to rustle, or to "spur" away and to be "reined" in by a society that supervises his movement—so this promotion saddles the Virginian with a social commitment that prevents him from leaving the ranch to pursue a cowboy's nomadic adventures. The "boy" who loves to "jingle his spurs" must now abandon the cowboy group and the irresponsible life of a drifting adolescent, and instead submit to "the rein and curb" of Judge Henry (94). The narrator notes that the Virginian is forced to grow up or to "grow out" of the cowboy group. "His appearance was changed. Aged I would scarcely say, for this would seem as if he did not look young. But I think that the boy was altogether gone from his face" (94). At last, the judge offers the full-time foreman's job to the cow-"boy" turned grownup, who has matured to the point that he can appreciate and handle the benefits and responsibilities of manhood. The job means "everything" to the Virginian: "recognition, higher station, better fortune, [and] a separate house of his own" (145).

The Virginian becomes more detached from the drifting cowboy group as he becomes more accustomed to the security of a stable career, a permanent home, and a respected position in domestic society. Eventually, he betrays the cowboy group by assuming the function of a livestock detective and by turning against a group of cowboys who have resorted to rustling. The Virginian hunts down the cowboy criminals and kills the members of "his own species" (247) without giving them the benefit of a formal trial by jury. He defends his actions by denying his cultural connection to cattle thieves and by privileging his economic allegiance to Judge Henry instead. Referring to one of his victims, he says that you "leave other folks' cattle alone, or you take the consequences, and it was all known to Steve from the start. Would he have me take the Judge's wages and give him the wink?" (258). The betrayal of the cowboy group's culture occurs not only with this new economic bond, but with this new social commitment to law enforcement. Now the Virginian works for a cattleman "judge" and, as a stock detective, answers to the "judicial" branch of an informal western system of justice. He also develops a reproductive bond with society by wedding the schoolteacher, Molly,[53] who introduces him to the works of Shakespeare, Sir Walter Scott, and Jane Austen before agreeing to marry him. Molly simultaneously courts and educates the Virginian, preparing him for marriage by making him into a literate citizen in a book-reading culture. She understands his attraction to livestock-detective work and therefore begins her instruction by lending him a "detective story" to read (86), in an effort to show him that reading and working are compatible in literate mainstream (noncowboy) culture.[54]

The livestock detective's social conversion is engineered in Owen Wister's account of the cowboy, as well as in Dashiell Hammett's later short story. In "Corkscrew" (1925), Hammett—a former Pinkerton detective himself—has a Continental operative investigate the smuggling of illegal aliens over the Arizona–Mexico border. In the process of looking for clues, the Continental operative interrogates the cowboys in Corkscrew, Arizona, and the owner of the Circle H.A.R. Ranch while making friends with Milk River, one of its hired hands. The ranch foreman fires Milk River when he chooses to work for Hammett's detective and to betray the cowboy group by investigating the motives and alibis of its members, who are suspected of having murdered a gambler (269). But although Milk River leaves the cowboy group, he initially refuses to obligate himself to the detective or to abide by society's laws: "I ain't going to be no deputy myself. I'll play around with you, but I don't want to tie myself up, so I'll have to enforce no laws I don't like" (271). Milk River, like the Virginian, however, abandons the cowboy group for a temporary career in western law enforcement before integrating himself into society by accepting the detective's advice to settle down, wed, and have children (301–2).

Here and in Walter Van Tilburg Clark's examination of mob violence and tyranny, the cowboy resists working with and committing himself morally to a detective agency or to a mob of vigilante frontiersmen. In *The Ox-Bow Incident* (1940), Croft unwillingly goes along with the town mob and hangs a band of suspected cattle thieves. While narrating the novel, he notes differences between the rest of the mob and himself: for instance, one man's posture on a horse is "too slumped for a cowboy" (100), and his gun belt is fitted with a flap holster "like a cowboy would never wear" (88). Croft denies his involvement with murdering, self-appointed *detectives* by suggesting that they don't act like *cowboys* and by asserting that *he* does. Other mob members refer to the pursuit and killing of men as a "roundup" (56) of suspects; they also distance themselves from livestock-detective work by euphemistically describing it as labor performed on a cattle ranch.

In "Corkscrew," euphemisms are also used to translate detection into a representational system of "cowboying." Milk River's decision to "head" off the human suspects or cattle, to "cut into the canyon," and to catch the men before they pick up "speed" (286) or arrive there before him reveals his identification with the cowboy's work culture through psychological association and word choice. Milk River expertly ties up the cattle-men when he catches them, having worked "with ropes" on the Circle H. A. R. Ranch, and he binds them together "back to back on the ground" (288), as though they were the pursued objects in a steer-roping contest. Having earlier told the detective that he would refuse to "tie" *himself* up or to bind himself to the law, Milk River now abides by the law and delivers bound-up lawbreakers to the Continental operative.

The detective positions himself midway between the cowboy group and the society that employs him to pursue the cowboy group's rustlers and thieves. As a detective, he eradicates crime and compares the capture of the cowboy criminal to the roping and branding of livestock. Croft and the Virginian, for instance, both punish suspected cattle bandits who rebrand or rewound and reclaim the cattleman's stock by shooting, lynching, or killing bandits or by inflicting wounds to capture these outlaws. They transform cowboys themselves into cattle and *brand* bandits or equate their containment with injurious physical *wounds*. But detectives defer to their employers as well, and, in the course of their detective work, they themselves receive wounds that confirm their submission to social organizations that employ them to sleuth. The cattleman orders the cowboy to brand or wound the cattleman's stock, and the cattleman's stock association orders the detective to wound or kill rustlers, whom Milk River and Croft treat like cattle.[55] Their doing so illustrates the cattleman's ability to command the detective's allegiance, as he controls the cowboy's labor on the range and at home. Society forces Croft to play detective, for example, when he joins the mob that hunts down a group of alleged cattle thieves. It associates him with society's mob when it literally *wounds* him or when it allows him, in the line of duty, to be shot while pursuing his suspects and to acknowledge his participation in a mob that advocates violence (Clark 124, 130).

The intermediate cultural place that a cowboy detective occupies—located between a group of outcasts and an urban society—has its verbal analogue in the mediating voice that a novel's cowboy-detective narrator sometimes develops. Milk River's small part in "Corkscrew" indicates that the nineteenth-century cowboy's role in twentieth-century American culture has shrunk and that the "old days" have "failed" (294). But in *The Ox-Bow Incident,* Croft's inability to control the outcome of the action is balanced by his ability to control the point of view of the novel he narrates. Telling the story in retrospect permits him to repay a debt to the men whom he and the mob wrongly murdered—to accept blame for not stopping the murders and to make up for not voicing his protest by narrating his guilt now to the reader: "I wanted to say something that would square me [then], but I couldn't think what" (35).

Removed from much of the action, as Croft is, but enabled as a narrator to explain its importance, Willa Cather's cowboy detective also plays a decisive role in *The Professor's House* (1925). Professor St. Peter and his family fight over the patents to and royalties from the inventions of a deceased former student. In the novel's middle section, the author moves from a third-person omniscient account of this feud to the student's first-person description of a summer that he spent riding for a New Mexico ranch. While chasing cattle one day, Tom Outland discovers artifacts in the remains of an ancient Indian cliff dwelling. He relinquishes his control of the artifacts to a Dutchman, who takes them out of the country and sells them to European antique dealers and museum collectors. This story foretells the student's later fate, when the professor's friends and family claim their right to his scientific discoveries. And as this earlier episode in the cowboy group both shapes and anticipates the issue of human inheritance, so the cowboy's narration of his western experience provides the professor with a posthumous legacy. St. Peter takes the cowboy's diary, which recounts Tom's discovery of the Indian artifacts, and edits it for publication, reserving his right as the cowboy's literary executor to replace Tom's account of the adventure with the professor's own annotated scholarly substitute (171). The cowboy has since gone to war and lost his life fighting in Flanders, and now his only possession or text has been taken over by the academic establishment.

Unlike Croft and the Virginian, the cowboy detective plays a scientific role in this scholarly novel: as an amateur archaeologist, he "detects" the cliff dwellers' remains while chasing cattle through a New Mexico canyon.[56] But like these two other men, Tom Outland must choose between a cowboy's nomadic life and a citizen's stable social position. Tom Outland's last name suggests his place in the West, and his life reflects the itinerant function of a frontier worker as well. As a group of "mover people," his family crosses "Kansas in a prairie schooner"; and another mobile family, a "locomotive engineer" and his wife (115), later adopt Tom when his parents die. They allow him to take a job with the Sitwell Cattle Company before going to college, for trailing cattle permits the orphan to wander again and to discover the cliff dwellings that an Indian civilization once built. Tom learns that the dwellers paid dearly for their sedentary habits and comforts: they faced extermination at the hands of "some roving Indian tribe without culture or domestic virtues, some horde that fell upon them in their summer camp and destroyed them for their hides and clothing and weapons" (221).

Here Cather distinguishes between a deeply rooted culture and a "roving" group that destroys an unarmed, sedentary society. The drifting cowboy confronts his own extinction, as well, when he tries to choose in *The Professor's House* between a place in the domestic sphere and a wandering life on the range. Tom moves from his cradle in a covered wagon to the home of his adoptive parents, and later abandons this lodging for a job in the open. In the winter, he stays temporarily with his companions, Blake and Henry, who keep their cabin "shining like a playhouse" or like an adolescent's fantastic retreat. Henry assumes the housekeeper's role and at Christmas decorates the room with festive green boughs. He brings a sign of the external world into the workers' domestic space and transforms it into a wilderness nonhome for men. At other times, he makes the drifting cowboys' bunks feel like beds in a "Harvey House" (197), turning a potentially permanent home into a transient's room in a hotel saloon. Tom eventually leaves this room and returns to the cliff dwellings, but as a detective-archaeologist he can confirm the importance of the dwelling's artifacts only by returning to society or by taking the artifacts to the Smithsonian Institution in Washington, D.C. There he rents another room in a couple's home, but quits the domestic space again when he develops a distaste for "that kind of life" (232). Failing to interest the Smithsonian in his findings, Tom leaves the city and returns to the West, only to leave it again and go to college, where he lives in "the professor's house." The novel's title calls attention to this back-and-forth cycle of movement, for as a cowboy Tom prefers the freedom of the open frontier, but as a detective who locates an ancient *society,* he depends on society's approval of what he has found, or on museum and academic acknowledgment.

The tension between society and the individual appears in this representation of the cowboy detective and in Cather's other portrait of cowboys. Two years after issuing *The Professor's House,* Cather published *Death Comes for the Archbishop* (1927), in which one of her characters says that cowboys are sacrilegious hooligans or social outsiders. Father Joseph tells the bishop at one point that "drunken cowboys" either wander into the Catholic church and disrupt it or noisely "serenade the soldiers" at night after going out to intoxicate the Tesuque Indians (42). Cather illustrates in this scene and in her representation of the cowboy detective Tom Outland that she can imagine the cowboy only in one of these two extreme relationships to western society—in the role of a drunk and disruptive outsider, or in that of a social insider, with parents and a past, with a respect for religion and culture, and with Tom Outland's potential for academic and scientific achievement.

The cowboy convict is this disruptive outsider who accepts society's punishment and containment of him by disappearing inside his cell and by surfacing only to express himself indirectly through obliquely inscribed objects of labor. The cowboy detective has a more visible place in society and a more prominent role in its fiction, but like the uprooted convict he also has an insecure right to that claim. Prominently displayed, but romanticized in *The Virginian;* made more realistic, but pushed to the periphery of the hard-boiled cop's world in "Corkscrew"; or reclaimed in *The Professor's House,* but reduced in Willa Cather's canonical novel to a footnote in the professor's own text, the cowboy becomes the property of a writer's imagination and, hence, the symbol of a dispossessed class.[57]

Tom Outland belongs to this class, for he claims no property but that which he finds and no heritage but that which he yields. Hence Indian artifacts or property are found by the cowboy and then are taken away or sold to the Dutchman, whose money gives Tom a chance to pay for a college education and to leave the cowboy group by selling his heritage or inherited Indian artifacts (243). Entering society's educational system depends on Tom's departure from cowboy life and on his separation from his cowboy inheritance—from the relics that belong "to boys like [Blake and Tom], that have no other ancestors to inherit from" (242). Tom studies the *Aeneid* before going to college (251–53), for this epic ironically narrates a Roman's attempt to preserve his own culture or to privilege a thing that Tom has lost by going to college and by leaving behind the West and its relics.

The following chapter moves from the dilemma that develops in *The Professor's House,* and in other popular and canonical texts, to that which occurs in the cowboy's own literature. It deals not with a discussion of a single cowboy's inheritance, but with a documentation of the entire cowboy group's legacy and with the group's difficulty in bequeathing its culture to members who do not reproduce biological lines of inheritance.

CHAPTER FOUR

WHERE SELDOM IS HEARD A DISCOURAGING WORD
Orphanhood and Orality at Home on the Range

I

No author ever fooled his or her audience more successfully than Will James did when he published his autobiography. Already famous because of his work in the 1920s as a western illustrator, novelist, and short-story writer, James capped his career in 1930 by issuing *Lone Cowboy* and by representing himself to the public as an orphan who had survived on his own in the West and had grown up to become a celebrity. In *Lone Cowboy* he wrote—and for a long time his readers believed—that his parents had sold their cattle in Texas at the turn of the century and that they had migrated north with the intention of relocating in Canada. In Montana, his mother had given birth to James, and his father had decided to raise his family there, instead of up north. His mother's death a year later and his father's death shortly thereafter had left James on his own, as the book's title, *Lone Cowboy,* suggested. However, his subsequent informal adoption by a French Canadian trapper named Bopy had enabled the young boy to survive and live in the West with the protection of a surrogate father. Referred to by James as "the Old Timer," the elderly man had introduced James to cowboys, mountain men, fur traders, and trappers while shepherding James through the Canadian and American wilderness. But according to James, the Old Timer had died in 1906, once again leaving James on his own as an orphan.[1]

Only later would scholars discover that the "orphan" had invented this myth— that the author had been born Ernest Dufault, that his parents had been a middle-class couple who had lived in Quebec, and that they had never crossed the Canada–

United States border or orphaned their child. Ernest Dufault *had* been born in 1892 (as his autobiography would later assert), but in 1907, at the age of fifteen, he had run away from home to become a "cowboy" and had temporarily traveled through Alberta and Saskatchewan before moving to America and changing his name to Will James. He had worked with livestock and at one time had stolen cattle in the American West, for which he had served a one-year sentence in the Nevada State Prison. After winning a pardon from the parole board, he had wandered aimlessly around the frontier, sketching pictures of cowboys and livestock. By the 1920s, he had begun to publish his sketches in American magazines and to develop a reputation in the United States as a promising artist. At the same time, he had continued to conceal his profession, his success, and his alias from family members who had been led to believe—by Ernest Dufault's correspondence—that the artist had gone to Montana to work, to save enough money to purchase a ranch, and to provide a new home for his parents.

Lone Cowboy forced James to continue this ruse, for it made the acknowledgment of his parents impossible. It attributed the authenticity of his western art and of his cowboy short stories and novels to the wilderness orphan's acquaintance with cowboys and to his separation from society since infancy. In 1934, James returned briefly to Canada, fearing that his parents would read his best-seller, expose his true background, and risk his status as a western celebrity. In desperation, he convinced his mother, who knew nothing of her son's deception and lies, to burn letters from him that were signed "Ernest Dufault" and that could link him to his family in Canada. He confessed to a sibling, who reluctantly agreed not to tell James's parents and other siblings about James's new name and life as an artist out West.[2]

Although Will James changed the facts of his life to ensure his success as a *mainstream* celebrity artist, he also used the orphan myth to establish his identity as a *marginal* cowboy outsider. Before *Lone Cowboy* appeared, oral poems had already defined "orphans" such as Will James as the only men who had rights to belong to a marginalized work culture of cowboys. The lyrics of the nineteenth-century oral poem "Poor Lonesome Cowboy" had therefore become an anthem for a group of male vagabonds, drifters, and loners who perceived themselves as separated from families and loved ones.

> I ain't got no father,
> I ain't got no father,
> I ain't got no father,
> To buy the clothes I wear.
>
> I'm a poor, lonesome cowboy,
> I'm a poor, lonesome cowboy,
> I'm a poor, lonesome cowboy,
> And a long way from home.
>
> I ain't got no mother,
> I ain't got no mother,
> I ain't got no mother,
> To mend the clothes I wear.

> I ain't got no sister,
> I ain't got no sister,
> I ain't got no sister,
> To go and play with me.
>
> I ain't got no brother,
> I ain't got no brother,
> I ain't got no brother,
> To drive the steers with me.
>   (Lomax and Lomax 290–91)

The poem seems intent only on demonstrating the evidence to support its premise—"I'm a poor, lonesome cowboy." With an insistence that borders on passion and with the fervor of a religious devotee, the poet persists in the notion that cowboys are orphans, repeating—almost chanting—the first three lines in each stanza as though they were a mantra that, in the process of reciting "Poor Lonesome Cowboy," transports orphaned men into some kind of culthood.

Preaching to the converted, oral poets influenced a congregation of cowboys who responded to such recitations by perversely embracing and taking pride in the notion that they were, in a real or an imagined sense, cut off from the mainstream. The mainstream, however, did not warm to the cowboy's self-portraits as much as it did to its own notion of cowboy heroes and outlaws. In the late nineteenth and early twentieth centuries, Wild West shows, dime novels, and films focused not on the cowboy's aloneness, but on his violent, exciting, and entertaining conflicts or involvements with train robbers, bandits, and Indians. These representations of cowboy life captured the public's imagination and gathered such cultural weight that they made the mainstream impatient with "dull" accounts of real working cowboys, who had a hard time dramatizing their social isolation and performance of mundane and repetitive tasks, such as protecting, branding, and castrating cattle.

Overwhelmed by their competition with Wild West shows, dime novels, and films, cowboy artists had to defend the importance of their work or suffer by comparison with counterfeit but more popular icons. Ironically, Will James chose to defend the cowboy fiction that he wrote by claiming that it was authentic. In 1922 he stated emphatically that "he was a real cowboy who [had] lived cowboy life extensively, as few other writers did."[3] And eight years later, *Lone Cowboy* attempted to back up that boast by recounting the life of Will James, growing up as an orphan out West. To some extent, there was truth in the myth and in the account that James gave of his childhood. To be a "real" cowboy, a man had to orphan himself, at least metaphorically: he left his family and friends, moved out West, and made do with men who could not wed or have children as long as they lived with and worked for a cattleman. Having no parents, no siblings, no wife, and no children surrounding him, a cowboy compensated himself for his loneliness, enforced isolation, or curtailed visits with noncowboy outsiders by mythologizing and celebrating the "orphanhood" that was, in fact, a prerequisite and sometimes a penalty for participating in the cowboy's work culture. Therefore, in order to be *authentic* in his depiction of cowboys, James paradoxically had to embrace the *myth* of the orphan's autonomy. But in ardently hugging the myth close to him, he squeezed out the few drops of truth

a

The orphan myth has enhanced the perception that cowboys were loners, but at the same time they were involved in labor that was clearly a collaborative enterprise. As a result, historical photographs usually show cowboys toiling in groups. Pictures that portray ranch hands as existing alone almost always seem posed. (a) Men employed by the Jennings and Blocker Cattle Company effect a crossing near Langtry, Texas, in 1914. (Photography Collection, Harry Ransom Humanities Research Center, University of Texas at Austin) (b) Lone cowboy R. K. Perry waters a herd in a photograph that appears perfectly framed and composed. (Barker Texas History Center, University of Texas at Austin)

b

*If cowboys were thought of as loners when they were really members of com-
plexly structured societies, it was partly due to the fact that the West was
perceived as an emptiness when, in fact, it was filled with activity. In this
amazing shot, taken in Beaver County, Texas, at the turn of the century, more
than 90 percent of the photograph is effectively void. But in the thin horizontal line that cuts the picture in half, 5,000 head of cattle belonging to the CCC
herd are compressed in a group and partially camouflaged as they blend
into the grass. (Barker Texas History Center, University of Texas at Austin)*

that it had in it. *Lone Cowboy* held the public's attention because it took outrageous
license with truths that were myths—which, in James's book, were lies. The author
could earn the mainstream's acceptance only by doing what the mainstream's Wild
West shows, films, and dime novels had done—sensationalizing aspects of cowboy
life, for the benefit of James's self-aggrandizement.

Other cowboys acknowledged but played with the myth that Will James so
obsessively cherished.[4] Will Rogers, for instance, wrote *Letters of a Self-Made
Diplomat to His President* (1926) and skewered the orphan myth four years before
James published *Lone Cowboy*. When New York port authorities tell Rogers that he
cannot get a passport to travel to Europe unless he can prove that he is an American
citizen, Rogers claims—tongue in cheek—that he is an orphan, or invisible resident.
Born on an Indian reservation in Oklahoma Territory, and not in the states, to a
mother and father who died before filing his birth certificate with the United States
government, Rogers says that his birth was a "private affair" (11) that no written
record or human witness can verify. The cowboy orphan, with no public proof of his
birth or American parentage, authenticates himself for his audience, becoming a
self-made diplomat in the process, as the title suggests. Having his passport photo-

graph taken, he commits his previously undocumented existence to film and acts out his self-preservation for the sake of posterity (13).

Rogers argues that the idea of the cowboy-as-orphan is viable, even though it is pliable or susceptible to parody. In spite of the comic confusion that reigns in the text, he is clear about one thing—cowboys are different from members of mainstream (reproductive) society in that they are not forced to verify their biological or genealogical origins. Equipping himself with a lasso and defining himself as a cowboy outsider, the author *symbolically* orphaned himself from the mainstream and spent much of his life, as a cowboy stand-up comic in costume, making fun of its culture and politics. Here he shows a cowboy outsider's contempt for political nonsense by critically distancing himself from the red tape that bureaucracies such as the passport office proliferate, and by *literally* orphaning or distancing himself from the bureaucratic process as well. Having no biological bonds with mainstream reproductive society, the orphan therefore has no social contract with institutions in New York or elsewhere. According to Rogers, a reproductive society calls on cowboys to testify to their genealogical origins, or ancestries; according to James, however, no such proof is demanded of cowboys in a work culture made up solely of orphans. When James appears alone in the West, for the first time after the Old Timer dies, he is seen by cowboys as a "gift from Above" (69) whom God has dropped on the earth to fend for himself without parents or family. He is understood to be part of a group that defines its orphanhood as a sign of divine will or as a mythologically "normal" state of affairs.

Because they seldom had wives or (legitimate) offspring, cowboys often interpreted orphan myths to mean that they had neither parents nor children. Fictional family constructs sometimes took the place of these claims, but economic factors often undercut their reality. The ties between cattle*men* and cow*boys,* for instance, were phrased as bonds between fathers and sons, or as signs of family duty and kinship. But when cattlemen faced depressions or hard times in the winter, they fired expendable cowboys quite easily; likewise, when cowboys received better offers from elsewhere, they left cattlemen to work for higher wages and benefits.

Oral poems sometimes hinted that cowboys were not only "sons" to ranchers, but "fathers" to ranchers' livestock as well. Cowboys often recited their poems at night to soothe cattle and to prevent cattle stampedes, and during the day to entertain cattle on trail drives. They compared cowboys to parents and cattle to offspring whom parents soothed by singing relaxing nursery-rhyme lullabies.[5] "Get Along, Little Dogies" makes this comparison clear[6] by repeating a song that the narrator once heard a "cow-puncher" sing on the open range to a cattleman's herd.

> Whoopee ti yi yo, git along, little dogies,
> It's your misfortune, and none of my own.
> Whoopee ti yi yo, git along, little dogies,
> For you know Wyoming will be your new home.
> (Thorp 70)

In cowboy slang, the word *dogie* means "orphan."[7] In the poem, the cowboy singer therefore projects his own orphan status on dogies, identifying and bonding with calves in a union that resembles the relationships between fathers and sons (71)

The terms "cowboy" and "cattleman" indicate that a manual laborer who worked for a menial wage might be perceived as socially and economically diminished in stature, while a ranch owner might be thought of as having matured into a position of power, even though that power could be disguised as a form of loving paternal control, as the son and father terms illustrate. But a "cowboy" was sometimes just that. This photograph from the 1890s shows a boy and two men working the B horse herd somewhere in the Texas–Oklahoma Panhandle area. (A. A. Forbes Collection, Western History Collections, University of Oklahoma Library)

Folklorists have shown that the melody in "Get Along, Little Dogies" is the same as that in three other earlier songs about adoptions, father-figures, and orphans: it stems from a Dakota Territory cowboy oral poem about an old man rocking an infant to sleep in his arms, from a Michigan lumberjack ballad about a single man nursing a little boy "that was none of his own," and from a comic Irish sing-along about a baby abandoned by its mother and discovered by an unnamed male narrator.[8]

It is important to note, however, that the cowboy's identification with the animal orphan is transitory and purely fictitious. Most cowboy nonfiction prose, and even some poems, define "dogies" not as personified children, but as consumable beef in a western cattle economy. Although he asks the reader to sympathize with his plight as an orphan, for instance, Will James never solicits the dogies that make up a cattleman's herd—even he finally deals with reality. "If a cowboy sings on a nightherd," says James, "it's only because he wants to, and not at all to sing any cattle to sleep" (*Lone Cowboy* 168) because livestock are not children, "just beef" (59).[9] And although "Get Along, Little Dogies" begins by equating the herd with a nursery, it ends by predicting that the herd will become a collective carcass of meat:

"Git along, git along, little dogies, / You're goin' to be beef steers by and by" (Thorp 71).

Cowboys, in a nonreproductive society made up of bachelors and orphans, understand children as James portrays calves in *Lone Cowboy*—at best as irrelevant, and at worst as irritating distractions. In their poems, cowboys sometimes die or martyr themselves in the process of rescuing children from runaway horses and stampeding cattle,[10] but in nonfiction accounts of "reality," cowboy authors type children as contemptible by-products of mainstream reproductive society. In *The Log of a Cowboy* (1903), for instance, one of Andy Adams's characters tells the story of a baby contest held in a cowtown. The teller says that he and other cowboys entered a black baby in the contest in order to mock those who claimed that blacks were "as good as" white townspeople (354). When the cowboys voted and the black baby won by a landslide, the speaker says that the white audience became visibly outraged (356). He notes the town's hypocrisy or opposition to racial equality, as well as nonreproductive cowboy society's opposition to mainstream reproductive communities. Members of an unassimilated group of bachelors and orphans subvert a reproductive society's ritual, disrupting a "baby contest" that rewards people for marrying, parenting, and parading their children in public.

Cowboys who read Andy Adams's account of this contest were so powerfully influenced by it that they were compelled to repeat it—and take credit for it—in their autobiographies. In *Cowboys and Cattleland* (1937), for instance, H. H. Halsell says that the baby contest occurred in Dodge City, Kansas, and that he entered the baby when "some Easterners defended social equality" for black Westerners (218). But in *The Cowman's Southwest* (1953), Oliver Nelson claims that the contest took place in Caldwell, Kansas (92), and that he and his friends engineered it themselves. Originally, Andy Adams used this anecdote, in his novel, to illustrate the cowboy's tendency to tell exaggerated campfire tales. But autobiographers of the West later used it to show tensions between cowboys and reproductive societies, turning Adams's fiction or lies into myths and then into truths that gained ground with each cowboy writer's retelling.[11]

Will James burning the letters that he had written to his mother in Canada, Will Rogers applying for a passport to travel to Europe, cowboys in oral poems driving "dogies" to market, and men distorting Andy Adams's account of a beauty contest for babies—these seemingly randomly floating and jaggedly excerpted fragments of texts have a true kaleidoscopic causality. They fall into their colorful places and make up a crazy-quilt pattern of myth that cowboy "orphans" stitched into their narratives. James calling himself an orphan when, in truth, he was not, Rogers comically lamenting the fact that his parents were dead, cowboys adopting and plaintively singing to stock and then cheerfully sending them to slaughter at meat-packing plants, and men maliciously upstaging a reproductive society's ritual—all these acts in some way attest to the absence, loss, or disruption of real or imaginary and temporary biological bonds.

The next section is concerned with ways in which those biological bonds were *invented* by noncowboy writers who dwelled in mainstream reproductive society. With the fencing of range land, the intrusion of railroads out West, and the down-swing in the cattle economy, cowboys moved to town, married, and took jobs as merchants and businessmen. Noncowboy writers simply mirrored this mainstreaming process, begun in the late nineteenth and early twentieth centuries. In short stories and novels, they started to domesticate men and attack the myth of the cowboy's autonomy. In works by Louisa May Alcott, Frank Norris, Owen Wister, John Steinbeck, and others, the idea of bachelors gave way to the notion of cowboys with wives, children, and claims to posterity; the myth of orphans gave way to the representation of cowboys with parents and traceable ancestries. In the kind of fiction that began to predominate—and eat away at the fiction that cowboys were "free"—these writers annexed orphans and bachelors to reproductive cultural sites that were held together by relational biological links—to families, neighborhoods, cities, and states that composed the urbanizing North American continent.[12]

Noncowboy writers ensnared cowboys within the web of their fiction both by fabricating biological ties between cowboys and reproductive society and by spinning out cultural threads between cowboys and institutions of learning. Before they settled down, married, and produced offspring, bachelors stopped singing songs that dealt with the cowboy's work culture and began reading books that noncowboy authors had written (in *The Virginian*); they contributed to the writing of poems instead of to the preservation of cowboy oral discourse and song (in *The Octopus*). Before finding adoptive or biological parents to care for them, orphans were educated—forced to read books and to think of their teachers as mothers or substitute parents (in *Little Men, Jo's Boys,* and *The Pastures of Heaven*). The mainstream's intertwining of cultural and biological bonds reflected that the cowboy's representations of orphanhood had first started in oral poems such as "Get Along, Little Dogies" and "Poor Lonesome Cowboy." Oral poetry was an appropriate medium for addressing notions of the cowboy's autonomy in that orphans and bachelors were single men who could never be claimed by mainstream reproductive society. Oral poems embodied the cowboy's elusiveness in that they were elusive forms of invisible discourse: they were orally transmitted among cowboy insiders and were never written down, published, and read by noncowboy outsiders who lived in a book-reading culture that privileged literacy instead of orality. Just as reproducing daughters and sons is a way of ensuring a race's survival, so writing and publishing books are means of preserving culture for the sake of posterity. Therefore, reading and writing were surrogate acts for the cowboy's becoming part of a family, for all actions led to an equal identification with "heritage"—with a culture's literary tradition or with a family's genealogical history.

In *The World, the Text, and the Critic,* Edward Said isolates these two different forms of identity. If "biological reproduction is either too difficult or too unpleasant," he asks, "is there some other way by which [celibate men, orphaned children, and others] can create social bonds" and form familylike units? Lacking *filiation* with or blood ties to others, these people have only their *affiliation* with "institutions, associations, and communities whose social existence [is] not in fact guaranteed by biology" (17). Lacking families, cowboy orphans and bachelors formed work groups that used oral discourse to sing about workers who lacked filiation with mainstream reproductive society. Noncowboy writers challenged the affiliation of cowboys with such work groups, emphasizing the blood ties of cowboy parents and children. At the same time, they dissociated cowboys from modes of communication that privileged certain notions of singlehood, linking cowboys with institutions of learning that taught them to read, write, and participate in the dominant discourse of literate and acculturated American citizens.

II

In the mid-nineteenth century, cowboys orally co-composed and recited their songs for an audience of other cowboy insiders. In the late nineteenth century, they started submitting written versions of oral poems that they knew to western magazines, journals, and newspapers. And by the early twentieth century, they had begun to write their own individual poems and publish them.[13] While making the transition from the oral perpetuation of culture to the written production of poems, cowboys have nevertheless maintained ties to the tradition of singing in the middle and late twentieth century by reciting their verses on records and videos, on television and radio, and at Cowboy Poetry Gatherings in Elko, Nevada.[14] Even mainstream American culture has fostered these ties in its own way: country music and films from the 1940s and 1950s—starring singing cowboys such as Roy Rogers, Gene Autry, and others—have distorted but sustained notions of the early cowboy's orality.

Literature produced by the mainstream, however, does *not* tend to dwell on the cowboy's orality. While films, for example, have aural dimensions that easily lend themselves to the recitation of songs, written works have relations with oral texts that are competitive instead of compatible. Hence works by Richard Henry Dana, Owen Wister, and the playwright Sam Shepard—written before, during, and after the cowboy's oral tradition held sway in the West—show inscribed and recited words competing for the right to document culture in both cowboy and noncowboy society.

In 1834 Richard Henry Dana left Harvard College in Cambridge and traveled to California by ship. As a sailor on the *Pilgrim,* he collected cattle hides from Mexican *ranchos* and worked with other sailors to cure, tan, and transport them back East. The work cited in *Two Years Before the Mast* (1840) prefigures the labor that cowboys later enacted out West. In *Two Years Before the Mast,* for instance, sailors live on an all-male ship, as cowboys would later live in a camp on the range or in a bunkhouse at the cattleman's ranch. The ship's captain and cook head the chain of command, as the ranch foreman and chuckwagon cook would later function as the cowboys' authorities. The sailors periodically sing songs about beef that the ship's cook prepares, as the cowboys would later sing oral poems about beef that they would eat on the cattleman's ranch or at the chuckwagon's campsite. Dana footnotes one of these songs, in which seamen complain about food that they eat by comparing their tough beef to horse meat (282–83).

Marginalizing or textually footnoting the notion that cattle inspire oral recitations or songs, Dana instead chooses to privilege the conceit that cattle contribute to a sailor's symbolic bookmaking process. He notes that in order to transport a cattle hide from the coast to the ship, a sailor folds over one side of the hide and carries this less cumbersome object on top of his head. He conserves space in the cargo hold of the ship by unfolding the hide and inserting other folded-over hides between the sides of the waiting receptacle: he makes "books," Dana notes, by placing hides, or "leaves of a book" (258), between the "covers" of a book (138), or unfolded hide. A seaman's learning to bind and make "books" is a skill that other sailors compare to a student's education in a book-reading culture or college. The ship's second mate, for example, ridicules Dana's instruction at an Ivy League college by pointing to men with hides on their heads and by telling Dana that this labor does not look like "college [work], does it? This is what I call *'head work'* " (60). Originally Dana had left Harvard because a measles infection had weakened his eyesight and prevented him from reading his textbooks. In California, he adopts the second mate's metaphor and learns to think of his vacation or education in a cattle economy as a substitute act for his reading books in a college that no longer holds him.

Two Years Before the Mast predates the cowboy's work culture, but shows oral discourse already giving way to representations of bookmaking. Set in the late nineteenth century, *The Virginian* (1902) spotlights the cowboy's work culture, but also reveals reading books to be more important than reciting songs on the range. *Vilifying* the oral tradition—as he would again later, in his musical adaptation of *The Virginian* in 1904, by assigning to the *villain* Trampas a new "song" he would write[15]—Wister gives the hero an indecent lyric to sing in the novel and allows other cowboys at the end of each stanza to "take up each last line, and keep it going three, four, ten times, and kick holes in the ground to the swing of it." Wister lets the inappropriate song air only on the range, for its obscene language can be voiced only in "round-up" (212) or in the cowboy's environment, as he later has the school-teacher Molly acknowledge. He forces the oral recitation to come to an end when the workers enter a schoolyard, approaching a classroom that promotes education through reading and writing. An educated and civilized "neighborhood" poaches on the "wilderness" of the untutored cowboy and therefore encroaches on his crude oral culture (60). The Virginian's song in Chapter 18 articulates this notion that cowboys have no acquaintance with books and therefore no place in an educated book-reading culture. Trespassing and peeping into the classroom, the cowboy in this poem has an unauthorized and tangential relation to learning:

> Great big fool, he hasn't any knowledge.
> Gosh! how could he, when he's never been to scollege?
> Neither has I.
> But I's come mighty nigh;
> I peaked through de door as I went by. (134)

This second song suggests another reason that cowboy poems are offensive to a predominantly white population. The song embraces a black oral tradition and dialect, hence arousing white society's fear that cowboy poems are not only obscene, but also aligned with other oral traditions that combine with cowboy poems to reproduce a murky ethnicity.[16] Imagining the cowboy as an Anglo-Saxon knight errant on horseback, the author must therefore purge the Virginian of the half-breed's illiterate influence by exposing the cowboy to Molly and to the written texts that the white teacher has read: *David Copperfield, Othello,* and *Emma.* In wedding his teacher and in reading these texts, the Virginian abandons the cowboy group's unacceptable oral tradition, accepting white society and its literary canon or heritage.

Two Years Before the Mast and *The Virginian* focus on time periods preceding and coinciding with the North American cowboy's appearance, while *True West* (1980) examines orality and the role that it plays during the postmodern era. In Sam Shepard's play, Lee tries to rival his brother Austin's success as a screenplay scenarist. Austin has an East Coast education and a reputation as a writer in Hollywood, while Lee has only his experience of life in the desert to fuel his imagination with concepts for films. He convinces a producer, however, to abandon Austin's new script and to purchase a western that Lee has pitched but not yet written or outlined (*Seven Plays* 35). The pitch succeeds only because Lee recites it out loud. "I'm not a man of the pen. . . . I can tell ya' a story off the tongue but I can't put it down on paper" (18), he says. Having earlier antagonized his brother by jealously interrupting his work, Lee must now downplay his success at his brother's expense and persuade Austin to commit Lee's verbalized screenplay to paper: "use all yer usual tricks," he tells Austin—"Yer fancy language. Yer artistic hocus pocus" (50), or talent for translating ideas into print. Austin writes down Lee's talk, but the working relationship between the mutually envious, resentful, and competitive brothers breaks down at last, in the play's final scene, when the two men fight and seek to hurt each other physically. Shepard's examination of sibling rivalry is the most explicitly detailed analysis of the cowboy's oral culture in contemporary American drama. Contrasting an educated artist's reliance on the written word with a desert cowboy's dependence on the oral tradition, Shepard turns the confrontation between Austin and Lee into a contest between competing forms of cultural discourse.

Elsewhere Shepard maintains that his own collaborations or plays are hybrids of two forms of language, as is the screenplay that the brothers compose in *True West*. In his preface to *Tongues* (1978), for example, he notes that the talk between his coauthor, Joseph Chaikin, and Shepard was "translated verbatim, written down on the spot, turned into monologue or dialogue, trance poem or whatever" (*Seven Plays* 300). Later in the introduction to *Savage/Love* (1981), Chaikin says that he verbally improvised, rehearsed, and dictated the play and that Shepard wrote it down as he spoke it (320)—that this play, like *Tongues,* was based on a text that was both verbal and written.[17]

Two Years Before the Mast, The Virginian, and *True West*—spread throughout the framework of historical time and arrayed across the spectrum of precowboy, cowboy, and postcowboy culture—show forms of writing suppressing or competing with notions of western orality. Transforming cowboys such as the Virginian and Lee into readers, writers, or coauthors of texts and assimilating them into a dominant written system of discourse is one way of establishing *cultural* bonds between cowboys and mainstream society, which perpetuates its culture by reading and writing in English. One way of constructing *biological* ties is by linking orphans and bachelors with families, which perpetuate themselves by producing their heirs. In *The Virginian,* and elsewhere in nineteenth- and twentieth-century fiction, orphans find parents to raise them in families and bachelors move from all-male frontier locations to town, settle down, marry, have children, and embrace domesticity.

Cultural and biological bonding sometimes take place at the same time: in works by Louisa May Alcott, John Steinbeck, Frank Norris, Owen Wister, and Larry McMurtry, the "civilizing" force of society both educates and domesticates cowboys by schooling orphans and bachelors and then pairing them off with parents or wives and children to care for them.

A "cowboy" orphan, for instance, must choose between living out a western fantasy and belonging to a family and school in *Little Men* (1871), by Louisa May Alcott. Jo Bhaer tries to make her home and classroom at Plumfield more appealing to the orphan Dan Kean by allowing him to tame a colt and to play with it in Mr. Laurie's pasture next door. Jo channels Dan's unharnessed physical energy into a disciplined extracurricular project: she domesticates a restless "cowboy" who threatens to disrupt her classroom by permitting him to domesticate a pet of his own. "I am taming a colt too, and I think I shall succeed as well as [he will] if I am patient and persevering," says Jo. Dan vows not to "jump over the fence and run away" (241), but to stay with the colt in the pen and to spend his time away from his pet in the classroom. He binds himself to the school and family at Plumfield not only by educating himself, but by accepting himself as Jo's "son." Jo decides to possess the dispossessed orphan and to adopt Dan informally, sealing her decision "with a kiss that made Dan hers entirely" (180). In replacing the real frontier with a pasture next door and in placing the would-be cowboy in it with a colt of his own, Jo turns the drifting orphan into a slightly more pacified pupil. And in combining her teacher's supervision with a mother's love for her surrogate son, she transforms a difficult student at Plumfield into an educated, obedient boy.

Jo tries to reform the orphan as Alcott strives to educate her young reading audience—to teach children the difference between good conduct and improper behavior by giving them two examples to choose from: bad little cowboys and good "little men." Alcott's sequel continues the lesson by letting readers see what happens to Dan when he deserts his family and academic environment. In *Jo's Boys* (1886), he grows up, leaves Jo and her family at Plumfield, and travels out West, where he hopes to become a cowboy at last. Jo's friends interpret the frontier either as an extension of their East Coast society or as a culturally barbarous habitat. Mr. March, for example, imagines it as a territory for educated New England missionaries to conquer—a space in which to build a college and to "educate the heathen" Indians and ruffians. But Mr. Laurie defines it as a place in which to find "prairies and cowboys" (60)—a barren, uninviting, but exciting foreign environment. Dan agrees with Mr. Laurie, the mentor who once allowed him to play cowboy by riding a colt and who now tells him to go West and live out his fantasy. But in the following chapters, Alcott illustrates the fatal consequence of becoming a cowboy. On his way to a job at a ranch, Dan accidentally murders a man and then serves a sentence in prison, acting out the fate that social outcasts or cowboys are doomed to meet up with in *Jo's Boys*. Alcott continues to isolate Dan and to punish him, once he leaves prison and returns to the West, by forcing Dan to live as an outcast, or Cain, and to die as an unloved, unmarried man. The cultural and biological bonds that were formed between Dan and the mainstream in *Little Men* are broken in *Jo's Boys*, as Dan drifts away from his moorings at Plumfield and shipwrecks on the deserted island of orphanhood.[18]

Noncowboy authors force an orphan to choose between cowboy life and a classroom environment. But unlike Louisa May Alcott, John Steinbeck suggests that a classroom may not serve an orphan as well as a cowboy father or guardian. In an untitled short story in *The Pastures of Heaven* (1932), a drunken cowboy goes into the California desert and finds a baby abandoned and hidden under the sagebrush. He takes it back to the ranch and tells his boss that the baby has an unknown and mysterious origin (48). The rancher doubts the orphan ''myth'' (47) or the claim that the baby has been dropped from the skies, as the cowboy suggests, but he admits that the boy has a stunted intellect and, at the same time, a precocious artistic talent. He and the cowboy informally adopt the autistic savant and keep him at home on the ranch. They agree that Tularecito can never learn in a traditional classroom, but that he can develop his artistic talent by painting, sketching, and sculpting images of the ranch animals that he encounters outdoors.

Society's laws dictate, however, that children must receive formal education until they reach the age of eighteen. The rancher and cowboy therefore send the orphan to school, where the teacher, Miss Morgan, prevents her socially malad-justed student from sketching in class—and from disrupting his peers—by reading to him from a collection of children's short stories. She gets his attention by telling him that the characters in the fairy tales that she reads provide clues to his origin—that the fairies and gnomes are his parents, but that they have gone off and left him with cowboys so that they can pursue their own business unhampered. This written text explains the cowboy orphan's parentage in a reproductive, book-reading culture. Miss Morgan notes that after ''the bare requisites to living and reproducing, man wants most to leave some record of himself, a proof, perhaps, that he has really existed'' (56–57). Culturally and biologically binding the orphan to the rest of mankind—which tries to ensure its survival not only by reproducing its race, but also by producing and preserving texts for the sake of posterity—Miss Morgan weaves the two bonds together by making Tularecito see a record of his *birth* in the *text* and by referring to him as a *text* that she has, in a sense, given *birth* to. ''Here was a paper on which to write . . . a lovely story'' (58), she thinks, as she compares her invention of the orphan's fairy-tale mother and father to her narration of a fictitious tale. She cannot predict the tragic conclusion of the story that she has authored, however. For when he learns that he has been abandoned by figures in a children's short story, Tularecito attempts to return to them by digging a tunnel in a farmer's backyard and by crawling through it to reach the underground fairies. When the farmer attempts to stop this trespasser from destroying his property, Tularecito attacks him and ends up in a mental institution instead, not in the fairies' under-ground burrow. The school takes the orphan away from a rancher and cowboy. It gives him a teacher and ''mother''—Miss Morgan—who instructs and ''authors'' the orphan, giving him faith in the notion that orphans should read books and know that they have parents and ancestries.

Conflicts between the cowboy group and society end tragically with the violent madness of Tularecito or with the death of Dan Kean. Compromises between these two groups end peacefully with cowboys accepting mainstream reproductive soci-eties and their conventional literary establishments. In *The Octopus* (1901), for example, Frank Norris reads the assimilation of all outsiders through the life and career of a man who is both cowboy and Indian. At various points in the novel, Vanamee works with wheat, sheep, and cattle, and falls in love with the daughter of a deceased woman whom he had once planned to marry. When he engages himself to the daughter—who has the slanting eyes of an "Oriental," the full lips of an "Egyptian," and the blond braids of a Viking (32)—he becomes a symbol for all forms of cultural, social, and economic compression. As a wheat-ranching, sheep-herding "cowboy" (356), he represents all work groups in a western economy. As an Indian and as a relation by marriage to a woman with Asian and European physical markings, he serves as an Everyman in an American melting pot or as a blend of all possible bloodlines. As an orphan and as a family man, whose wife is the daughter of the woman whom he had once planned to marry, he becomes part of a romantic triangle that is almost incestuous.[19]

Vanamee not only is ensnared by the "octopus" bonds that link "cowboys" with families in an ethnically diverse western society, but also is caught up in the literary career of Presley, the novel's protagonist. Presley cannot imagine the scope or define the tone of the epic poem that he wishes to write until Vanamee tells him what a poet's artistic purpose and subject matter should be, in a series of intellectual discussions. Vanamee tells Presley that he should write about the American West— "the heat of the desert, the glory of the sunset, the blue haze of the mesa and . . . canyon" (35–36). He adds that Presley should publish the epic not in the popular "monthly periodicals," but in the daily press: "such a poem as this of yours, called as it is, *'The Toilers,'* must be read by the toilers. It *must be* common; it must be vulgarized. You must not stand upon your dignity with the people, if you are to reach them" (265). Presley must infuse an ancient oral form or an epic with life by writing on issues that interest present-day readers out West. In the same sense, Norris must break down the economic, social, and cultural boundaries that separate an American author's stratified audience in order to make his own epic, *The Octopus,* accessible. He does so, in part, by giving the reader a compressed symbol of assimilation with which to identify. As Everyman, Vanamee embodies all workers, all races, all social and family relations, and all cultural perspectives and forms of expression. Having grown up as a cowboy and Indian, Presley's literary adviser and muse has untutored, but trustworthy artistic instincts that let him respond to Presley's writing subjectively. Having gone to college (32), he also has refined, sharpened skills that permit him to understand conventional aesthetic standards and to judge Presley's poem objectively.

Norris published *The Octopus* in 1901, and after reading *The Virginian,* which appeared in the following year, he wrote an essay in which he argued that novels should represent cowboys as respectable members of obedient, law-abiding societies, not as antisocial, irreligious, and violent frontiersmen. He praised *The Virginian* for envisioning cowboys as fathers to children[20] and as friends to domiciled and civilized citizens—for exploring a frontier that *The Octopus* had begun mapping out in the preceding year: a New World that was populated by more daddies than dogies. Ironically, as the novel begins, the Virginian sings a feisty song that ridicules parenthood. When he meets a cowboy who has married and started a family, however, he stops singing the song, for he knows that it would horrify the cowboy, his wife, and their family. For the same reason, Wister edits out the last verse of the song, knowing that readers in a reproductive society—who believe in "baby worship," as Anthony Trollope once called it—would not be amused by the poem's final lines. The Virginian sings the following lyrics from the nineteenth-century oral poem, "Lulu":

> If you go to monkey with my Looloo girl,
> I'll tell you what I'll do:
> I'll cyarve your heart with my razor, AND
> I'll shoot you with my pistol, too. (60)

But Wister permits the cowboy to quit before mentioning Lulu's attempt to murder her unwanted offspring—an attempt that, according to editors of cowboy poetry anthologies, occurs in the poem's final verse:

> Lulu had twin babies,
> Born on Christmas Day;
> She mashed one's head with a rollin' pin,
> The other one got away.
>   (Lomax and Lomax 263–64)

Familiar with an extensive collection of poetry, Wister had traveled out West to Wyoming, met cowboys, and transcribed their poems in his journals before writing his novel in 1902. He probably knew how "Lulu" ended and chose it in order to contrast the Virginian's rollicking dismissal of children with a former cowboy's marriage and love for his baby boy, Christopher.

Tensions between orphaned and reproductive societies, and conflicts between oral and written traditions, combine in this novel and represent two related aspects of the same ongoing issue. Hence the Virginian learns to respect biological bonds between parents and children, as well as cultural ties that link people who read the same literature. The cowboy must acknowledge the difference between oral poems and written texts that he reads, for if "Lulu" persuades him that the murder of children is a lighthearted subject for song, then *Othello* instructs him that the act of murder is morally wrong and criminally outlawed. After reading of Desdemona's death, the Virginian says that he has heard of a worse man even than the wife-murdering Shakespearean hero—an Arizona rancher who "killed his little child as well as his wife"—but he adds that "such things should not be put down in fine language for the public" to read (174). Studying a *literary* classic has made the Virginian appreciate *children:* two statements in the cowboy's comment about the Arizona rancher make this comparison clear. First, reading a play reminds him that killing a child and its mother is even more reprehensible than killing a wife (Desdemona). Then, it reminds him that written texts such as *Othello* are different from bawdy works such as the oral poem "Lulu." Recitations about infanticide ("Lulu") are acceptable in a bachelor's society; "such things," however, "should not be put down in fine language for the public" to read, because books express values that mainstream reproductive society cherishes.

Here the Virginian begins to consider the feelings of children and the reactions of a reading audience to an account of violent and immoral behavior. In the next chapter, the author contrasts *Othello*'s representation of murder with *The Rime of the*

Ancient Mariner's moral. Again Wister contemplates the effect of a written text on the minds of young children, condemning the albatross's murderer by citing the following lines of the poem—"He prayeth well who loveth well / Both man and bird and beast"—and by arguing that these lines are "good to teach children; because after the children come to be men, they may believe at least some part of them still" (179). Comparing the child's moral and educational evolution into adulthood with the tutored cowboy's admission into society, Wister connects the cowboy with a book-reading and sexually reproducing community, writing about children who read and about a cowboy who reads, like a student, under the schoolteacher Molly's literary auspices.

The Virginian accepts society's educational supervision by submitting to Molly's instruction and to the teacher's treating him like one of her students. Later he redefines this student–teacher relationship as a courtship by using his enthusiasm for Molly's recommended novels and plays to express his love for her. Bluntly equating literary discourse with sexual intercourse, Wister indicates that a cowboy can make love to a woman only by first gaining intellectual access to her through an acquaintance with canonical fiction. The *consumption* of reading material before marriage leads to the *production* of children afterward: these two sides of the author's equation between a literary culture and a reproductive society explain the presence of cultural and biological bonds and the significance of the novel's last line. Referring to the Virginian's children, the author ends the novel by stating that the "eldest boy rides the horse Monte; and, strictly between ourselves, I think that his father is going to live a long while" (317). In a novel about the cowboy's reproducing and reading, Wister ends with a sentence that examines genealogical and literary relationships: he notes the blood ties between the Virginian—or "father"—and son, as well as the intimate literary ties between the reader and Wister—"*strictly between ourselves,* I think that his father is going to live a long while" (emphasis added).[21]

Emphasizing the cultural and biological bonds between cowboys and mainstream society, the author argues that the Virginian's fame and immortality in the American West will be matched by his family's longevity. Larry McMurtry makes the same point about cowgirls or *Buffalo Girls* (1990), fictionally reconstructing the life of the little-known but legendary Calamity Jane. Throughout the novel, Martha Jane Canary writes letters to her daughter, Janey. Only near the end of the novel does the mother confess that she made up the correspondent with whom she alleged to communicate. A cross-dresser (341) and suspected hermaphrodite (350), Calamity Jane could never bear children and invented a daughter to recompense herself for her loneliness. But McMurtry hints that the buffalo girl's fabrication of a biological bond is intertwined with her wish for some cultural form of continuance—that her yearning for fame is caught up with her quest for posterity. Calamity Jane notes that she first thought up Janey when Ned Buntline advised her to record her adventures and exploits. Buntline, who in real life wrote dime novels and used them to sensationalize and sell the West to the American public, now thinks that Calamity Jane's autobiographical jottings will translate well into lurid pulp fiction. Buntline's taste buds not only respond to the public's hunger for reading, but also whet the cowgirl's literary appetite for long-lasting remembrance. But when she sits down to compose, she says that "I started to write 'Dear Diary' and I wrote 'Darling Jane'" (343). In order to perpetuate history, she adopts a written form of expression and attempts to move from her isolation out West into the literary American marketplace. She tries to record both her text and her family, but preserving the latter finally takes precedence.

If Calamity Jane bonds with her fictitious daughter, then children also bond with cowboys and cowgirls in mainstream reproductive society. In coloring books and children's short stories, they read about those who once appeared to be outcasts but now seem to be familiar heroes and heroines. Although moving from adult fiction to portraits of cowboys and cowgirls in children's literature may seem a leap that is too great to make, it is nonetheless logical. The association of cowboys and cowgirls with written systems of discourse, on the one hand, and with children who are products of sexually reproducing communities, on the other, comes into focus when cowboys and cowgirls finally pop up in *texts* that are written for *children*.

Children are able to bond or identify with cowboys because they are taught, in coloring books that they look at, that belonging to a particular race, gender, or class is not a good reason for excluding anyone from the cowboy's society. Adult novels, histories, and autobiographies seldom mention roles that black cowboys and vaqueros played in shaping the West. But David Rickman's coloring book *Cowboys of the Old West* (1985) begins with an account of the American cowboy's Moorish and Spanish ancestors (1). Ubet Tomb's coloring book *Cowboys* (1987) includes lengthy discussions of vaqueros (1) and black cowboys such as Nat Love (13) and Bill Pickett (23). *The Adventures of the Negro Cowboys* (1965), by Philip Durham and Everett L. Jones, illustrates, compresses, and simplifies stories of black cowboys for children. Rewriting American history, these authors suggest that the West was not simply the white cowboy's domain: they allow readers in the twentieth-century American mainstream—comprising more immigrants and people of color—to relate to cowboys by highlighting Nat Love, Bill Pickett, and other ethnic and minority role models.

Cowgirls (1987), Ubet Tomb's coloring-book companion to *Cowboys,* privileges gender as other texts emphasize race and ethnicity: it offers little girls role models such as Annie Oakley and Belle Starr.[22] Other works focus on the permeable boundaries that allow members of every occupation and class to infiltrate the group and become cowboys and cowgirls. Tomb's two books, for instance, include stories of people who belong to the working class and to the economic stratosphere of well-known performers such as Roy Rogers, Dale Evans, Will Rogers, John Wayne, and Gene Autry. The cow-"person" is not only a manual laborer who works for a menial wage, but also a rodeo athlete, recording artist, or highly paid movie star—one of the mainstream's pop heroes or heroines, one of the entertainment industry's icons.

These books weave cultural bonds between the cowboy group and society, stitching cowboys and cowgirls into the fabric of Hollywood's music, movie, and television industries, sewing them into the tapestry of mainstream America's ethnically and racially diversified heritage. The books also fabricate surrogate biological bonds by addressing themselves to both parents and children. Many coloring books and children's short stories, for example, are filled with terminology and historical facts that are clearly aimed at adults, as Marie and Douglas Gorsline's

A drawing of the black ranch hand Nat Love. While the text makes an issue of race, the picture in this coloring book erases that point, for the sake of crayon-wielding children leaving everything blank. (From Ubet Tomb, Cowboys. Picture by Quickdraw Conkle. Bellerophon Books, Santa Barbara, Calif.)

Cowboys (1978) indicates.[23] *Cowboys* explains the aerodynamics of the lariat (14), the exact length of the Chisholm Trail (19), and the etymology of the word *cowpoke* (26), offering dense intellectual arguments and other adult information not to children, for whom the texts are allegedly written, *but to parents who read the texts to their children*. A line on the book's inside cover confirms that adult and young readers collaborate—that children process only what their parents narrate to them. "This is my book. My name is _____. Will you read it to me?"

Like this selection from *Cowboys,* the information in Tomb's *Cowgirls* seems to be offered to an adult (sometimes "adult-rated") audience. For example, will parents explain to their children that Ella Watson, alias Cattle Kate, was a prostitute? Will they let them puzzle out the significance of the following euphemism: "In 1888 [Jim] Averill set his old friend Ella Watson up in a home near his store, where she entertained lonely cowboys" (9) in exchange for payment? Will they divert children away from the text and let them color the picture of Cattle Kate, which appears to the left of the narrative? The image to fill in shows her lynched by a mob for having rustled its livestock, and the sobering caption below shrieks that "I wish that I had listened to Mother!" Proving the text correct when it claims that the ranchers "did a sloppy job" of hanging the rustler and prostitute, the picture depicts Kate in the noose, with her glazed-over eyes bulging out of their sockets and her limp tongue lolling outside her mouth, as if inviting some child to color it.

Sometimes the bonds between parents and children are tested by lines such as these. "I wish that I had listened to Mother!" suggests a relationship between parents and children that is based on admonishment and punishment; hence Cattle Kate's last words are a lesson to girls who toy with the idea of disobeying their mommies' advice. Jon Bowerman also plays with the notion that children are pests, underscoring the fact that his book is about parents who are comically annoyed by their offspring. For example, in his preface to *Cowkids, Colts and Peanut Butter Bulls* (1986), he asks what children have in common with hornets in a cattleman's outhouse, and answers: it sure doesn't take long for either one of them to get his "attention" (1).

Equating this description of children with an image of defecation and pain is only slightly more innocuous than comparing the implied fate of all naughty children with the picture of dead Cattle Kate, and only slightly more brutal than representing a cowgirl's bad relationship with her father in *White Dynamite and Curly Kidd* (1986), by Bill Martin, Jr., and John Archambault. In this illustrated children's short story, a young girl goes to watch her father ride a bull at the rodeo. As he waits to get on White Dynamite, she tries to engage him in a series of one-sided dialogues; each comment she makes and each question she asks him meets with a dismissive one-word response: "Yep" (9). This ostensibly entertaining short story is almost painful to read, not only because a cowgirl tries hopelessly to strike a conversational chord with her father (almost a caricature of the laconic cowboy of yore), but also because she attempts to win his approval by assuming his name, which he finally withholds. The daughter—who remains unnamed in the text—tells her father, Curly Kidd, that she would like to be called "Curly Kidd's Little Kid" when she becomes an adult. "Do you like that, Dad?" she asks. "Nope," he replies (6). This is certainly not "Home on the Range," where seldom is heard a discouraging word, but a broken home and broken-down system of discourse.

Cowboys and cowgirls strengthen their cultural links to the mainstream by appealing to the biological bonds between parents and children. In a sexually reproducing and book-reading culture, young people and adults respond equally to texts about cowboys and cowgirls. Hence in *White Dynamite and Curly Kidd,* the daughter uses her father's name to suggest her affiliation with the world of adults, and the

*I wish that I had
listened to Mother!*

*What happens to girls when they're naughty, as witnessed by this portrait of
a lynched Cattle Kate. Instead of a halo, a grim epitaph hovers over her
head, suggesting where girls go when they're naughty as well. (From Ubet
Tomb,* Cowgirls. *Picture by Nancy Conkle. Bellerophon Books, Santa Barbara, Calif.)*

father uses his nickname (Kidd) to suggest his childlike qualities: both generations
want to saddle themselves with the cowboy's or cowgirl's mystique. Writers also
indicate the Westerner's rope-hold on both parents and children by textually illustrating the importance of language. In *Cowkids, Colts, and Peanut Butter Bulls*, Jon
Bowerman says in his preface to parents that cowboys and children resemble each
other in their speech patterns. Listening "to cowboys talk is somewhat like listening
to small children" whose conversation is "sprinkled with attention getting words"
and obscenities (1). The cowboy's immature manner of speaking, however, is not

readily accessible to children, who learn it—in Bowerman's text—by parroting a quatrain in rhymed verse for each letter in the coloring book's alphabet. (To teach the letter *V* to young readers, for instance, the author writes:

> Vaquero is English for buckaroo,
> Vista's the Spanish word for view.
> Verse of a cowboy's a mix of the two,
> Very few use big words when small ones'll do.

Here cowboy poetry serves as another example of the cowboy's simplified language—''Very few [poems] use big words when small ones'll do.'') Authors have a hard time defining their audience. If cowboys really do speak and behave like children, as Bowerman argues, then they must speak to children more directly than they do to adults. But if they perform the work—and, in the case of Cattle Kate, the sexual acts—of adult men and women, then they must appeal to ''parents and other adults'' as well as to children (1).[24] Authors therefore attempt to interest both parents and children by making ''cute'' and diluting the significance of cowboys and cowgirls and, at the same time, exploring their importance with adultlike approaches to sex, economics, and history.

III

In the nineteenth century, cowboys used poems such as ''Poor Lonesome Cowboy'' to indicate ways in which the cowboy group differed from mainstream society. The orphan myth acted out the cowboy's isolation from family, and the recitation of that myth in ''Poor Lonesome Cowboy'' called attention to the cowboy's reliance on oral, not written, forms of expression. When the dismantling of the cowboy's oral culture and the reshaping of the West's cattle economy began, at the turn of the century, authors as varied as Owen Wister, Frank Norris, John Steinbeck, and Louisa May Alcott—and writers of coloring books and children's short stories— began, in their works, to mirror changes that were taking place as cowboys started assimilating, taking part in family life and in new modes of discourse. Their texts reflect hard facts that cowboys, in real life, run into when the old ways of life pass them by and the new truths of the twentieth century, on a collision course with myth and history, approach them.

Today cowboys are likely to move to town, marry, and give up their jobs at ranches as the West becomes more densely populated, settled, and urbanized. Alternatively, they are apt to commute from their jobs to split-level homes in the suburbs, riding home at the end of the day in pickups instead of on horseback. In other words, they are hard pressed to write about their alleged ''orphan'' status or bachelorhood when, in fact, they string fences on ranches that sit next to minimalls and join their wives and children on weekends at drive-ins that sell corn dogs and slurpies. The notion of cowboys as urban family men slowly begins to develop, to crop up in poems, and to hold sway in western circles of influence. The 1991 Cowboy Poetry

Gathering in Elko, Nevada, for instance, made cowboy families its theme and chaired special sessions on poems that were written by wives and children of cowboys.[25] As they head toward the twenty-first century, both cowboy and noncowboy authors are therefore more apt to question myths that once waltzed around, partnering cowboys with other single men in their work culture.[26]

When the cowboy group and its oral tradition began to disappear in the late nineteenth and early twentieth centuries, some cowboys began to write poetry and publish it publicly. Oral poems such as ''Poor Lonesome Cowboy'' had been jointly composed and designed by early cowboy coauthors to reflect democratic consensus—to highlight a series of group myths. But poems in the 1920s, 1930s, and 1940s—individually written by Bruce Kiskaddon, Badger Clark, Omar Barker, and others—now dealt with a wide range of topics, *not* with a series of myths that conveyed a sense of the cowboy group's unanimity. Written texts reflected the individual opinions or viewpoints of poets who no longer lived in and wrote for a tightly knit group, which had long ago given up its claims to ideological agreement and historical unity.

In the 1920s, 1930s, and 1940s—and again in the 1950s, 1960s, and 1970s—poets seemed unsure whether they should cling to group myths that had united cowboys in the nineteenth and early twentieth centuries or examine new issues while addressing themselves to a new group of men—rodeo athletes, urban cowboys, and ''dudes,'' all of whom called themselves ''cowboys'' in spite of their efforts to hook up with mainstream society. Poets in the 1980s and 1990s illustrate their wavering uncertainty even more graphically. Therefore, they serve as test cases in the rest of this chapter, in that they are more representative. Writing at the end of the twentieth century, they are even more apt to wonder whether they should write for the book-reading mainstream or orphan themselves from ''reality,'' writing for ''cowboys'' who seem to have retreated even farther into the tunnel of the nineteenth century's far-distant past.

Instead of reciting their work exclusively to the cowboy group's audience, modern poets write for cowboy and noncowboy readers. Sometimes poets even bond exclusively with noncowboy readers, comically dismissing cowboys and myths that nineteenth-century oral poets in the cowboy's work culture privileged, or revising those myths for new noncowboy readerships. For instance, Wallace McRae's ''Reincarnation,'' one of the most popular cowboy poems of the 1980s, mocks the branding myth of religious salvation and literally makes cowboys out to be pieces of shit.

> ''What does reincarnation mean?''
> A cowpoke ast his friend.
> His pal replied, ''It happens when
> Yer life has reached its end.
> They comb yer hair, and warsh yer neck,
> And clean yer fingernails,
> And lay you in a padded box
> Away from life's travails.''

α

As the West becomes more settled, it becomes harder to think of the cowboy as a social outcast or loner. The 1991 Cowboy Poetry Gathering in Elko, Nevada, acknowledged this fact by showcasing poems and songs about family life. (a) The Flying J Wranglers from Riudoso, New Mexico, feature the wife-and-husband team of Cindy and James Hobbs. (b) A young poet on stage. (c) The Braun Brothers, comprising Muzzie Braun and his sons. (C. J. Hadley, Carson City, Nev.)

"The box and you goes in a hole,
That's been dug in the ground.
Reincarnation starts in when
Yore planted 'neath a mound.
Them clods melt down, just like yer box,
And you who is inside.
And then yore just beginnin' on
Yer transformation ride."

"In a while, the grass'll grow
Upon yer rendered mound.
'Till some day on yer moldered grave
A lonely flower is found.
And say a hoss should wander by,
And graze upon this flower,
That once wuz you, but now's become
Yer vegetative bower."

"The posey that the hoss done ate
Up, with his other feed,
Makes bone, and fat, and muscle
Essential to the steed.
But some is left that he can't use,
And so it passes through,
And finally lays upon the ground.
This thing, that once wuz you."

"Then say, by chance, I wanders by,
And sees this on the ground.
And I ponders, and I wonders at,
This object that I found.
I thinks of reincarnation.
Of life, and death, and such.
I come away concludin': Slim,
You ain't changed, all that much."
(It's Just Grass and Water 28–29)

Nineteenth-century branding poems gave reincarnated cowboys a place in the after-life; McRae's poem, however, pokes fun at cowboys, their poems, and their hopes for Christian salvation while enshrining itself in the literary American marketplace. Proudly proclaiming that "Reincarnation" has been "heard on *A Prairie Home Companion* and *The Johnny Carson Show,"* the book advertises two strategies at work in *It's Just Grass and Water.* Comically insisting that cowboys are "just grass and water" manure (with the emphasis on the modest word *just*), McRae distances himself from the myths of the nineteenth-century cowboy's work culture and cozies up to the twentieth-century mainstream's book-reading audience, hoping that those who heard his poem and liked it will buy it in paperback.[27]

Comic poems are more common today than they were in the nineteenth century, suggesting perhaps that contemporary cowboys are more prone to puncture their pretensions and disparage themselves in their poetry. But comic poems are often more complex in their intentions than that, for they tend to simultaneously resurrect and deflate myths. While making fun of cowboys, poems entertain and solicit only *parts* of the mainstream, closing out readers in other parts and severing cultural ties to parts of their audience. The orphan myth, which once argued for the oral poet's autonomy, still rings out in written works that are read by the book-reading main-stream. But today poets wonder whether they should orphan themselves from the mainstream or address their written works to the noncowboy public and, if so, to what part of it.

Comic poems, for example, target a mass anti-intellectual audience, not an-other section of the book-reading public—an academic elite that decides which works of culture to canonize. In *A Feedbag of Cowboy Poetry* (1987), Bob Chris-tensen ends every poem with a punchline or pun, including one about male and female grizzly bears that have eaten a Czechoslovakian. Two men track, kill, and skin the bears for their pelts, only to discover what Christensen notes in the poem's final lines:

[They] opened up those grizzlies
And now we can end this tale
You really won't believe it, but
The Czech was in the male. (43)

Christensen—in addition to dealing here with ignoble forms of reincarnation, as Wallace McRae does—sports with images of feces elsewhere in his book, as if to suggest, on the surface, that cowboys work in the stable and that cowboy poets therefore have a barnyard mentality: they do not shy away from discussing unpleasant natural acts, as if to reinforce their earthiness. On another level, however, scenes of defecation suggest when and where to read poetry. Christensen writes that his poems should be read in "the outhouse." If a reader accidentally drops the book down the hole, then he or she should write to the poet and ask to receive a replacement copy "post haste" (54). Defending himself against academic misreadings of poems that the cowboy has composed, Christensen apologizes to critics for his poems' lack of intellectual content and begs them not to judge cowboy discourse by what he has written, for most cowboy poems are "pretty good" stuff (54). Bad stuff can perhaps be purchased by red-necked K-Mart shoppers who only want something to laugh at and wipe with. Canonized poems or high culture reside in the main house; cowboy poems or low culture make off to the outhouse, not to experience literary traditions, but movements of some other kind. And if readers drop their books down the hole in the outhouse, then they act out the prophecy written on the back of Christensen's book jacket: "Cowboy Poetry Reduced to Its Lowest Level," it jokes, tongue in cheek.

If some poems set out to slay high-minded readers, then other poems set out to capture them. Zeroing in on environmental and political issues, they aim at convincing mainstream readers that cowboys are concerned not only with local western affairs, but with national and international happenings. At the same time, however, they shove aside those who want to read comic poems, moving from the outhouse to the White House in poetry.[28] Like Wallace McRae, they sometimes try to move back and forth between these two houses and have it both ways, making light of the cowboy poet's purpose at one point and equating his function with that of a political oracle elsewhere. Although McRae uses "Reincarnation" to empty the brand of religious importance, he uses the square-dance call to convey a political message in "Put That Back . . . Hoedown." Lines from the poem—berating the "Supercollider, M H D, / and coal-fired powerplants. / The fiddles croon; sweet is the tune. / Now everybody dance" to the harangue against progress (32)—appear in *Things of Intrinsic Worth* (1989), a book whose title hammers home the high-minded importance of poetry. In *Up North Is Down the Crick* (1985), McRae chastises the Bureau of Land Management, which destroys the environment while looking for new sources of energy. "Eminent Domain," the most widely known poem in the collection, contrasts the cowboy's preservation of the public range with strip-mining operations, which leave the landscape in ruins.

Many writers mainstream themselves by moving from the West to the international front in their poetry. In *Where Old Trails Meet the New on Oregon's High Desert* (1988), for instance, Ramona Turmon laments the high "price of hay" and then free-associates, complaining about the "Arabs and their darn oil / The price of

Wallace McRae—author of Up North Is Down the Crick, It's Just Grass and Water, *and* Things of Intrinsic Worth—*is known for taking up environmental and ecological concerns in his poetry. He is seen here at the 1990 Cowboy Poetry Gathering in Elko, Nevada. (C. J. Hadley, Carson City, Nev.)*

fuel can make your blood boil'' (30). Lona Tankersley Burkhart, the coauthor of this collection of poems, also writes about the high ''price of hay'' (37) and, in the same piece, about global conflict and warfare:

> So sadly we watch the agony,
> of Beirut, Poland and Afghanistan.
> And of all this war torn world,
> how blessed is our land. (38)

Allusions to the Middle East may seem like referential non sequiturs, somehow slipped into the hermetically sealed West of regional poetry. They represent attempts by poets in the 1980s and 1990s, however, to update their work and to write for an audience that cares more about United States foreign policy than it does about preg-testing cattle in Idaho.[29]

These poems, because they are written by women, illustrate another principle by which mainstream ''cowboy'' poetry operates. Twentieth-century cowboys assimilate not only by discoursing on nonwestern themes, but by letting outsiders share their discourse and practice an art form that once featured male poets exclusively. But again, the role of women is tenuous, suggesting that cowboys—while reaching out—also draw back and resist changing their art form, making noncowboys conform to traditions that cowboy poets have followed for more than a century, instead of revising traditions to make room for twentieth-century noncowboy poets. Women, for instance, are inclined to conceal their ''otherness,'' obscuring their gender or adopting the voices of men by using one of five strategies. First, they narrate their poems from a male (not a female) perspective.[30] "I'm just a lonely cowboy," says the speaker in one piece, written by Lona Tankersley Burkhart (Turmon and Burkhart 10). I'm one of the "boys," insists Betty Lynne Grue's protagonist, in "Rain on the Tent Fly," attempting to insert herself into a group that does not include women (Grue 11). Second, narrators take on neutered identities, if not disguising themselves as cowboys, then passing as unidentified first-person speakers in Yula Sue Hunting's "A Fall" (Edison 43), in Turmon's "High Sierras," and in Burkhart's "The Cowman's Love of the Land" (Turmon and Burkhart 83, 17).[31] Third, cowgirl characters sometimes appear in poems that these

Recently women have been accepted as poets. Here, Mrs. Ted Egan performs at the 1990 Gathering in Elko, Nevada. (C. J. Hadley, Carson City, Nev.)

"cowboys" narrate, but never compete with cowboys or threaten their dominance. So, in "Cowgirls," Turmon demurs and writes: "Cowgirls aren't as good as cowboys with big, rank colts / But they ride what they can and live with the lumps and jolts" (Turmon and Burkhart 56). Fourth, they work with cowboys only reluctantly, preferring, in Tina Burke's "The Wink," to shop at a white sale at Sears instead of cutting livestock with men (Burke 3). Fifth, when they can, they leave ranch work to men and do housework. But in "Ranch Wife," Turmon writes about female feebleness, indicating that cowgirls cannot even clean house, much less do ranch work, without manifesting the weaker sex's timidity. "Just last week I saw / Another creepy little mouse," says a *Hausfrau* plaintively (Turmon and Burkhart 34).

Simultaneously expanding and contracting the boundaried definitions of what constitutes "poetry," cowboys permit men, as well as women, outside the circumscribed circle of cowboys to practice and diversify poetry, and to write it for a noncowboy audience. Still, at the same time, they call these works "cowboy" poems, even though they are not written by or for cowboys. Even though they swim in the mainstream, letting noncowboys read and write poetry, cowboys still refuse to be carried away by the tide of mainstream American literature, swimming out of the mainstream, crawling up on shore, drying off, and calling works "cowboy" poems—defining them as belonging, like a separate genre, to a unique subcategorical form of expression. According to Wallace McRae, for instance, the ranch and wildlife photographer Mike Logan writes "cowboy" poetry. In the preface to *Bronc*

People of color seldom write poems about cowboys or cowgirls. As a result, minority voices seldom sing out at these gatherings. Hank Real Bird, a Native American poet, recites his work at the 1990 Gathering in Elko, Nevada. (C. J. Hadley, Carson City, Nev.)

Widening its cultural scope, the 1990 Gathering examined Australia's aboriginal poetry. Here, Ted Egan sings a song while country-music star Charlie Daniels looks on. The 1992 Gathering featured Spanish, Mexican, Tex-Mex, Chicano, and Chicana verse as well as its usual sample of cowboy poems. (C. J. Hadley, Carson City, Nev.)

to Breakfast and Other Poems (1988), McRae notes that even though Logan is not a cowboy, he is still a master of cowboy poetics: his "rhyme is not only on target, but a bullseye every time" (9). It is instructive to note that as men assimilate and become part of the book-reading mainstream, the term *cowboy* no longer refers to one who works on a ranch and recites oral poems: it means one who writes and successfully imitates art forms, passing on his poems—with McRae's letter of introduction—to a book-reading audience. As a genre, cowboy poetry began to dry up when cowboys left the group at the turn of the century. It continues to define itself as an existing tributary of American discourse, not as part of the mainstream, only by drinking in as "cowboys" those literary infiltrators who trickle in from the outside and who replenish the cowboy poet's evaporating applicant pool. Hence the last fight for the water hole.

The annual Cowboy Poetry Gatherings, which began in 1985 in Elko, Nevada, illustrate the cowboy's tendency to hark back to old days and, at the same time, to look forward to new ways of marketing and publicizing his poetry. On the one hand, the Gatherings reclaim the nineteenth-century oral tradition by allowing people to "gather" and hear songs sung or poems recited from manuscripts. Returning to the primal scene seems to bring out the best in those who wish to preserve the nineteenth-century oral poet's autonomy: whole poems are written by people who praise Cowboy Poetry Gatherings and their alleged marginality. In "The Cowboy Poetry Gathering," for instance, Baxter Black says that he

> . . . went to the first annual ever
> convention of cowboy bards.
> (I woulda said poets, but poet's a word
> that sure makes a rhymer's job hard).
> (*Coyote Cowboy Poetry* 18)

Black can identify with "bards," oral singers, but not with writing "poets," who seem more pretentious than modest; he modestly notes that he can't be a poet because he can't even rhyme the word *poet* with another word in the cowboy bard's limited lexicon. In "One to Long Remember," Jim Ross insists that Gatherings are not like Broadway musicals or other spectacles that take place in the mainstream. They are exclusive functions that are held to express western "fellowship"; only cowboys can gather here and truly appreciate one another's poetry (Ross 50). In "To be or not to be—a Cowboy," Tina Burke writes about this "elite, select group of people, / To which I'd like to belong," even though she knows that she would be ostracized. She confesses, in a preface, that she composed the poem for an uncle who warned her, when she tried to enter a writing competition, that she "wouldn't qualify, because [she] wasn't *really* a cowboy" (Burke 9). In "To Elko and the Gathering Staff," Lona Tankersley Burkhart seems to think that she has a right, but that other outsiders don't have the credibility, to appear at the Gathering: "Can't you just see, a group of plumbers gathered here" to recite "cowboy" poems, she thinks, seeming to find this distortion somehow more comic than other "cowboy" permutations that operate (Turmon and Burkhart 43). But Ramona Turmon, in "The Old and the New," questions even her right to sing what used to be (and sometimes still is) thought of as discourse engaged in only by men. Only fathers, not mothers, should teach "cowboy rhymes" to their children; keep the flame burning and pass on the torch of tradition, she stipulates (Turmon and Burkhart 1). Cowboy Poetry Gatherings take place on the margins in that they revive the oral tradition, renounce the modern poet's pretensions, and define his art form as one that does not allow men and women in the mainstream to practice it.

On the other hand, these events meet with mainstream acceptance in that they draw a national and international audience, and attract men and women of all ages and from all walks of life.[32] Poems from the Gatherings are published in book form, sold, and publicized. Poets such as Waddie Mitchell and Baxter Black promote Gatherings, appearing on PBS specials, "The Tonight Show," video, and radio to make mainstream readers aware of their poetry. Popping up in different contexts and venues, they make one aware of the springiness and pliability that is a sign of their amorphous art form. In Elko, their work might seem to be an example of regional folkloric poetry; on "The Tonight Show," as a piece of pop culture or kitsch; on PBS, as an odd adjunct of high culture, coming on—as it might—after an episode of "Masterpiece Theatre."

Waddie Mitchell, author of **Christmas Poems,** *has appeared on "The Tonight Show" and has become one of cowboy poetry's most popular writers and reciters of verse. He is seen at the 1990 Gathering in Elko, Nevada. (C. J. Hadley, Carson City, Nev.)*

Neither poets nor critics know whether this writing should be defined as an amateur hobby, as an unskilled art form, or as a refined intellectual exercise. In "Comments on Cowboy Poetry Criticism," for example, Wallace McRae rails against those who reject his work *and* against those who embrace it, providing a

> . . . caution to those who'd dismiss us;
> or praise our work as sublime
> And heap too much praise, or too little,
> upon a cowpuncher's rhyme.
> *(Things of Intrinsic Worth* 71)

Academics stake out the equally unsatisfactory, critical middle ground by proposing, on the one hand, to abolish interpretation and remain true to cowboy poetry's apparently anti-intellectual roots while attempting, on the other, to remain faithful to interpretive strategies that come naturally to critical readers of literature. Judith K. Winzeler and Wilbur S. Shepperson, in their article "Cowboy Poetry," ask "whether cowboy poetry should be studied as poetry per se" or whether it should be seen merely as an "extension of cowboy life" (199)—that is, an example of amateur artistry. What is instructive to witness is the anguish that they act out as they vacillate. First they decide, like New Critics, to look for value in poems by searching for sophisticated metrical rhyme schemes or other complicating factors that might somehow make the poems seem less obvious. Unfortunately, they find nothing

Cowboy poets alternately envision themselves as a dying breed and as practitioners of an art form that gains in sophistication, recognition, and influence with each passing day. Between takes, Baxter Black, America's most
famous cowboy poet, mugs for the camera while filming a video of his poem
"Anonymous End." The poem deals with the death of a ranch hand, but here
Black clearly mocks death not only by winking in its face, but by giving his
poem life after "death." Transferring poems onto film and selling cassettes in
the marketplace allow artists to reach even more readers and viewers and to
profit even more from their repackaged work. (Darrell Arnold, La Veta, Colo.)

"irregular" (201), not even one paradox worth pondering. Brewing over this absence, they conclude that perhaps less is more—that cowboy poems should be praised for their simpleness. Winning the battle but losing the war, Winzeler and Shepperson are unsatisfied with the conclusion that these allegedly simple poems are examples of "folk art," but they are also unable to claim that the poems are complexly operating examples of high art. When the turf of culture is staked out and boundaries are set up to demarcate high art, low art, and every other conceivable "level" of art, within the city limits of literature, poets such as Wallace McRae—as well as critics such as Winzeler and Shepperson—are unable to determine whether cowboy poetry resides in respectable neighborhoods or on the wrong side of the tracks, on the poor side of town. On the one hand, McRae wants to live in the mainstream, seeking critical recognition of his poetry and condemning interpreters who dismiss his work with "too little" praise. On the other hand, he wants to maintain his place on the margins, encouraging the public's misunderstanding of his poetry and rejecting "too much" sympathetic support for his artistry.

It is useful to note that cowboys do not tend to write novels, as Larry McMurtry does; they do not tend to write plays, as Sam Shepard does; they tend to write *poems,* and it is necessary to understand why. Cowboy poems *are* simple in that they are quickly constructed; they therefore make simple demands on people who write as a pastime, not as a full-time profession.[33] A cowboy, a cowgirl, or anyone else who writes "cowboy" poems can come up with a verse while pitching hay to the cattle, filing briefs at a law firm, or engaging in any other professional activity. However, one cannot compose the first chapter of a book or the first act of a play in one's head and keep it there, only to write it down after going home from work, eating dinner, and taking the dog out for a walk in the neighborhood. Rhyme, as well as brevity, makes the composition and remembrance of verse possible. In the oral tradition, rhymes were mnemonic devices that enabled cowboys to hear songs once and commit them to memory. Now they facilitate the writing, as well as the memorization, of poetry. Like rap music, poems theoretically can be tossed off by anyone who is able to make words at the end of lines rhyme with each other, no matter how awkwardly. In "Puncher Poet Plague," for example, Wallace McRae attributes the plague or proliferation of poets to factors such as rhyme and, hence, says that being a "poet's plumb easy" (*Things of Intrinsic Worth* 8). In the nineteenth century, works could be practiced, performed, and accepted only by the increasingly fewer number of men who had access to the oral culture of cowboys. In the twentieth century, however, any literate person can write cowboy poems, read them, and value them.

What may not appear, at first glance, is the complex bargain that is struck with the gods in order to achieve this simplicity. Perhaps one should say that only an *illiterate* person can write cowboy poems, read them, and value them, for faked illiteracy is one of the earmarks of poems that are written by "cowboys" in the twentieth century, many of whom have formal educations and access to standardized discourse.[34] In "Dressin' Up," Baxter Black writes that the "dress code for everyday cowboys / Ain't changed since Grandpa got wise" and that all one needs is a "good pair of boots, yer Sunday hat," and "yer levis" to act out one's ties to the nineteenth-century cowboy's work culture in ways that are both linguistically and physically manifest (*Croutons on a Cow Pie* 4). To achieve the illusion that cowboys are simple sojourners, trekking down the road of tradition—that things "[a]in't changed since Grandpa got wise"—one must complexly transform oneself into the ur-cowboy of yesteryear. Paradoxically, costumes or dress codes are signs of Black's authenticity; saying "yer" instead of "your" and "Ain't" instead of "Isn't" and dropping the *g* at the end of his words are indications of his regional dialect, linguistic tokens of membership in a group of semiliterate or untutored cowboys, all of which make one forget that Black, in fact, has several college degrees and a license to practice veterinary medicine. Although nineteenth-century oral discourse has died out, Black preserves it by reminding his readers that cowboy poets are not prone to write well. Their words, like the language of dialect, seem out of place on the page, better suited to speech and better savored when recited out loud.[35]

Reviewing the Cowboy Poetry Gatherings in Elko, Nevada, Edward Hoagland wrote that cowboys "don't really write poetry any better than lawyers play golf, but one can learn a good deal about lawyers by how they play golf."[36] Cultural historians are less concerned with aesthetics—how well cowboys write poems—and more concerned with why they write them or, more importantly, how they think of them. The orphan myth held sway in the nineteenth century, when cowboys metaphorically orphaned themselves both from mainstream (reproductive) society and from mainstream (written) communicative discourse. At the turn of the century, the orphan myth lost force as cowboys mainstreamed, substituting marriage for singlehood and reading and writing for western poetic forms of orality. The myth lost force or changed shape and came back, in the twentieth century, disguised as a veiled philosophy. Some cowboys disclose that philosophy, admitting that it influences how they look at their poetry. Should they "orphan" it, not letting members of mainstream society practice it; not letting other people publish, publicize, market, and "gather" it; and not letting critics trumpet its virtues, including it in their canonized syllabi?

The orphan myth—and the branding, castration, and drifting myths—attempt to answer these questions by asking whether cowboys should separate from noncowboy society and set up their own cowboy work culture, or should mainstream and give up the distinguishing myths that their separate work culture privileges. The branding myth argues that cowboys should fight against ranchers who use cattle brands and barbed-wire fences to displace cowboys who work for them. On the open ranges of heaven, branded ranch hands define themselves as members of God's chosen race and, in doing so, isolate and elevate men who belong to the cowboy's work culture, branding livestock as one of their work functions. The castration myth also sets apart and privileges geographically isolated, sexually abstinent, and metaphorically castrated cowboys, suggesting that castrating cowboys are potent men, not girls and women on ranches or castrated steers at square dances held in noncowboy society. The branding and castration myths empower men, paradoxically using signs of the cowboys' perceived disadvantages and stigmatized differences to mythologize—to elevate to the religious status of demigods and to compare to the equivalent of sexual satyrs on horseback—ranch hands who participate in a distinct cowboy work culture. The drifting and orphan myths, on the contrary, cope with what happens when a cowboy work culture ceases to operate. When unemployed cowboys abandon their group and sign on as detectives with livestock associations in order to continue working out West, or when rustlers go to prisons in cities, forced as cowboy detectives are to mainstream or reform themselves; when orphaned oral poets move to town, marry, start families, assimilate, and begin to write poetry, selling their commercial publications to book-reading noncowboy outsiders—when all these events unfold, cowboys try to reconcile roles that they once played in the cowboy's work culture with functions that they currently act out in noncowboy society. In the cowboy's *work culture,* branding, castration, drifting, and orphan myths perform important *cultural work,* instilling nineteenth-century cowboys who manually labored for menial wages out West with a sense of labor's meaning and urgency, and providing twentieth-century men who inherit the cowboy's legacy with a sense of work's mythic context and coherent heritage—assurances that give cowboys purpose as they round themselves up, regroup, and head off into the frontiers of the uncertain twenty-first century.

NOTES

Introduction

1. "Bucking Horse in Mexico Throws Reagan."
2. "Baldrige Recalled as Honest Cowboy."
3. "Bush Eulogizes Baldrige as 'Noblest Work of God.'"
4. John-Thor Dahlburg, "It's Just 'Glasnost,' Soviet Says of Anti-American Publications."
5. Here I draw on earlier statements that critics of popular culture have made. Michel de Certeau writes, in *The Practice of Everyday Life,* that popular culture "invents itself by *poaching* in countless ways on the property of others" (xii)—in this case, on the dominant system of thought. In *Understanding Popular Culture,* John Fiske compares this "poaching" to a "military strategy" or a form of "guerilla" tactical warfare (19). It is "the process by which the subordinate make their own culture out of the resources and commodities provided by the dominant system, and this is central to popular culture, for . . . the only resources from which the subordinate can make their own subcultures are those provided by the system that subordinates them" (15). He notes that the same process reverses itself when the dominant system borrows back from the subcultures in turn.
6. Jane Tompkins, *West of Everything: The Inner Life of Westerns.*
7. In *The Negro Cowboys,* Philip Durham and Everett L. Jones first suggested that as many as five thousand black cowboys worked in the West after the Civil War (44). But in *The Cowboy Hero: His Image in American History and Culture,* William W. Savage, Jr., has refuted this long-held assumption. Savage notes that the earlier authors arrived at this figure by accepting the claims of a cattleman who had no facts or statistics to support his impressions (7). Savage goes on to say that "there is no such thing as cowboy demography" or ethnography either: "no one knows how many cowboys there were, or how they were distributed by age, ethnic origin, or geographical location. The life of cowboys hardly lent itself to careful observation by outsiders, to say nothing of statistical analysis by anybody, and cattlemen in search of profits in an opportunity-oriented business environment seldom kept personal records about their employees, most of whom were hired on a seasonal basis" (6). Nobody "counted cowboys, but people did try to count cows" (7), which were worth more than expendable men.

Unfortunately, recent scholars have accepted Durham and Jones's claim for five thousand cowboys as historical fact. In *The Negro in Texas 1874–1900,* Lawrence D. Rice says that "about five thousand Negro cowboys . . . rode the trails northward during the great cattle drives" (196). William Loren Katz, in *The Black West,* echoes that "five thousand men helped drive cattle up the Chisholm Trail after the Civil War" (146).

8. Other than rephrasing the claims that Durham and Jones have made, scholars seldom introduce new information concerning black cowboys and the work that they did. In *Blacks in the West,* W. Sherman Savage observes that black chuckwagon cooks played a role on the cattleman's ranch (87); and in *The Negro on the American Frontier,* Kenneth Wiggins Porter says that black cooks "were on the average better workers than the available whites" (504). But in examining a group about which little is known, many writers permit the category of "black cowboys" to include men and women who worked in the West without enacting the cowboy's labor routines. Thus Katz lists the rodeo performer Bill Pickett and a woman named Mary Fields, who carried the United States mail and who later worked in a laundry, in his chapter on "cowboys."

Chapter 1

1. For a detailed account of the procedure and a discussion of the political process, see Walter Baron von Richthofen, *Cattle-Raising on the Plains of North America* (1885), quoted in William W. Savage, Jr., *Cowboy Life: Reconstructing an American Myth* 41–47.

2. For an extended description of branding on the open frontier, see Mark H. Brown and W. R. Felton, *Before Barbed Wire* 181–89. Today, the brand is usually placed on the animal's left flank (David Dary, *Cowboy Culture* 157).

3. A vent brand is a "cattle brand placed upon an animal that has been given an ownership brand and later sold. It has the effect of canceling the ownership brand, thus serving as the acknowledgment of a sale. It is usually placed on the same side of the animal as the original brand. . . . From the Spanish *venta,* meaning *sale*" (Ramon F. Adams, *Western Words: A Dictionary of the American West* 337).

4. A road brand is a "special brand of any design for trail herds as a sign of ownership en route. Such a brand helped the herders to keep from mingling their herd with outside cattle and spiriting off their home range those animals of disinterested ownership" (Adams, *Western Words* 252).

5. Here, as elsewhere, I have given hypothetical examples in order to avoid infringing on the real or existing brands of other people.

6. I base my discussion of language and my use of terms on *Course in General Linguistics* (1916), in which Ferdinand de Saussure distinguishes between two systems of writing: the ideographic system, "in which a word is represented by some uniquely distinctive sign which has nothing to do with the sounds involved," and the phonetic system, in which syllables or alphabetic letters "represent the sequence of sounds as they occur in the word" (26). I argue here that the two systems of writing combine or occur together during the branding process.

7. An exception to this rule appears in the Colorado Brand Book of Arapahoe County (1887), in which descriptions of brands coexist with their pictures. But again, as later books demonstrate, the authors have made no attempt to *name* the brands they describe (Maurice Frink, W. Turrentine Jackson, and Agnes Wright Spring, *When Grass Was King: Contributions to the Western Range Cattle Industry Study* 242–43). For a documentation of early brand books that lack pictures and/or descriptions, see, for example, Richard Goff, Robert H. McCaffree, and Doris Sterbenz, eds., *Centennial Brand Book of the Colorado Cattlemen's Association* frontispiece.

8. Will Rogers died in 1935. *The Autobiography of Will Rogers* first appeared in 1949 and included essays and editorial pieces that had been written and published during his lifetime.

In addition to Rogers, other artists and writers have indicated ways in which brands can be altered and made to yield different meanings. See, for example, Frederic Remington, "Cracker Cowboys of Florida" (1895), in Peggy Samuels and Harold Samuels, eds., *The Collected Writings of Frederic Remington* 208–12.

9. A maverick is an "unbranded animal, usually a motherless calf, of unknown ownership" (Adams, *Western Words* 191).

10. I do not mean to suggest that branding today is unnecessary. I merely mean to distinguish between branding and alternative proofs of ownership that exist in the twentieth century. As fencing now allows the owner *physically* to separate his stock from that of other owners, so legal bills of sale now write out and *document* ownership when a cattleman sells his stock to a buyer or when he transports it across county lines and state borders. Hence although branding still plays an important role in western culture and law, it no longer functions as the *sole* means of determining ownership.

11. Oren Arnold and John P. Hale illustrate the significance of the brand as a commercial artifact by suggesting that the mark most frequently registered in the United States is the dollar sign (*Hot Irons: Heraldry of the Range* 62).

12. The Transamerica Title Insurance Company is the successor to the Security Abstract and Title Company in Colorado. The text of the preface is taken from the abstract of the Hitch Rack Ranch, now owned by Rose Mary Allmendinger of Colorado Springs, Colorado.

13. Like Joseph McCoy, Mark Twain examines America's system of writing by comparing it with early Egyptian society's. In "Simplified Spelling" (1906), Cadmus makes the transition from hieroglyphics—as they are used to describe cattle and other livestock—to Arabic numerals (Bernard DeVoto, ed., *Letters from the Earth* 131–34).

14. For a discussion of stories in which Mormons allegedly branded their wives, see Arnold and Hale, *Hot Irons* 188–89.

15. In Steinbeck's Americanized version of this biblical myth, even Joseph's name suggests the way in which the economic advancement of a society is built on top of its religious and moral foundations, for like his namesake in the Old Testament, Joseph is both a religious prophet and an economist: a man who guards the produce of the land, prepares for famine, and portions out food to Egyptian society.

16. "The Parson's Round-Up," *Denver Tribune-Republican,* 3 December 1884, in Clifford P. Westermeier, ed., *Trailing the Cowboy: His Life and Lore as Told by Frontier Journalists* 245.

17. The owner's conception of the brand is utilitarian and functional. It becomes what Roland Barthes will later call a "sign-function"—a semiological system derived from the objects of daily use or "a substance of expression whose basic essence is not to signify" (*Elements of Semiology* 41). The brand is made from such objects of daily use and it is interpreted by the cattleman in its simplest sense—as a transparently clear symbol of ownership, not as an indication of religious salvation or an example of the deep, metaphysical meaning that can be read into texts.

18. Cowboy poetry originates in oral song: in pieces brought by younger sons of aristocratic families, who came from England and Scotland to the West, looking for new adventures; in poems that cowboys clipped from newspapers, altered, transformed, and carried by word of mouth from camp to camp; or in new creations, composed over a period of time, performed verbally, and passed within the group from singer to singer (Douglas Branch, *The Cowboy and His Interpreters* 163). N. Howard Thorp collected these poems for the first time in *Songs of the Cowboys* (1908). His anthology was followed by John Lomax and Alan Lomax, comps., *Cowboy Songs and Other Frontier Ballads* (1910), and by John Lomax, comp., *Songs of the Cattle Trail and Cow Camp.*

Concerning the notion that cowboys sang songs to soothe cattle at night and during the day to prevent cattle stampedes: this assertion has been challenged ever since cowboys, folklorists, and historians began writing about the American West. I accept the likelihood of this allegation if only because cowboys tend, for the most part, to accept the claim instead of refuting it. In *Adventures of a Ballad Hunter* (1947), John Lomax insisted that he had witnessed the cowboys singing to herds (20, 45), but in *Pardner of the Wind,* N. Howard Thorp and Neil M. Clark denied that the cowboy ever sang to the cattleman's stock (29). Lomax and Thorp were the early twentieth century's two foremost critics of the cowboy's work culture, and even they could not agree concerning the likelihood of this long-held assumption.

19. Quoted in Savage, *Cowboy Life* 186.

20. For an introduction to brands, and a brief description of their history and connection with cowboy names, see Arnold and Hale, *Hot Irons;* Manfred R. Wolfenstein, *The Manual of Brands and Marks.* For a cowboy's first-person account, see W. S. James, *Cow-Boy Life in Texas, or 27 Years a Mavrick* (1898), quoted in Savage, *Cowboy Life* 108.

21. James H. Cook, *Fifty Years on the Old Frontier as Cowboy, Hunter, Guide, Scout, and Ranchman* 109.

22. For John T. Irwin, "Adam's naming" involves an interweaving "of God-given natural forms into a language of signs, gestures, and pictures—a human language that is continuous with the language of nature because its elements are borrowed from that language" (*American Hieroglyphics: The Symbol of the Egyptian Hieroglyphics in the American Renaissance* 33).

23. R. W. B. Lewis has defined the American Adam as a mythic hero, living in nature, creating language, and using it to name "the elements of the scene about him" (*The American Adam: Innocence, Tragedy and Tradition in the Nineteenth Century* 5). It is possible to see the brand as a manifestation of this language and to see the branding mark as an articulation of the worker's special standing, for as early as 1898, W. S. James noted that the cowboy receives an education in "the school of nature." He learns his letters on the range, puts them in the brand, and writes them on the animals in the cattleman's pasture (Savage, *Cowboy Life* 108).

In cowboy culture, salvation songs indicate the way in which the poet takes the economic meaning of this language and transforms it to his own advantage, using the brand to give members of his group an access to the mythic pastures of the heavenly range. This poetry makes use of the salvation myth that Northrop Frye discovers in pastoral representations of range life. In *Anatomy of Criticism,* Frye notes that an attention to animal nature appears not only in "the sheep and pleasant pastures" of the idyllic, but in "the cattle and ranches" of the West, and that animal nature combines with myth to illustrate the biblical theme of salvation (43). But in branding poems, the myth that writes itself on the "animal nature" or cattle hide also necessitates an economic restructuring of the relationship between employer and worker.

Occasionally noncowboy writers acknowledge the cowboy's religious interpretation of branding. Alfred Henry Lewis, in *Wolfville,* describes the cowboy evangelist Short Creek as a man who "ain't workin' with no reg'lar religion round-up; he's sorter runnin' a floatin' outfit, criss-crossin' the range, prowlin' for mavericks an' strays on his own game. But what of that? He's shorely tyin' 'em down an' brandin' 'em right along" (184). Bob Burleson, in "Welded Stainlessteel," writes that nineteenth-century cowboys "burned horny butts with the runic meaning found in Texas cattle brands, a faith in more than survival that comes from unseen sky selves till they boom and light up to let you know where they are" (*Runic Meaning in Texas Cattle Brands: Dramatic Essays and Illusions of the Organic Theatre* 107).

24. Rollins assumed that cowboys were "religiously asleep," and almost every scholar since Rollins has clung to that mistaken assumption. See, for example, *Cowboys of the Americas,* in which Richard W. Slatta writes that nineteenth-century cowboys "seemingly worried little about theology" (227).

In fact, a belief in Christian salvation bound cowboys together and expressed itself in a series of branding signs, much like what cultural anthropologists mention when they write about emblems that other societies used to illustrate group beliefs and forms of social cohesiveness. Claude Lévi-Strauss says that the permanence and continuity of a clan require "only an emblem, which may be . . . an arbitrary sign, so simple that any society whatever . . . may conceive of it" and he attributes the creation of this sign to the "instinctive tendency . . . to paint or incise on the body images which recall this community of existence." An analysis of branding coincides with his study of writing in other cultures, in that it culminates like these other writing systems in an "affective theory of the sacred" (*Totemism* 61, 71). Don D. Walker has argued that "the cowboy's world seemed closed, marked by monotonous routines and binding group loyalties" (*Clio's Cowboys: Studies in the Historiography of the Cattle Trade* 86–87). I argue, instead, that poetry enables the cowboy to free himself from the monotonous aspects of branding and to fashion the brands into what Clifford Geertz would call "a historically transmitted pattern of meanings embodied in symbols, [into] a system of inherited conceptions expressed in symbolic forms by means of which men communicate, perpetuate and develop their knowledge about and attitude towards life" (*The Interpretation of Cultures* 89).

25. Recent poems have even pessimistically envisioned the afterlife as a filthy city or spiritual wasteland. In "Cowboy Heaven," for example, Baxter Black says that "men get recycled like cans / And eventually wind up in Heaven / After wearin' numerous brands" (*Croutons on a Cow Pie* 12). He compares the expendability of the worker in the city to the refuse that the city is responsible for—to a beer can, which is discarded when the alcohol is consumed, or to a brand, whose meaning is lost when the cattle are slaughtered and are eaten by urbanites.

26. For a discussion of barbed wire and its effect on the cattle industry, see Walter Prescott Webb, *The Great Plains* 270–318; Wayne Gard, *The Chisholm Trail* 207, 225; Edward Everett Dale, *Cow Country* 82–85; Walter Gann, *Tread of the Longhorns* 104–6; Henry D. McCallum and Frances T. McCallum, *The Wire That Fenced the West*.

27. Umberto Eco says that the "nature of the sign is to be found in the 'wound' or 'opening' or 'divarication' which constitutes it and annuls it at the same time" (*Semiotics and the Philosophy of Language* 23).

28. Lewis Atherton says that the "brand mark demonstrated that *property* concentrated itself in herds of cattle. . . . In the 1880s and after, *property* concentrated itself more in land, and fenced-in acreage became a mark of ownership" (*The Cattle Kings* 181). Joe B. Frantz and Julian Ernest Choate, Jr., have suggested that with the development of barbed wire, branding became "more of a preventative measure against rustling and a compliance with demands of legal ownership [rather] than a method for establishing ownership among cattle on the open range" (*The American Cowboy: The Myth and the Reality* 59).

29. McCallum and McCallum, *The Wire That Fenced the West* 22; Webb, *The Great Plains* 290–95.

30. McCallum and McCallum, *The Wire That Fenced the West* 42.

31. Ibid., 31–74; Webb, *The Great Plains* 298–309.

32. Cordia Sloan Duke and Joe B. Frantz, *6000 Miles of Fence: Life on the XIT Ranch of Texas* 6. McCallum and McCallum note that when an agent for the Barb Fence Company came to Texas, his purpose was not "to demonstrate fencing as a means of keeping cattle out of a plot which [the buyer] wished to cultivate but as a means of keeping them in the feeding grounds allotted to them" (*The Wire That Fenced the West* 117).

33. McCallum and McCallum, *The Wire That Fenced the West* 31.

34. Webb, *The Great Plains* 309.

35. J. Evetts Haley, *The XIT Ranch of Texas and the Early Days of the Llano Estacado* 88.

36. English novels also sometimes equate the cattle brand with the barbed-wire fence. In *The Boy in the Bush* (1924), for example, D. H. Lawrence portrays Jack Grant as a branded cowboy-figure—"a sinner, a Cain" (10)—who is expelled from an English school and transported to the bush in Australia, where he is forced to earn a living and repair the reputation of his family back home. Lawrence, like Conrad Richter, equates the brand with the fence and defines both as symbols of shame. Jack's sinful behavior leads to his expulsion from school. His moving from Britain's domesticated and virtuous realm to the sinful outback that cowboys and other drifters inhabit is described as an escape from a fenced-off enclosure, within which domesticated animals live, and as a journey onto unrestricted new ground. Jack is portrayed as having crossed over the line or as having jumped over the "fence" that distinguishes between "sin and virtue" in civilization (12). Jumping over that fence, he has traveled into morally dangerous territory and has therefore earned the brand of a sinner.

37. The opposition between the cattle brand and the barbed-wire fence is evident even in the language that is used today to describe a ranch that is owned by one of pop culture's icons. Designer Ralph Lauren, who has marketed his clothes and perfume by playing off the cowboy's mystique, recently built the Double R L Ranch in Ridgeway, Colorado, in order to develop a "brand" of designer beef. In "Ralph Rides the Range," originally published in the *Denver Post,* reporter Jim Carrier notes that Lauren "has placed his brand on this land—just as he has on fashion—in a way that is at once new and old, trendy and traditional." Carrier defines the ranch as "traditional" because Lauren has worked to re-create the look of a nineteenth-century "spread"; he identifies it as "trendy" because Lauren has replaced the "traditional barbed wire" fence on the highway with fifteen miles of "four-rail pine." The Double R L Ranch is an ironic example of the way in which culture sometimes mistakenly works to pinpoint its traditional heritage, for the barbed-wire fence was itself a trend that supplanted the wooden rails the reporter describes. Unwittingly, Lauren acknowledges the brand's even earlier precedence by dispensing with the fence that led to its untimely demise and by emphasizing his "brand" of designer beef at the expense of the fence that confines his beef cattle.

Chapter 2

1. Grace McClure, *The Bassett Women* 101–2.

2. According to McClure, Haley never specified the technique that his cowboys used to spay heifers. A common procedure at that time, however, was performed on the left or right flank of the animal. After shaving the hair on the flank, one made a diagonal incision below the transverse process of the lumbar vertebrae. Using a knife, one then cut through the skin, subcutaneous connective tissue, fascia, external and internal oblique abdominal muscles, and peritoneum. Inserting a hand into the heifer and locating the uterus, one followed its right cornu upward and backward with the hand, finding the right ovary and then severing the ovary from its attachment at the head. Going back to the left cornu and from there to the other ovary, one performed the action again and then brought out the ovaries. The fibers of the internal and external oblique abdominal muscles came together naturally and anatomically closed the wound. Once the external incision was sewn up, scar tissue built up on the surface skin, indicating where one had made the incision. (George Ransom White, *Animal Castration: A Textbook for the Use of Teachers, Students and Practitioners* 161–68). Thus Haley's claim— though unsubstantiated—is credible. Although the reproductive organs of the heifer are *internal,* their removal is accomplished through means which are apt, in the process, to leave an *external* wound.

3. For verification of the branding and castration process, as they occur together, see Dary, *Cowboy Culture* 157; Arnold and Hale, *Hot Irons* 3, 79.

4. Brown and Felton, *Before Barbed Wire* 189.

5. McClure, *The Bassett Women* 102.

6. Ibid., 177–78.

7. Historians agree with Atherton, who says that "the labor force on most ranches consisted almost wholly of unmarried men" (*The Cattle Kings* 96), but they disagree on the reasons for this phenomenon. Branch suggests that the cowboy was self-centered: that marriage and family were distasteful to him because "nothing in the cowboy's society was more important than the cowboy himself" (*The Cowboy and His Interpreters* 157). Philip Ashton Rollins says that the cowboy was independent: that "marriage meant almost always for the man of gentle birth a return to the East, or to England, and usually for the man of more ordinary blood retreat from the open country and settling either in some town or upon a fenced farm near it" (*The Cowboy* 35). In his article "The Cowboy and Sex," Clifford P. Westermeier seems to agree with Branch. "Married cowboys in the early days," he writes, "were not the rule, because wanderlust, extended absence, the somewhat arrogant attitude of self-importance, and a poor wage did not lend themselves toward domesticity" (Charles W. Harris and Buck Rainey, eds., *The Cowboy: Six-Shooters, Songs, and Sex* 90). Although critics argue whether bachelorhood was enforced or self-imposed, they agree that the economic consequences of marriage were debilitating to the profession. Jack Weston, for instance, says that married men "would have to give up cowboying for wages, because no provision was made for wives of workers on the range or trail" (*The Real American Cowboy* 18–19).

8. A line camp is a tent, an "outpost cabin or dugout on a large ranch in which line riders are housed" (Adams, *Western Words* 178). Line riders follow a ranch's fences or boundaries and maintain order on the borders of a cattleman's property.

9. As a topic, castration is considered taboo and, as Walker notes, "rarely if ever" has it been cited by cowboys or scholars as part of cowboy work. This chapter, in part, takes up Walker's suggestion that an "interesting study could be made of the evasion" as it operates in recent scholarship (*Clio's Cowboys* 196). Duke and Frantz illustrate that this evasion takes place—even in historical reconstructions of range life—when they write that in working a calf, two men "use the knife (for earmarks and so forth)" (*6000 Miles of Fence* 14). In a parenthetical apology to the reader, they allude to the fact that the knife is also used to castrate the calf ("and so forth"). Their discretion typifies the reluctance to comment on the cowboy's castration of animals.

10. Adams, *Western Words* 86.

11. J. Marvin Hunter, "Cowboy Life in West Texas," in Hunter, ed., *The Trail Drivers of Texas* 329–30.

12. For a discussion of homosexual cowboys, as they are portrayed in works written by noncowboy outsiders, see Westermeier, "The Cowboy and Sex," in Harris and Rainey, eds., *The Cowboy* 95–105.

13. For a definitive account of the cook and the role that he plays, see Ramon Adams, *Come an' Get It: The Story of the Old Cowboy Cook.*

14. For a discussion of race and ethnicity, as worked out in the histories of chuckwagon cooks, see Durham and Jones, *The Negro Cowboys* 50–56.

15. In fiction written by noncowboy outsiders, the "effeminate" cook can even be portrayed as having latent or manifest homosexual yearnings. See, for example, Gretel Ehrlich's *Heart Mountain* (1988), in which the Asian-American cook at a Wyoming cattle ranch remembers a homosexual encounter that he participated in during his youth (118–121). Ehrlich's representation of a cook illustrates Frank Chin's complaint, in "Confessions of the Chinatown Cowboy," that white writers tend to portray Asian men as effeminate (66).

16. Durham and Jones define the "wedding feast" as "a wedding of dinner and supper"—an especially large banquet thrown on special occasions—but other citations of gen-

dered phrases, which proliferate in their text, suggest that this term actually fits into a system of language that can best be described as a sexual lexicon (*The Negro Cowboys* 53). In *Yellow Back Radio Broke-Down* (1969), Ishmael Reed uses that lexicon when Mustache Sal, a prostitute, rings the "come-and-get-her-while-she's-juicy-and-hot" bell and calls the ranch hands to "dinner" (111).

17. Adams, *Come an' Get It* 166.

18. Adams says that the testicles "were not served with the meals, as the cook seldom prepared them, but were generally roasted on the coals of the branding fire until they popped open. They were salted and eaten there at the fire as a between-meal-snack" (*Come an' Get It* 114).

If eating castrated testicles seems like a strange, isolated occurrence to dwell on, it is useful to note that noncowboy writers were aware of this dimension of cowboy life and frequently described it in their works. In *Life on the King Ranch,* Frank Goodwyn noted that behind the castrator "comes a little boy or otherwise useless person with a bucket in which he puts the testicles of the castrated calves" (121). These organs were then handed over to cowboys who roasted them. In *Giant,* Edna Ferber's Bick Benedict tells Leslie (in a scene that Rock Hudson and Elizabeth Taylor would later act out on film) that a Mexican boy picks up "the testicles of the castrated calves. The tumbadores [men who throw calves] roast them on the coals, they burst open and they eat them as you'd eat a roast oyster, they're very tasty really and the vaqueros think they make you potent and strong as a bull" (205). And in *The Rounders* (1960), Max Evans's cowboy, Wrangler, fries calf "balls" for Dusty and himself to eat, after rounding up and castrating cattle (46).

19. Even in a recent article, "Uncommon Myths About Beef," the cowboy poet and essayist Baxter Black notes the myth that the "consumption of bull meat increases libido," although he facetiously adds that it has never yet helped the author himself.

Noncowboy writers have also attributed the male's sexual potency to his consumption of the bull's castrated testicles. In *A Cool Million* (1934), for instance, Nathanael West satirizes Wu Fong's attempts to redecorate and update his brothel by turning it into an all-American house of ill-fame. Wu Fong designs each prostitute's bedroom to reflect the ambiance of a different locale—New England, the Midwest, the Southwest. Powder River Rose's apartment is a replica of a Wyoming "ranch bunk-house," with "spurs, saddle blankets, straw, guitars, quirts, pearl-handled revolvers, hay forks, and playing cards" strewn about the room in calculated confusion (*The Collected Novels of Nathanael West* 333). Customers can eat "mountain oysters" (334), or bull testicles, before copulating with Rose, in order to enhance their performance.

20. Mari Sandoz, *The Cattlemen* 96. For another description of the same surgical process, see J. Evetts Haley, *Charles Goodnight: Cowman and Plainsman* 446–47.

21. Adams, *Come an' Get It* 114; Adams, *Western Words* 201, 236.

22. Even recent cowgirl poets have reinforced the cowboy's age-old castration myth. In "Oyster Power," Gwen Petersen writes that "mountain oysters," or bull testicles, function as male aphrodisiacs (Gwen Petersen and Jeane Rhodes, *Tall in the Sidesaddle: Ranch Woman Rhymes* 27).

> For like the oysters in the ocean
> They give a cowboy lovin' notions.
>
> And when he meets a gal in town
> Well, hell, cain't keep that feller down.
>
> Now he's got urgings strong and stout
> And oyster power to carry them out.

Now I've known cowboys—quite a few—
And near as I can tell,—that's true.

Noncowboy writers also suggest that "oysters" reinforce manhood. Examples are Ferber, *Giant* 205, and James Welch, *Winter in the Blood* (1974), in which the Native American Long Knife, who comes "from a long line of cowboys," feels that his mother challenges his reputation as a cowboy and undoes his manhood by roasting testicles after castrating calves: "She made a point of eating the roasted balls while glaring at one man, then another—even her sons, who, like the rest of us, stared at the brown hills until she was done" (24).

23. In his study of different societies, Bruno Bettelheim determines that, in combat or war, "castration appears in much earlier times as the toll exacted by the victor from his defeated enemy. . . . The victor's main purpose was to gain for himself the masculine power of his victim" (*Symbolic Wounds: Puberty Rites and the Envious Male* 90). Cowboys symbolically illustrate this conquest of male animals by castrating them, as "The Castration of the Strawberry Roan" indicates. Both in Baxter Black's version of this poem (Text A) and in Dallas "Nevada Slim" Turner's version (Text B), a cowboy attempts to punish a roan horse that he cannot ride by castrating it. But the enemy victimizes his aggressor instead by castrating the *cowboy*—by biting off (Text A) or by grabbing (Text B) his testicles (Guy Logsdon, comp. and ed., *"The Whorehouse Bells Were Ringing" and Other Songs Cowboys Sing* 86–96).

The cowboy castrates the male animal not only to subdue it, but to illustrate what Freud has suggested—that "in absorbing parts of the body of a person through the act of eating we also come to possess the properties which belong to that person" (*Totem and Taboo: Resemblances Between the Psychic Lives of Savages and Neurotics* 107). That the act of eating can be understood as a sexual metaphor is made clear in *The Raw and the Cooked,* in which Claude Lévi-Strauss notes that some primitive tribes use the same verb to describe the acts of eating and sexual intercourse (269). See also Lévi-Strauss, *The Savage Mind* 105. I only argue that the cowboy's consumption of the bull's testicles is a sign for the sexual act and a strategy for increasing his sexual potency.

24. For accounts that discuss the cowboy's predilection for raw meat and his equation of meat consumption with sexual prowess, see F. M. Osbourne, "Sargent's Rodeo" (1880), quoted in Westermeier, ed., *Trailing the Cowboy* 18. See also Samuel Dunn Houston, "A Trying Trip Alone Through the Wilderness," in Hunter, ed., *The Trail Drivers of Texas* 85; Frank Collinson, *Life in the Saddle* 42.

25. The link between the consumption of meat and the increased sexual powers of men who consume it is made in works on the cattle trade, and sometimes in writings on buffalo hunting (Stanley Vestal, *Queen of Cowtowns: Dodge City* 67). It is not mentioned, however, in accounts of the sheep industry or in literature about the American shepherd (Ivan Doig, *This House of Sky: Landscapes of a Western Mind* 159–65).

26. For an early, nonfiction account of cowboys who are surprised to see women eat "oysters," see Dan Moore, *Shoot Me a Biscuit: Stories of Yesteryear's Roundup Cooks.* Moore describes castrating cattle on a northern Arizona ranch at the turn of the century. When the wife of his Mormon employer and her two visiting women friends come to the roundup, they are "skittish about trying this sample of Western ranching fare; but after Mrs. Jones had persuaded [her two friends] to 'try just a bite,' they nobly overcame their aversion and dived in for second helpings, just as though they had been eating calf nuts all of their lives" (94).

27. Estrogenic compounds include compudose; nonestrogenic ones include zeranol (M. E. Ensminger, *The Stockman's Handbook* 226, 284).

28. "The implant site is subcutaneous, between the skin and cartilage on the back side of the ear and below the midline of the ear. The implant must be placed in the middle one-third of

the ear, no closer to the head than the edge of the auricular cartilage ring farthest from the head.'' Implanting in the veins ''may cause too rapid absorption. Implanting the cartilage or skin may decrease absorption because pellets may be walled off'' (*Ralgro Implants*). I am indebted to Stephen A. Ellis, of Pitman-Moore Inc., and to Ralgro, a company that produces a nonestrogenic compound, for providing this information.

29. Baxter Black, ''The Cabbage Patch.'' The cattle industry has attempted to dispel this fear by demonstrating that an 8-ounce portion of beef contains only 2.8 nanograms of estrogen (1 nanogram equals one-billionth of a gram), whereas an 8-ounce glass of milk contains 34 nanograms of estrogen; an 8-ounce helping of peas, 340 nanograms; and a comparable portion of cabbage, 2,050 nanograms. Hence the cattle industry argues that the estrogen levels for beef are lower than those found in other foods. It should be noted that this information was provided by Ralgro, a company whose continued success is clearly tied in with that of the beef industry's.

30. ''Magnum CP-20: New Controlled Pressure Design, Implants Right the First Time.''

31. In fiction, the cowboy's gun has often been represented as a phallic symbol and as a means of castrating others. In *The Brave Cowboy: An Old Tale in a New Time* (1956), for instance, Edward Abbey describes Jack Burns's hands not as resting near the gun in his holster, but as pointing to his groin and testicles: ''His hands, big and long-fingered like those of a flutist or a good plank-stacker, and hard, brown, leather-skinned, rested like a pair of lifeless tools on his lap, on his groin and genitals'' (13–14). In John Herlihy's *Midnight Cowboy,* Joe Buck imagines a cowboy as a man with ''legs apart, pelvis thrust forward, . . . in the act of turning a big gun on you. The barrel of it was coming at you thick and gleaming, and it was about to go off'' (97). The cowboy manifests his potency by wielding his gun and by using it to injure or metaphorically castrate his victims.

32. Haley, *The XIT Ranch of Texas and the Early Days of the Llano Estacado* 242.

33. Arnold and Hale, *Hot Irons* 150–51.

34. J. Frank Dobie, *Cow People* 68.

35. For further historical citations of the cowboy's cross-dressing, see Philip D. Jordan, ''The Pistol Packin' Cowboy,'' in Harris and Rainey, eds., *The Cowboy* 76–77. Jordan mentions a newspaper article in the November 3, 1885, edition of the *Bismarck Daily Tribune* written by a reporter who describes cowboys costumed as women descending on Bismarck and shooting off guns.

36. Betty Casey, *Dance Across Texas* 54.

37. Lloyd Shaw, *Cowboy Dances: A Collection of Western Square Dances* 123. In such films as *My Darling Clementine* (1946) and *She Wore a Yellow Ribbon* (1949), director John Ford used reel dances to illustrate western forms of social behavior as well.

38. Glenda Riley, *The Female Frontier: A Comparative View of Women on the Prairie and the Plains* 203–4. In separate appendixes, Riley lists the number of men and women who lived in the plains states (Kansas, Montana, Nebraska, North Dakota, Oklahoma, South Dakota, and Wyoming) between 1870 and 1910, and the number of men and women who lived in the prairie states (Illinois, Indiana, Iowa, Minnesota, and Missouri) between 1830 and 1870.

39. Casey, *Dance Across Texas* 31; Rollins, *The Cowboy* 189. Logsdon also describes ''stag dances'' for men in which cowboys took women's places by wrapping ribbons and scarves around their arms and by designating themselves as female substitutes (*''The Whorehouse Bells Were Ringing'' and Other Songs Cowboys Sing* xiv).

40. In *Reminiscences of a Ranchman,* Edgar Beecher Bronson says that, at a saloon where there were ''not enough gals to go round'' (268), a ranch foreman once dressed up as a cowboy's female dance partner by wearing a white skirt with a pink waist sash over his boots, spurs, and chaps (269–70). Both the cowboy and the foreman treated the incident as a

practical joke, for unlike the square dance, at which the foreman ordered his cowboys to wear "heifer brands," the saloon dance enabled men to mock the conventions that held precedence in "civilized" society. Here the cowboys could hold their own frivolous dance, and the foreman could make fun of himself, by satirizing the measures that society's square dancers enacted in order to compensate for the absence of women.

Similarly, in *Monte Walsh,* Jack Schaefer writes that Monte and his friend, Chester Rollins, go to a town dance, having first "raided a nearby store and arrayed themselves in feminine apparel. . . . They never lacked for enthusiastic partners the entire evening and . . . there were several vigorous encounters between jealous suitors anxious for their favors" (365).

41. C. C. Walsh, "The Old 'Square Dance' of the Western Range," in Hunter, ed., *The Trail Drivers of Texas* 992–93.

42. Zane Grey also associates dancing with work in *Code of the West* (1934). Here Cal's boxing steps are defined as a form of "queer dancing" (119) and the square dance in Chapter 10 is graphically and extensively described as a form of labor in which "physical exhaustion for both sides [is] the outcome" (141).

43. Dancing as a form of male competition and displacement also operates in Larry McMurtry's *Leaving Cheyenne* (1963). Gideon Fry's and Johnny McCloud's competition for Molly is defined as a variation on the western dance, for the title of the novel is taken from the traditional dance song "Old Paint" ("Good-bye, Old Paint, I'm a-leavin' Cheyenne"). Ultimately, neither Gideon nor Johnny marries Molly or wins her away from his rival. Instead, they negotiate with each other for the right to share her sexually (Thorp, *Songs of the Cowboys* 118).

44. Robert R. Dykstra, for instance, describes the dance hall in Dodge City, Kansas, as a long frame building with bars and a dancing room in front, and with sleeping rooms in the rear. The proprietor of the saloon hired prostitutes to dance with men and to sleep with them in rooms at the back (*The Cattle Towns* 106).

45. See, for example, Dykstra, *The Cattle Towns* 105. Joseph McCoy, one of the cattle industry's early biographers, also remarked on the costume that a cowboy wore in the barroom. In *Historic Sketches of the Cattle Trade of the West and Southwest* (1874), he writes that a "cow-boy enters the dance with a peculiar zest, not stopping to divest himself of his sombrero, spurs or pistols, but just as he dismounts off his cow-pony, so he goes into the [dances]" held in Abilene, Kansas, saloons. With "the front of his sombrero lifted at an angle of fully forty-five degrees [and] his huge spurs jingling at every step," he called attention to himself by wearing the articles that square dances often made him take off (Dary, *Cowboy Culture* 216).

46. Agnes Morley Cleaveland, *No Life for a Lady* (1941) 172.

47. For instance, in "A Border Affair," the poet equates the cowboy's spurring of a horse with his conquering of the opposite sex. The cowboy leaves the ranch, rides into town at night, and has an illicit rendezvous with an unmarried woman. She listens for his spurs and calls his name, and as the lover rides toward her, spurring his steed, he hears her words in the hoofbeats of his galloping horse (Thorp, *Songs of the Cowboys* 10–11).

48. Anne M. Butler, *Daughters of Joy, Sisters of Misery: Prostitutes in the American West, 1865–90* 8–9.

49. As cowboy oral poems were composed with the consent of the group, and with the intention of keeping the cowboy group's interest, so square-dance calls often reflected the caller's attempts to modify his oral texts and to do so as a means of engaging his audience. Shaw says that there will always be "distractions" for the caller: "Someone always wants to talk to the caller in the very middle of his call. And even though he does not listen he is severely distracted. Fast sets, slow sets, new arrivals, little accidents, all tend to distract him"

(*Cowboy Dances* 41). The caller must suit his text to the needs of the group, in the same way that the bard must tailor his oral text to please the members of his audience. In his account of oral poetry, Albert B. Lord writes that the factor that most influences the form is the "variability and instability of the audience." It "requires a marked degree of concentration on the part of the singer in order that he may sing at all; it also tests to the utmost his dramatic ability and his narrative skill in keeping the audience as attentive as possible" (*The Singer of Tales* 16).

50. Square dances have other social dimensions, one of which is that callers often identify dancers by name and at intervals engage dancers in dialogues (Shaw, *Cowboy Dances* 41). For a fictional account of interchanges between callers and dancers, see, for example, Grey, *Code of the West* 140–41.

51. Casey, *Dance Across Texas* 22–23.

52. Thorp says that Belle Starr, of the "Indian Territory, was a member of a notorious gang of outlaws, but a very big-hearted woman. I knew her well" (*Songs of the Cowboys* 14).

53. Having someone edit or coauthor a cowboy's autobiography used to be common practice in the publishing world. See, for example, *The Cowman's Southwest, Being the Reminiscences of Oliver Nelson* (1953), edited by Angie Debo, and *Nothing but Prairie and Sky: Life on the Dakota Range in the Early Days*, "recorded" by Walker D. Wyman from the original "notes" of Bruce Siberts.

54. Feminist revisions of frontier American history seldom mention women and roles that they played in the cowboy group. See, for example, Sandra L. Myres, *Westering Women and the Frontier Experience, 1800–1915;* Julie Roy Jeffrey, *Frontier Women: The Trans-Mississippi West, 1840–1880;* Susan Armitage and Elizabeth Jameson, eds., *The Women's West* 19–34; Butler, *Daughters of Joy, Sisters of Misery*.

55. Fred M. Mazzula and William Kostka discuss the different biographies of Mountain Charley and contrast Guerin's account with a story in the *Colorado Transcript,* published in Golden, Colorado, in 1885 (*Mountain Charley: Or the Adventures of Mrs. E. J. Guerin, Who Was Thirteen Years in Male Attire* vii–xii, 63–112). Guerin's cross-dressing is less well documented than Calamity Jane's (Duncan Aikman, *Calamity Jane and the Lady Wildcats* 57).

56. *The Friendly Young Ladies* (1949) is a British variation on this representation of "cowboy" lesbians. Mary Renault's novel, originally published as *The Middle Mist*, contrasts the inferior "cowboy" fiction written by a lesbian, Leo, with the more authentic novels authored by Joe, who grew up on an American cattle ranch. Her nationality and gender define Leo as an outsider whose fiction can never match Joe's, while her sexual orientation stigmatizes her as someone who can never have a heterosexual cowboy's romantic companionship. As a lesbian hack, Leo has neither an access to cowboys nor a right to call herself a true cowboy novelist.

57. Sometimes heterosexual women accept the rodeo's sexist conventions more easily than lesbian writers do. In *The Solace of Open Spaces* (1985), for instance, Gretel Ehrlich writes about rodeos and the roles that male and female competitors act out in them, without condemning barrel racing as "the one women's event" (94), a point that Judy Grahn makes in her article. Ehrlich's heterosexual contact with men provides a context for her description of rodeos, perhaps inclining her to view them more kindly because she has sexual contacts with the opposite sex, unlike lesbians. In her autobiographical collection of essays, Ehrlich writes about being introduced to the rodeo by her husband after their honeymoon. As a noncowboy outsider who has married a Wyoming rancher, or insider, Ehrlich feels almost privileged to witness a western (nearly all-male) athletic event, not offended to observe that women have been reduced to subordinate places in rodeos. Her honeymoon's initiation rite involves not only an intimate contact with the opposite sex, but an acceptance of its male-oriented leisurely pastimes.

Cyra McFadden's *Rain or Shine* (1986), however, illustrates the heterosexual female author's frustration with men such as her father, who announced rodeos and ignored her because he deemed her less important than rodeos and the men who performed in them. Noting that western women are still "admired for how well they imitate men" (231), she says that she left home loathing a system that privileged manhood and made light of womanhood (9).

Chapter 3

1. In *The Drifting Cowboy,* the artist and novelist Will James says that the cowboy "drifts and hunts for new cow countries; the call from new ranges still makes him run to his saddle and pack horse and hit out; he often takes the train in drifting that way nowadays . . . but *wherever* or however he goes his saddles, ropes and chaps go with him" (vi). In *The Cattle Kings,* Atherton suggests, in a less romantic fashion, that cowboys simply "degenerated, drifted [or] disappeared, [but] where they disappeared to remained a mystery" (108). He notes, for example, that of the 901 hands who worked on the Spur Ranch in Texas between 1885 and 1909, "only 3 percent worked as many as five seasons and 64 percent remained for only one" year (16).

The uprooted cowboy's attraction to drifting can be understood by reading almost any older or more recent account of the West. Even Louis L'Amour's autobiography testifies to the migratory life of a cowboy, as the title—*Education of a Wandering Man*—indicates.

2. For a complete list of nineteenth-century American cattle trails, see Harry Sinclair Drago, *Great American Cattle Trails* 50–51.

3. Quoted in Kent Ladd Steckmesser, *The Western Hero in History and Legend* 71–72.

4. For a more recent analysis of the relationship between the vampire and Billy the Kid, see the discussion of the motion picture *Billy the Kid versus Dracula* (1966), in Stephen Tatum, *Inventing Billy the Kid: Visions of the Outlaw in America, 1881–1981* 75.

5. *Tick Eradication: A Program Chronology.*

6. Quoted in Fawn Vrazo, "USDA's Cowboys Hunt a Deadly Little Outlaw."

7. *Animal Health Technician.*

8. Many records from western state and territorial prisons were lost or destroyed when the original prisons were razed and replaced by new facilities at different locations. The remaining documents are now often held in the archives and museums at state capitals. Statistics for this chapter were obtained from the Wyoming State Archives in Cheyenne, from the New Mexico State Records Center and Archives in Santa Fe, from the Nevada State Library and Archives in Carson City, from the Montana State Archives in Helena, and from the Utah State Archives and Records Service in Salt Lake City. Incomplete data and statistics reflect the scarcity of extant archival texts and not my intention to mislead the reader by presenting only a partial portrait of cowboy work programs in prison.

9. *Wyoming's Annual Reports of the Board of Charities and Reform, 1892–1898.*

10. An index entitled "Classification by Occupation" appears in *New Mexico's Report of the Board of Penitentiary Commissioners, 1902,* and ranks New Mexico's prison inmates according to their former professions. Notice the number of "cowboys."

Blacksmiths	8
Barbers	3
Bookkeeper	1
Butcher	1
Bricklayers	2
Cooks	9
Clerks, railroad	1

Clerks, office	1
Cowboys	19
Cigar makers	1
Engineers	4
Electricians	1
Engraver	1
Farmers	17
Hostlers	2
House-keepers	4
Herder, sheep	9
Herder, goats	2
Laborers	90
Laundrymen	1
Laundress	1
Machinist	1
Machinists, helper	1
Marble polisher	1
Miners	21
Musicians	3
Merchants	3
Painters	2
Plumbers	1
Plasters [*sic*]	1
Printers	1
Railroad men	1
Ranchmen	5
Shoemakers	4
Sailors	1
Stone masons	4
Teamsters	5
Telegraph operators	1
Waiters	1
Total 235	(15–16)

Similar indexes appear in the reports for earlier and later years.

11. *New Mexico's Biennial Reports of the Board of Commissioners and Superintendent of the New Mexico Penitentiary, 1893–94* 48, and *New Mexico's Report of the Board of Penitentiary Commissioners, 1902* 15–16. The latter report includes an index entitled "Classification by Crime, of Convicts in Confinement Nov. 30, 1902" and lists fourteen convicts who were charged with rustling or "larceny of cattle."

12. Annual and biennial *Reports of the Warden of the Nevada State Prison* (1865–1878).

13. *Nevada's Biennial Report of the Warden of the Nevada State Prison 1879–1880* 37.

14. *Nevada's Biennial Report of the Warden of the Nevada State Prison 1881–1882* 17.

15. Table 15, "Number of Convicts," in ibid., 60.

16. *Nevada's Biennial Report of the Warden of the Nevada State Prison 1887–1888* lists the "Previous Occupation of Convicts" in Table 17. Notice the number of "vaqueros."

Artificial flower maker	1
Blacksmiths	1
Butchers	3

Bartenders	1	
Bakers and painters	1	
Baker and tailor	1	
Boilermakers	1	
Book-keepers	1	
Clerks	3	
Carpenters	2	
Cooks	7	
Coopers	1	
Confectioners	1	
Druggists	1	
Farmers	5	
Farmer and miner	1	
Gardners [*sic*]	2	
Housekeepers	2	
Horse trainers	1	
Joiners	1	
Laborers	18	
Laundrymen	1	
Miners	12	
Merchants	1	
Moulders [*sic*]	1	
Musicians	1	
Machinists	2	
Machinist and Blacksmith	1	
None	13	
Painters	5	
Plumbers	1	
Packers	1	
R.R. Brakeman	1	
Saloonkeepers	2	
Stockmen	2	
Stewards	1	
Stone cutters	1	
Sailors	1	
Tailors	3	
Teamsters	9	
Tinsmiths	1	
Vaqueros	11	
Whitesmiths	1	
Shoemakers	1	
Waiters	3	
Total	132	(52)

17. *Montana Prison Description Sheets, 1880–1894.*

18. Gail S. Funke, Billy L. Wayson, and Neal Miller, *Assets and Liabilities of Correctional Industries* 5.

19. Ibid., 25. Nineteenth-century American prisons used labor not only to punish their inmates, but to invest them with social virtues—"to instil habits of industry, obedience,

perseverance, and conformity'' (Donald R. Cressey, ''Limitations on Organization of Treatment in the Modern Prison,'' in Social Science Research Council, ed., *Theoretical Studies in Social Organization of the Prison* 85). Michel Foucault has also defined prison labor as the community's attempt to create an economically successful citizen and has suggested that, if ''the work of the prison has an economic effect, it is by producing individuals mechanized according to the general norms of an industrial society'' (*Discipline and Punish: The Birth of the Prison* 242). This attempt became so important at the end of the nineteenth century that the American government's prison commission stated emphatically in 1900 that industrial training was ''the only way'' to make convicts ''industrious and useful members of society,'' that the ''severest punishment that can be inflicted on a prisoner is to *deprive* him of labor'' (emphasis added) (*Report of the Industrial Commission on Prison Labor* 21).

20. For a complete list of prison labor systems and the distinctions among them, see Funke, Wayson, and Miller, *Assets and Liabilities of Correctional Industries* 9–12.

21. The Utah State Prison maintained a ''Cinches and Switches'' department in the late nineteenth and early twentieth centuries. The *Reports of the State Board of Corrections for the State of Utah* indicate that the prison accounted for the production of 375 dozen cinches in 1896 (*Biennial Report of the State Board, 1897–98* 20). The 1899–1900 *Biennial Report* lists 325 dozen in its inventory (23); the 1901–1902 report, 365 dozen (8); the 1907–1908 report, 106½ dozen (32); and the 1909–1910 report, 4½ dozen (37). In some of these reports, the prison refers to the ''Cinches and Switches'' department as ''Department D.''

22. R. M. Hall, a bit maker and amateur western historian in Jolon, California, provided me with an oral history of this bit in telephone interviews conducted on July 12 and September 14, 1988.

23. Margaret Kuehlthau, ''Plaited Horsehair Bridles.''

24. For a discussion of the cowboy's role in the Cuban invasion, see Theodore Roosevelt, *The Rough Riders*.

25. I am indebted to Linda Kohn of Los Angeles, who provided the information about this bridle's alleged background.

26. For a discussion of the spur and for a diagram of the instrument's general parts, see Fay E. Ward, *The Cowboy at Work;* Sandra Kauffman, *The Cowboy Catalog*.

27. These spurs were donated to the ProRodeo Hall of Fame and Museum of the American Cowboy by Ralph Ardourel of Lakewood, Colorado. They are now housed in the museum's warehouse.

28. I am indebted to Dr. J. S. Palen of Cheyenne, Wyoming, and to Jane Pattie of Fort Worth, Texas, for this information. The text of this chapter argues that prisons attempted to erase the identity of the spur maker by replacing his signature on the spurs with a number or series of signs. The cowboy's identity was tied in to these spurs not only because he made them in prison, but because other cowboys bought them in the outside world and used them to inscribe signs of their presence in nature. Wayne Gard, for example, notes that many cowboys ''used their knives or spurs to carve initials or brands on the soft rocks'' in the wilderness or near the tracks of a trail drive. ''Men on the trail could see the markers for 10–15 miles in either direction'' and use them to identify the men who had made them (*The Chisholm Trail* 79).

29. Hannah Arendt argues in *The Human Condition* that an object of labor leaves ''nothing behind''—that it is ''almost as quickly consumed as the effect [in creating the object] is spent'' (76). Prisons reduced spurs to such a status by defining them as disappearing products of labor and by allowing them to circulate anonymously in the outside world without bearing the permanent, enduring names of their creators.

30. This picture's negative was discovered in the archives of the Local History Center at the Cañon City Public Library, Cañon City, Colorado.

31. *Report of the Industrial Commission on Prison Labor* 63, 85.

32. Funke, Wayson, and Miller, *Assets and Liabilities of Correctional Industries* 15.

33. Elinor M. McGinn, "Trying to Profit: Inmate Labor at Cañon City, 1872–1927," 17.

34. Anthony Amaral, *Will James: The Last Cowboy Legend* 4–13.

35. I am indebted to the Nevada State Library and Archives, which provided copies of Will James's correspondence in the Nevada State Prison.

36. *So You'd Like to Adopt a Wild Horse . . . or Burro?; Colorado Wild Horse–Inmate Program;* Barry Noreen, "Mustangs Shipped East After Stay at Prison."

37. "'Elite' Horse–Inmate Program Enlarged."

38. Quoted in *Colorado Wild Horse–Inmate Program.*

39. John Lemons, "Inmate Paints History Lesson on Wall of Centennial Facility."

40. *Fifty-Fourth Annual Texas Prison Rodeo Program* 36.

41. The Texas Prison initiated its annual rodeo in 1931 and discontinued it in 1986.

42. *Fifty-Third Annual Texas Prison Rodeo Program* 33.

43. Ibid., 23.

44. *Fifty-Fourth Annual Texas Prison Rodeo Program* 22; *Fifty-Third Annual Texas Prison Rodeo Program* 46.

45. For a discussion of cattlemen's associations and their employment of livestock detectives, see Ernest Staples Osgood, *The Day of the Cattleman* 118–19, 149–58. For a discussion of western vigilante movements, see Richard Maxwell Brown, *Strains of Violence: Historical Studies of American Violence and Vigilantism* 101–10; W. Eugene Hollon, *Frontier Violence: Another Look.*

46. In *Bandits,* Eric Hobsbawm notes that the structure of rural politics first "fosters, protects and multiplies, bandits" and then integrates these men "into the political system" (82). The American frontier produced cattlemen bandits—who rustled other cattlemen's stock—and then integrated these men into a political system, similar to the one that Hobsbawm describes: livestock associations that represented the law and enforced it.

47. Quotations from the court transcripts are taken from Dean F. Krakel, *The Saga of Tom Horn: The Story of a Cattleman's War* 135–36. Krakel's book reproduces the transcripts in their entirety.

48. Ibid., 140.

49. J. Frank Dobie, "Bibliography of Siringo's Writings," in Charles Siringo, *A Texas Cowboy, or Fifteen Years on the Hurricane Deck of a Spanish Pony* xxxix.

50. Mark Twain, autobiographical dictations, August 11, 1906, in Bernard DeVoto, ed., *Mark Twain in Eruption: Hitherto Unpublished Pages About Men and Events* 49.

51. Mark Twain, "The Hunting of the Cow," autobiographical dictations, October 18, 1907, in DeVoto, ed., *Mark Twain in Eruption* 7–14. Richard Slotkin suggests that Tom Sawyer also plays this "cowboys and Indians" game and that he "gets his sense of the game from [James] Fenimore Cooper" (*The Fatal Environment: The Myth of the Frontier in the Age of Industrialization, 1800–1890* 19–20). Twain's unfinished fragment "Huck Finn and Tom Sawyer Among the Indians" (1884) mocks the "noble savage," as he appears in Cooper's Leatherstocking series, and argues that Indians are barbarous cretins who slaughter the members of a pioneer family and kidnap one of its women. Tom comes closest to adopting the cowboy detective's role when he hunts for these Indians in Twain's unfinished fragment (Walter Blair, ed., *Mark Twain's Hannibal, Huck and Tom* 81–140).

52. For information about Wister's friendship with Roosevelt and about Roosevelt's influence on Wister's work, see Owen Wister, *Roosevelt: The Story of a Friendship, 1880–1919;* Fanny Kemble Wister, ed., *Owen Wister Out West: His Journals and Letters.*

53. On August 6, 1885, Wister wrote in his Wyoming journal: "[cowboys are] a queer

episode in the history of this country. Purely nomadic, and leaving no posterity, for they don't marry" (Wister, ed., *Owen Wister Out West* 39). In *The Virginian,* the cowboy symbolically abandons the cowboy group, first, when he accepts a job, refuses to drift, and rejects nomadic life, and, second, when he marries Molly and reproduces for posterity's sake.

54. In " 'When You Call Me That . . .': Tall Talk and Male Hegemony in *The Virginian,*" Lee Clark Mitchell works out the significance of the novels that Molly gives the Virginian to read, but he can't account for the first one's importance. While he argues that the detective story apparently has nothing to do with the "issues raised by [*The Virginian*]" (75), I believe that it forms a symbolic bond between Molly and the cowboy detective. His distaste for detective fiction (*The Virginian* 86) only underscores his ironic relationship to it and in no way undermines the connection that Wister means us to notice.

55. In a controversial section of *The Virginian,* Wister allows the cattleman judge to defend the detective's decision to lynch cattle thieves. "I see no likeness in principle whatever between burning Southern Negroes in public and hanging horse-thieves in private. I consider the burning a proof that the South is semi-barbarous, and the hanging a proof that Wyoming is determined to become civilized. . . . [I]n Wyoming the law has been letting our cattle-thieves go for two years. We are in a very bad way, and we are trying to make that way a little better until civilization can reach us. At present we lie beyond its pale. The courts, or rather the juries, into whose hands we have put the law, are not dealing the law. They are withered hands, or rather they are imitation hands made for show, with no life in them, no grip. They cannot hold a cattle-thief. And so when your ordinary citizen sees this, and sees that he has placed justice in a dead hand, he must take justice back into his own hands where it was once at the beginning of all things. Call this primitive, if you will. But so far from being a *defiance* of the law, it is an *assertion* of it" (272–74).

56. Geological markings and cultural ruins have always fascinated the cowboy. See, for example, Lincoln Lang, *Ranching with Roosevelt;* Bronson, *Reminiscences of a Ranchman:* "geology is the only branch of science that could have held me in its active, persistent pursuit" (3). The archaeological excavation or discovery of an ancient (usually Indian) society also motivates the action in many "cowboy" novels, including Zane Grey's *Riders of the Purple Sage* (1912) and Louis L'Amour's last novel, *The Haunted Mesa* (1987).

57. In fiction, the cowboy can be equated with, and sometimes displaced by, the livestock detective. For example, Larry McMurtry's *Anything for Billy* (1988) points out that late-nineteenth-century dime novels gradually phased out cowboy heroes in favor of detective protagonists. At one point the narrator, himself a dime-novel writer, has one of his cowboy dime novels rejected by an editor, who says that "readers won't tolerate cowboys now; what we want are detectives, Pinkertons especially" (404).

Chapter 4

1. At first, James seems depressed by the Old Timer's absence: "I was all alone," he says. "Whatever I done now was all up to me." But he quickly accepts his new freedom when he realizes that "I could go anywhere I pleased and there wasn't a soul in the whole world . . . to answer to" (*Lone Cowboy: My Life Story* 139–40).

2. For a detailed account of James, his relationship with his family, and his intrigues, see Amaral, *Will James* 97–115.

3. Amaral, paraphrase of Will James's preface to "Bucking Horses and Bucking Horse Riders" (1922) (*Will James* 60).

4. For another comic interpretation of the orphan myth, see J. T. Crozier's autobiographical sketch at the end of his collection, *Cowboy: A Roundup of Verse* (1986). Crozier face-

tiously claims to have been separated from his parents during a camping trip and raised in the wilderness by a mountain lion (35).

5. In addition to "Get Along, Little Dogies," see, for example, "Dogie Song" (51–52) and "Night-Herding Song" (60–61) in Lomax and Lomax, *Cowboy Songs and Other Frontier Ballads.*

6. Thorp included "Get Along, Little Dogies" in *Songs of the Cowboys.* Lomax and Lomax assigned the title "Whoopee Ti Yi Yo, Get Along, Little Dogies" to the text in their later collection, *Cowboy Songs and Other Frontier Ballads.*

7. Adams defines a "dogie" as a "calf who has lost his mammy and whose daddy has run off with another cow." He also suggests that the word once referred to an orphaned animal's anatomy: the swollen stomach that an unweaned orphaned calf developed when it lost access to its mother's milk. During the roundup, "all orphan calves became known as *dough-guts,*" for their stomachs resembled a cook's flour sack when it was filled up with a batch of sourdough. Later "the term was shortened to *dogie,* which has been used ever since throughout cattle land to refer to a pot-gutted orphan calf" (*Western Words* 96).

8. Alan Lomax and Joshua Berrett, Introduction to Lomax and Lomax, *Cowboy Songs and Other Frontier Ballads* xxviii.

9. Mainstream American writers, as well as cowboy poets, sometimes use characteristics of a herd to reflect changes in the human condition. In *The Jungle* (1906), for instance, Upton Sinclair focuses on a Chicago stockyard where cowboys deposit their livestock at the end of a drive and on a meat-packing plant that employs Jurgis Rudkus, the novel's protagonist (32). Rudkus equates the economic exploitation and social subordination of the meat-packing plant's workers with the confinement and killing of cattle. Referring to his relationship with people, Rudkus says at one point that "he must take his chances with the common herd. Nay worse, he dared not mingle with the herd—he must hide himself, for he was one marked out for destruction" (281).

However, when he goes to the countryside and escapes from the evil that Chicago embodies (on the bodies of cattle that are marked out for slaughter), he encounters "a herd of cows, and a meadow full of daisies" (213)—a landscape across which both Rudkus and cattle can roam, no longer penned in by stockyards and industrial meat-packing plants. Now he attributes a restorative power to the pastoral life, distinguishing between the rancher's "cattle," which are slaughtered for meat, and the farmer's "cows," which are kept alive for the milk that they continually yield; between the city's prisoners, who are initially "marked out for destruction," and its escapees, who are temporarily revitalized by their contact with nature.

10. For example, in "Panhandle Cob" (105–10), a cowboy rescues a cattleman's daughter from an angry steer by throwing himself in front of it and receiving a fatal wound in the process. Again, in "Utah Carroll" (125–28), a cowboy saves a cattleman's daughter by distracting a stampeding herd and directing it instead toward himself (Lomax and Lomax, *Cowboy Songs and Other Frontier Ballads*).

The cowboy's tangential and temporary relations to children are born out in both cowboy and noncowboy texts. Waddie Mitchell's *Christmas Poems: A Cowboy Celebrates Christmas,* for instance, depicts cowboys acting as elves or assistants to Santa Claus, making gifts for cowboys and cowgirls, but then going away, like Santa Claus (who is a surrogate father to children), and returning, like Father Christmas, only at Christmastime.

Noncowboy writers and artists also use Christmas to contrast a cowboy's usual aloneness with his unusual sacrifice for children during a seasonal holiday. The film *Three Godfathers* (1936), deals with three cowboy outlaws who give up their chance for escape and return to town after finding a baby left alone in the desert. This Christmas film—a holiday classic—

works out the story of the three wise men, who travel through the desert to Bethlehem, hoping to witness Jesus Christ's birth. Based on an earlier silent film version, *Three Godfathers* so charmed American viewers that John Ford later remade it, with John Wayne, in the following decade.

11. In his discussion of the conventions that structure narratives about the cowboy as gunslinger, Warren J. Barker notes that the "hero's arrival from nowhere at the beginning of each adventure suggests the child's feeling of mystery and confusion about its own origin." No character in pulp westerns, however, may question the cowboy's orphanhood or express "any curiosity about the identity, origin, or parentage of the hero" ("The Stereotyped Western Story: Its Latent Meaning and Psychoeconomic Function" 276). The orphan myth plays a role in pulp fiction, as well as in cowboy texts that I discuss in this chapter. At the same time, the ambivalent relationship of the cowboy-father with "dogies" supports Walker's thesis that "the working relationship of a man to a cow . . . has limited significance," in that it operates in an inconsistent and irregular fashion (*Clio's Cowboys* 119).

12. American writers attribute successful parenting techniques to cowboys more frequently than to other workers who belong to nonreproductive male societies. In "The Luck of Roaring Camp" (1868), for instance, Bret Harte describes the short-lived attempt of gamblers, adventurers, and forty-niners to raise an "orphan" in a California mining camp. The child is the product of a reproductive society and a catalyst for the "work of regeneration" (107) that takes place when Roaring Camp's adoptive fathers reform themselves in order to conform to the image of socially acceptable parents. However, their metamorphosis into respectable men—and their concurrent transformation of the camp into a civilized town—is prematurely terminated by Harte when a flood destroys the camp, killing the bachelors and orphan (*The Outcasts of Poker Flats and Other Tales* 101–11).

13. For an account of the nineteenth-century cowboy's oral transmission of poetry and his later transcription of poems "on paper for a reading public," see Carol A. Edison, ed., *Cowboy Poetry from Utah: An Anthology* 9–11.

14. The first Cowboy Poetry Gathering took place in January 1985 in Elko, Nevada. As a result of the publicity generated by each Gathering, cowboy poets now appear on "The Tonight Show" each year, promoting the event and reciting their poetry.

15. For a discussion of Wister's knowledge of cowboy poetry and his own composition of songs, see "Owen Wister, Songwriter," in John I. White, *Git Along, Little Dogies: Songs and Songmakers of the American West* 27–37. Trampas's new song, "Ten Thousand Cattle Straying," includes a line—"I'm a lone man" (33)—that emphasizes the cowboy's connection to orphans. As the villain, Trampas can never marry and reproduce children. Only the hero, the Virginian, can do these things as a reward for leaving the cowboy group and entering mainstream society.

16. The idea that the cowboy's oral tradition is "tainted" by a preliterate or illiterate ethnic group's influence on it was suggested by Andy Adams, as well as by Wister. In *The Log of a Cowboy* (1903), written one year after *The Virginian,* Adams wrote that cowboy music is "a hybrid between the weirdness of an Indian cry and the croon of a dark mammy" (Dary, *Cowboy Culture* 193). Adams's supposition is worked out more clearly in *The Virginian,* which includes the hero's debate over whether another cowboy is "white" before the Virginian launches into a song (101).

17. In *Cowboy Mouth* (1971), Sam Shepard also examines the cowboy's orality. Dramas, as a genre, work out the notion of hybrid productions in that they are *written* texts that culminate in *oral* performances. In *Cowboy Mouth,* for instance, Slim's rambling monologues are controlled by the playwright, who writes the words and puts them in the cowboy's "mouth." The spontaneity of Slim's speech is therefore illusory, as is the "reality" of any theatrical artifice. Hence Cavele calls attention to the cues that Slim takes by linking his staged

performance with the cowboy's orality: "You're a performer, man. A rock-and-roll Jesus with a cowboy mouth" (*Fool for Love and Other Plays* 157).

18. In *Jo's Boys* (1886), Jo suggests that Dan would have been a terrible father. She imagines that his own father had been "a handsome, unprincipled, and dangerous man, with more than one broken heart to answer for," and she implies that if Dan had had a family, he would have abandoned it, just as his own father must have abandoned Dan and his mother. Jo finally decides that it is better for Dan to go to a "solitary" grave than to continue a tradition of poor male parenting (312).

19. Donald Pizer has suggested that Norris eventually envisioned an "increased social complexity [that] produces a widening social allegiance, from the family, to clan, to city, to nation, and—in the future—to humanity at large" ("The Writer and Society: The Novelist as American," in Pizer, ed., *The Literary Criticism of Frank Norris* 102). Vanamee's developing economic and domestic relations with the American mainstream are the result of this increasing "social complexity."

20. Frank Norris, "A Neglected Epic," in Pizer, ed., *The Literary Criticism of Frank Norris* 119–22.

21. Wister first blurs the distinctions between literary and biological relationships when he says, in the introduction to the first edition of *The Virginian,* that he knows real men such as the Virginian as well "as a father should know his [own] son" (x).

The Virginian initially denies the importance of parents, telling a friend that the world did not "beget" him (169) and that the cowboy must take care of himself. The Virginian also indicates that the cowboy has no use for children in a reproductive society. In an early chapter, he switches the babies at a local dance and confuses their parents in order to deny the allegedly indelible biological clues that enable parents to distinguish their children from others. By mistaking the children who are disguised in each other's clothes, the parents demonstrate that superficial familial bonds are unstable—that they are based not on genetic links, but on easily exchanged outfits or altered appearances (75–80).

Even before publishing *The Virginian* in 1902, Wister had begun working out the notion of orphanhood. In "The Evolution of the Cow-Puncher" (1895), he wrote that cowboys "sprang from the loins of no similar fathers and few begot sons to continue their hardihood" (Robert Murray Davis, ed., *Owen Wister's West: Selected Articles* 50).

22. Cowboy and cowgirl texts are aimed at a respective male and female audience and are therefore apt to promote models or sex roles for children. In his article "Can Playing 'Girl' Games Turn a Boy into a Homosexual?" Darrell Sifford interviews a professor of educational psychology at New York University. Dr. Lawrence Balter tells Sifford that if a parent encourages a boy to play with "feminine sex-role toys," then he or she causes "a child to wonder if he should be a boy. Maybe, he thinks, it's better not to be a boy, to be a girl instead. . . . I'd rather see a boy wearing a cowboy outfit than a cowgirl outfit. . . . It is less confusing during periods of uncertainty to have such clear markers." We know that cowboys and cowgirls have become potent symbols in children's imaginations and important players in American culture when they are seen as "clear markers" or examples of proper male and female sex roles.

23. In *Cowkids, Colts and Peanut Butter Bulls,* by providing a glossary in the back of the book for "parents" (1) who need to translate into standard English certain cowboy terms that appear in his text, Jon Bowerman indicates his awareness that his children's coloring book will be read by adults.

24. Cowboys appeal to adults who watch children's programming, as well as to those who read children's literature. "Pee-wee's Playhouse," for instance, had an adult following that first became acquainted with Paul Reubens's character by watching Pee-wee on late-night television talk shows and specials. Cowboy Curtis, one of the characters who appeared in the

"playhouse," also had an adult audience and a function that adults, unlike children, observed. As a black cowboy, he subverted television's depiction of cowboys as white and, hence, registered with adult viewers who understood the program's intended subversion of cultural and historical stereotypes. Young children were less apt to spot this subversion and more apt to respond simply to Cowboy Curtis's goofy antics each week.

25. Female poets more frequently tend to write for and about parents, children, relations, and acquaintances. In *Seven Hundred Miles from the Pecos River,* for instance, Tina Burke dedicates individual poems to her son (11), uncle (9), and neighbors (6, 13). In *Where Old Trails Meet the New on Oregon's High Desert,* Ramona Turmon writes one poem for her husband, Dennis (39), while her coauthor, Lona Tankersley Burkhart, writes one for her friend Ella Fisher (48). Unlike most cowboy poems, these works commemorate women's social and biological attachments to members of mainstream reproductive society.

26. Like Mitchell's *Christmas Poems,* stories about Christmas also examine the cowboy's problematic relations with parents and children. In "Stubby Pringle's Christmas" (1966), for instance, Jack Schaefer mocks the cowboy's theory of self-origination while describing the worker's decision to miss the yearly Christmas Eve dance and to help a nearby family prepare their children for Christmas. Stubby Pringle—the "son of the wild jackass," "orphaned at thirteen" (250)—chops down a Christmas tree for the family and thereafter becomes identified, in his imagination, as "Stubby Pringle, born an expert on Christmas trees, nursed on pine needles, weaned on pine cones" (256). He then carves gifts for the children out of wood and becomes "Stubby Pringle, born with feel for knives in hand, weaned on emery wheel, fed on shavings, raised to whittle his way through the world" (259). Each act of family "rescue" forces the cowboy to revise and exaggerate the folkloric dimensions of the "orphan" myth, making it both more insistent (through repetition) and, at the same time, more ludicrous. (Bill Pronzini and Martin H. Greenberg, eds., *The Western Hall of Fame: An Anthology of Classic Western Stories* 249–64).

27. With the exception of Black's "Cowboy Heaven" (*Croutons on a Cow Pie* 12), few modern branding poems equate brands with the cowboy's religious salvation. In "Brands," for example, the cowboy narrator explains the significance of cattle brands to a "lady driver" in a "Cadillac with New York plates"—a woman who represents interpretive outsiders—merely by listing the brands in the surrounding neighborhood and by defining them as nothing more than signs of economic ownership (Mike Logan, *Bronc to Breakfast and Other Poems* 26–30).

28. The cowboy's alternate interest in and withdrawal from the mainstream is evident everywhere, even in casual and sometimes comic discussions of mainstream American politics. On the July 30, 1987, broadcast of "20/20," for instance, reporter Bob Brown interviewed men who work on the I L Ranch in northern Nevada. Two cowboys, Jim Casper and Jim Koepke, cast doubt as to whether they knew who was running the country, noting that ranch labor sometimes prevents cowboys from keeping up with events that are recorded in newspapers:

> **Mr. Koepke:**   You can damn sure drift away from the real world real easily. What day is today, what's the date, doesn't really matter. It's another day you're going to get up and go to work. You're going to do it tomorrow and the next day, till the work's done.

> **Mr. Casper:**   Everybody here, you know, I think pretty much everybody votes. They sure care who the President of the United States is and stuff—what's his name? ("On the Range" 12–13)

(Transcripts provided by Journal Graphics, 2 John Street, New York, NY 10038).

29. These poems merely sample the great number of social, cultural, and political issues

that appear in late-twentieth-century cowboy poetry. See also, for example, Logan's treatment of the Los Angeles International Airport (62–63) in *Bronc to Breakfast and Other Poems,* and Baxter Black's discussion of computers (108), of federally subsidized farming programs and price freezing (166), and of vegetarians who attack the beef industry (188) in *Coyote Cowboy Poetry.*

30. Many women credit men—not other women—with inspiring them to do ranch work and write "cowboy" poetry. Georgie Connell Sicking, in the autobiographical preface to *Just Thinkin',* admits that her cowboy stepfather influenced her decision "to hold down a job on a cowboy outfit, in spite of being a girl. I studied the ways of the best cowboys I worked with and tried to copy them" (ii), and later wrote about this work in her poetry. In *Cowgirls: Women of the American West,* Teresa Jordan adds that most "cowgirls learned their skills from men—a father, a brother, or a husband. . . . Man's world encompassed the things many cowgirls liked most about their lives and they looked on it with true affection. Quite possibly they saw their history not so much unwritten as included in the history of men" (279). In *In a Narrow Grave: Essays on Texas,* Larry McMurtry makes the same point, but more pessimistically: "[The cowboy's] women, too, are victims, though for the most part acquiescent victims. They usually buy the myth of cowboying and the ideal of manhood it invokes, even though both exclude them. A few even buy it to the point of attempting to assimilate the all-valuable masculine qualities to themselves, producing that awful phenomenon, the cowgirl" (148).

31. Cowboy poetry's intolerance for a gendered female perspective is also seen in some male poets' contempt for the one segment of society that can *never* successfully become part of the West, male homosexuals, who appear despicable to heterosexual male poets because they seem to manifest effeminate qualities. See, for example, Black's "The Gay Cabellero" (36) in *Coyote Cowboy Poetry* and Wallace McRae's "Puncher Poet Plague" in *Things of Intrinsic Worth:* "Cow poets are sweepin' the country like the / scours, viral AIDS, and the flu" (8). Here AIDS is not only a sexually transmitted disease, but a sign for the literary and cultural contamination of poetry. One wonders whether lesbians escape the male poet's condemnation because they "blend in" and seem to become "masculine," or because they appear less threatening to a predominantly male group as a result of their perceived masculinity.

32. The statistics listed below have been taken from the polling data collected at the 1989 Cowboy Poetry Gathering by Tara McCarty, general manager of the Western Folklife Center in Elko, Nevada. With 6,000 people in attendance, McCarty polled 261 audience members and acquired the following information about the spectators' gender, age, place of residence, and choice of profession.

Place of Residence   [fewer than 10% lived within a two-hour driving distance from Elko, Nevada]

Nevada	26%
California	20
Idaho	12
Utah	12
Montana	6
Oregon	5
Wyoming	3
Washington	2
Canada	2
New Mexico	1

South Dakota	1%
Florida	1
Texas	1
Missouri	1

Other 4%   including West Germany
                            North Dakota
                            Oklahoma
                            Illinois
                            Arkansas
                            Massachusetts

Profession

Ranchers, cowboys, and farmers 40%
Other 60%, including, in order of popularity:
    Professionals (doctors and lawyers)
    Retirees and service occupations (tie)
    Education, business occupations, and blue-collar workers (tie)

Age [children not polled]

40–55	30%
30–40	27
Over 55	24
20–30	17
Other	2

Gender

Men	56%
Women	44

Instead of catering only to white male members of ranching and farming communities, Gatherings seem to appeal almost equally to people of both sexes and all ages, professions, and places of origin.

33. The following excerpt from the biography of the cowboy poet Jon I. Pentz suggests the central importance of poetic discourse as a form of communication and, at the same time, the definition of it as a marginal pastime that competes for Pentz's attention with his more important professional duties: "Whether he's writing a letter to his wife or one of his six children, or leaving a note for the boss, it's always in verse. For [Pentz], writing is a recreational activity. He often writes in his old wood sheep-camp either late at night after the sheep have all settled, or first thing in the morning while waiting for the coffee to boil" (Edison, ed., *Cowboy Poetry from Utah* 115).

34. This "faked" illiteracy is a strategy that distinguishes the cowboy's texts from other poems in American literature. It operates not only in poems, but in comic essays written by Will Rogers, the "cowboy philosopher," to name only the most famous example. Some of his essays were collected in *The Illiterate Digest,* a book whose title makes fun of the traditional cowboy's dysfunctional grammar. Poets also use "illiterate" language—on the printed page—as a constant orthographical reminder to the reader that the cowboy poet is uneducated and therefore set apart from the educated American mainstream.

35. The cowboy's preservation of his literary tradition often leads to considering cowboy poetry as part of "low culture." In *The Anxiety of Influence: A Theory of Poetry,* for instance, Harold Bloom defines "strong poets" (5)—or canonical authors who participate in forms of high cultural discourse—as men who reject the influence of their literary precursors by (in one

of six ways) misreading or misinterpreting a poetic tradition that has been passed down to them, and revising or rewriting the tradition in their own poetry (30). Bloom defines past poets as "fathers" (71) and their texts as "parent poems" (94); he envisions younger revisionist poets as rebellious "sons" in this "family romance" (64), which pits children against parents and which rewards poets for rebelling against their father-figures, muses, or literary influences.

It is this lack of literary experimentation or youthful rebellion that characterizes cowboy poetry. In "Dressin' Up," for example, Black privileges a past work culture and a paternal father-figure or ur-poet when he says that things "[a]in't changed since *Grandpa*" (emphasis added). While defining themselves as orphans in a reproductive society, poets at the same time are quick to revere a traditional male art form and to privilege it as a son respects his father or grandfather. The respect for a grandfatherly muse and the preservation of a male tradition prevents cowboy poets from experimenting with poems, from "improving" them (as Bloom would suggest), and from earning the respect of high culture's critics.

36. Edward Hoagland, "Buckaroo Poets: Whoop-ee-ti-yi-yo, Git Along, Little Doggerel."

BIBLIOGRAPHY

In the bibliography, the publication date listed for each cited work indicates either first publication or reprint date, depending on the edition I used in researching and writing *The Cowboy*. In the text and notes, the dates that are given in parentheses after the titles of works indicate the original date of each text's publication. Therefore, if one is interested in tracking down a source's first publication date, one should look for the information in *The Cowboy*'s chapters and notes.

Primary Sources

Histories, autobiographies, novels, short-story collections, and poetry written or orally composed by cowboys and cowgirls

Abbott, E. C. ("Teddy Blue"), and Helena Huntington Smith. *We Pointed Them North: Recollections of a Cowpuncher*. Norman: U of Oklahoma P, 1939.

Adams, Andy. *Cattle Brands: A Collection of Western Camp-Fire Stories*. Boston: Houghton Mifflin, 1906.

Adams, Andy. *The Log of a Cowboy*. Lincoln: U of Nebraska P, 1964.

Adams, Andy. *The Outlet*. Boston: Houghton Mifflin, 1905.

Adams, Andy. *The Wells Brothers*. Boston: Houghton Mifflin, 1911.

Black, Baxter. "The Cabbage Patch." *Arkansas Valley Journal* [La Junta, CO] 31 December 1987: 5.

Black, Baxter. *Coyote Cowboy Poetry*. Denver: Coyote Cowboy and Record Stockman, 1986.

Black, Baxter. *Croutons on a Cow Pie*. Denver: Coyote Cowboy and Record Stockman, 1988.

Black, Baxter. "Uncommon Myths About Beef." *Arkansas Valley Journal* [La Junta, CO] 31 August 1989: 5.

Bronson, Edgar Beecher. *Reminiscences of a Ranchman*. New York: McClure, 1908.

Burke, Tina. *Seven Hundred Miles from the Pecos River: A Collection of Wyoming Poetry*. Douglas: privately printed, 1986.

Cannon, Hal, ed. *Cowboy Poetry: A Gathering*. Salt Lake City: Peregrine Smith, 1985.

Christensen, Bob. *A Feedbag of Cowboy Poetry: A Sampling of Poems*. Preston: Citizen, 1987.

Clark, Badger. *Sun and Saddle Leather*. Tucson: Westerners International, 1983.

Clay, John. *My Life on the Range*. New York: Antiquarian, 1961.

Cleaveland, Agnes Morley. *No Life for a Lady*. Lincoln: U of Nebraska P, 1977.

Collinson, Frank. *Life in the Saddle*. Ed. Mary Whatley Clarke. Norman: U of Oklahoma P, 1963.

Cook, James H. *Fifty Years on the Old Frontier as Cowboy, Hunter, Guide, Scout, and Ranchman*. New Haven: Yale UP, 1923.

Crozier, J. T. *Cowboy: A Roundup of Verse*. Loveland: Chilmit, 1986.

Edison, Carol A., ed. *Cowboy Poetry from Utah: An Anthology*. Salt Lake City: Utah Folklife Center, 1985.

Fife, Austin, and Alta Fife. *Heaven on Horseback: Songs and Verse in the Cowboy Idiom*. Logan: Utah State UP, 1970.

Fletcher, Curley. *Songs of the Sage*. Salt Lake City: Peregrine Smith, 1986.

Gardner, Gail I. *Orejana Bull*. Prescott: Sharlott Hall Museum, 1987.

Grue, Betty Lynne. *Frost on the Fork Handle and Other Selected Verse*. Terry: Betty Lynne Grue and Tri-C Printing, 1987.

Guerin, Mrs. E. J. *Mountain Charley: Or the Adventures of Mrs. E. J. Guerin, Who Was Thirteen Years in Male Attire*. Ed. and intro. Fred M. Mazzulla and William Kostka. Norman: U of Oklahoma P, 1986.

Halsell, H. H. *Cowboys and Cattleland: Memoirs of a Frontier Cowboy*. Fort Worth: Texas Christian UP, 1983.

Hands Up! or, Twenty Years of Detective Life in the Mountains and on the Plains. Norman: U of Oklahoma P, 1958.

James, Will. *The Drifting Cowboy*. New York: Scribner, 1925.

James, Will. *Lone Cowboy: My Life Story*. New York: Scribner, 1930.

Kiskaddon, Bruce. *Rhymes of the Ranges*. Salt Lake City: Peregrine Smith, 1987.

Lang, Lincoln. *Ranching with Roosevelt*. Philadelphia: Lippincott, 1926.

Logan, Mike. *Bronc to Breakfast and Other Poems*. Helena: Buglin' Bull, 1988.

Logsdon, Guy, comp. and ed. *''The Whorehouse Bells Were Ringing'' and Other Songs Cowboys Sing*. Urbana: U of Illinois P, 1989.

Lomax, John, comp. *Songs of the Cattle Trail and Cow Camp*. New York: Macmillan, 1919.

Lomax, John, and Alan Lomax, comps. *Cowboy Songs and Other Frontier Ballads*. New York: Collier, 1986.

Love, Nat. *The Life and Adventures of Nat Love*. Englewood Cliffs: Prentice-Hall, 1977.

McFadden, Cyra. *Rain or Shine*. New York: Vintage, 1987.

McRae, Wallace. *It's Just Grass and Water*. Spokane: Oxalis, 1986.

McRae, Wallace. *Things of Intrinsic Worth*. Bozeman: Outlaw, 1989.

McRae, Wallace. *Up North Is Down the Crick*. Bozeman: Outlaw, 1985.

Mitchell, Waddie. *Christmas Poems: A Cowboy Celebrates Christmas*. Salt Lake City: Peregrine Smith, 1987.

Moore, Dan. *Shoot Me a Biscuit: Stories of Yesteryear's Roundup Cooks*. Tucson: U of Arizona P, 1974.

Nelson, Oliver. *The Cowman's Southwest, Being the Reminiscences of Oliver Nelson*. Ed. Angie Debo. Lincoln: U of Nebraska P, 1986.

Ohrlin, Glen, ed. *The Hell-Bound Train: A Cowboy Songbook*. Urbana: U of Illinois P, 1989.

O'Malley, D. J., and John I. White. *D. J. O'Malley: ''Cowboy Poet.''* Helena: Montana Folklife Project, 1986.

Petersen, Gwen, and Jeane Rhodes. *Tall in the Sidesaddle: Ranch Woman Rhymes*. Big Timber: P/R Press, 1986.

Ross, Jim. *Pull Up a Chair: Cowboy Poetry*. Stephensville: privately printed, 1987.

Siberts, Bruce, and Walker D. Wyman. *Nothing but Prairie and Sky: Life on the Dakota Range in the Early Days*. Norman: U of Oklahoma P, 1954.

Sicking, Georgie Connell. *Just Thinkin'*. N.p.: n.p., n.d.

Siringo, Charles. *A Cowboy Detective*. Chicago: Conkey, 1912.

Siringo, Charles. *A Lone Star Cowboy*. Sante Fe: n.p., 1919.

Siringo, Charles. *Riata and Spurs: The Story of a Lifetime Spent in the Saddle as Cowboy and Detective*. Boston: Houghton Mifflin, 1927.

Siringo, Charles. *The Song Companion of a Lone Star Cowboy: Old Favorite Cow Camp Songs*. N.p.: Norwood, 1975.

Siringo, Charles. *A Texas Cowboy, or Fifteen Years on the Hurricane Deck of a Spanish Pony*. New York: Umbdenstock, 1885.

Siringo, Charles. *Two Evil Isms: Pinkertonism and Anarchism*. Austin: Steck-Vaughn, 1967.

Stewart, Elinore Pruitt. *Letters of a Woman Homesteader*. Boston: Houghton Mifflin, 1914.

Thorp, N. Howard, comp. *Songs of the Cowboys*. Lincoln: U of Nebraska P, 1984.

Turmon, Ramona, and Lona Tankersley Burkhart. *Where Old Trails Meet the New on Oregon's High Desert*. Redmond: privately printed, 1988.

Histories, essays, letters, autobiographies, novels, short-story collections, films, children's literature, and coloring books written and produced by artists and authors outside the cowboy and cowgirl group

Abbey, Edward. *The Brave Cowboy: An Old Tale in a New Time*. Albuquerque: U of New Mexico P, 1977.

Alcott, Louisa May. *Jo's Boys*. London: Dent, 1982.

Alcott, Louisa May. *Little Men: Life at Plumfield with Jo's Boys*. London: Collier, 1962.

Austin, Mary. *The Land of Little Rain*. Boston: Houghton Mifflin, 1903.

Bowerman, Jon. *Cowkids, Colts and Peanut Butter Bulls: Cow Country Verse from A to Z for Little Cowboys, Cowgirls, and Buckaroos!* Antelope: Antelope Free P, 1986.

Burleson, Bob. *Runic Meaning in Texas Cattle Brands: Dramatic Essays and Illusions of the Organic Theatre*. Berkeley: Worksworth, 1983.

Cather, Willa. *Death Comes for the Archbishop*. New York: Vintage, 1971.

Cather, Willa. *The Professor's House*. New York: Vintage, 1973.

Clark, Walter Van Tilburg. *The Ox-Bow Incident*. New York: Signet, 1984.

Dana, Richard Henry, Jr. *Two Years Before the Mast*. Ed. Charles W. Eliot. Harvard Classics. Vol. 23. New York: Collins, 1937.

Doig, Ivan. *This House of Sky: Landscapes of a Western Mind*. New York: Harcourt, 1978.

Ehrlich, Gretel. *Heart Mountain*. Harmondsworth: Penguin, 1989.

Ehrlich, Gretel. *The Solace of Open Spaces*. Harmondsworth: Penguin, 1987.

Evans, Max. *The Rounders*. Albuquerque: U of New Mexico P, 1983.

Ferber, Edna. *Giant*. Garden City: Doubleday, 1952.

Gorsline, Marie, and Douglas Gorsline. *Cowboys*. New York: Random, 1978.

Grahn, Judy. "Boys at the Rodeo." *True to Life Adventure Stories Volume 2*. Ed. Judy Grahn. Trumansburg: Crossing, 1981.

Grey, Zane. *Code of the West*. New York: Pocket, 1982.

Grey, Zane. *Knights of the Range*. New York: Grosset, 1936.

Grey, Zane. *Riders of the Purple Sage*. New York: Pocket, 1980.

Hammett, Dashiell. "Corkscrew." *The Big Knockover*. Ed. Lillian Hellman. New York: Vintage, 1972.

Harte, Bret. *The Outcasts of Poker Flats and Other Tales*. New York: Signet, 1985.

Herlihy, John. *Midnight Cowboy*. New York: Simon and Schuster, 1965.

Hough, Emerson. *North of 36*. New York: Grosset, 1923.

L'Amour, Louis. *Education of a Wandering Man*. New York: Bantam, 1989.

L'Amour, Louis. *The Haunted Mesa*. New York: Bantam, 1988.

Lawrence, D. H. *The Boy in the Bush.* Harmondsworth: Penguin, 1974.

Lewis, Alfred Henry. *Wolfville.* New York: Stokes, 1897.

Martin, Bill, Jr., and John Archambault. *White Dynamite and Curly Kidd.* New York: Holt, 1986.

McMurtry, Larry. *Anything for Billy.* New York: Pocket, 1989.

McMurtry, Larry. *Buffalo Girls.* New York: Simon and Schuster, 1990.

McMurtry, Larry. *Horseman, Pass By.* Harmondsworth: Penguin, 1984.

McMurtry, Larry. *Leaving Cheyenne.* Harmondsworth: Penguin, 1984.

My Darling Clementine. Dir. John Ford. With Henry Fonda and Victor Mature. Twentieth Century Fox, 1946.

Norris, Frank. *The Octopus.* New York: Signet, 1982.

Pronzini, Bill, and Martin H. Greenberg, eds. *The Western Hall of Fame: An Anthology of Classic Western Stories.* New York: Morris, 1984.

Reed, Ishmael. *Yellow Back Radio Broke-Down.* New York: Atheneum, 1988.

Remington, Frederic. *The Collected Writings of Frederic Remington.* Ed. Peggy Samuels and Harold Samuels. Garden City: Doubleday, 1979.

Renault, Mary. *The Friendly Young Ladies.* New York: Pantheon, 1984.

Richter, Conrad. *The Sea of Grass.* New York: Ballantine, 1984.

Rickman, David. *Cowboys of the Old West: A Coloring Book.* New York: Dover, 1985.

Robbins, Tom. *Even Cowgirls Get the Blues.* New York: Bantam, 1984.

Rogers, Will. *The Autobiography of Will Rogers.* Ed. Donald Day. New York: AMS, 1979.

Rogers, Will. *The Illiterate Digest.* Ed. Joseph A. Stout, Jr. *The Writings of Will Rogers* Ser. 1, no. 3. Stillwater: Oklahoma State UP, 1974.

Rogers, Will. *Letters of a Self-Made Diplomat to His President.* Ed. Joseph A. Stout, Jr. *The Writings of Will Rogers* Ser. 1, no. 6. Stillwater: Oklahoma State UP, 1977.

Roosevelt, Theodore. *Ranch Life and the Hunting Trail.* New York: Bonanza, 1888.

Roosevelt, Theodore. *The Rough Riders.* New York: Scribner, 1902.

Schaefer, Jack. *Monte Walsh.* Boston: Houghton Mifflin, 1963.

Shepard, Sam. *Fool for Love and Other Plays.* New York: Bantam, 1984.

Shepard, Sam. *Seven Plays.* New York: Bantam, 1984.

She Wore a Yellow Ribbon. Dir. John Ford. With John Wayne. RKO Radio, 1949.

Silko, Leslie Marmon. *Ceremony.* Harmondsworth: Penguin, 1986.

Sinclair, Upton. *The Jungle.* New York: Bantam, 1981.

Steinbeck, John. *The Pastures of Heaven.* Harmondsworth: Penguin, 1982.

Steinbeck, John. *The Short Reign of Pippin IV.* Harmondsworth: Penguin, 1978.

Steinbeck, John. *To a God Unknown.* Harmondsworth: Penguin, 1982.

Stir Crazy. Dir. Sidney Poitier. With Richard Pryor and Gene Wilder. Columbia, 1981.

Stoker, Bram. *Dracula.* New York: Signet, 1981.

Three Godfathers. Dir. Richard Boleslawski. With Walter Brennan and Lewis Stone. MGM, 1936.

Tomb, Ubet. *Cowboys.* Santa Barbara: Bellerophon, 1987.

Tomb, Ubet. *Cowgirls.* Santa Barbara: Bellerophon, 1987.

Twain, Mark. *The Adventures of Huckleberry Finn.* New York: Signet, 1979.

Twain, Mark. *The Adventures of Tom Sawyer.* New York: Signet, 1980.

Twain, Mark. *A Connecticut Yankee in King Arthur's Court.* New York: Signet, 1975.

Twain, Mark. "Huck Finn and Tom Sawyer Among the Indians." *Mark Twain's Hannibal, Huck and Tom.* Ed. Walter Blair. Berkeley: U of California P, 1979.

Twain, Mark. *Letters from the Earth.* Ed. Bernard DeVoto. New York: Perennial, 1974.

Twain, Mark. *Mark Twain in Eruption: Hitherto Unpublished Pages About Men and Events.* Ed. Bernard DeVoto. New York: Harper, 1940.

Twain, Mark. *Roughing It.* Ed. Paul Baender. Berkeley: U of California P, 1973.

Twain, Mark. *Tom Sawyer Abroad and Tom Sawyer, Detective.* New York: Airmont, 1966.

Welch, James. *Winter in the Blood.* Harmondsworth: Penguin, 1986.

West, Nathanael. *The Collected Novels of Nathanael West.* Harmondsworth: Penguin, 1981.

Wister, Owen. *Lin McLean.* New York: Harper, 1897.

Wister, Owen. *Owen Wister Out West: His Journals and Letters.* Ed. Fanny Kemble Wister. Chicago: U of Chicago P, 1958.

Wister, Owen. *Owen Wister's West: Selected Articles.* Ed. Robert Murray Davis. Albuquerque: U of New Mexico P, 1987.

Wister, Owen. *Roosevelt: The Story of a Friendship, 1880–1919.* New York: Macmillan, 1930.

Wister, Owen. *The Virginian.* New York: Signet, 1979.

Secondary Sources

Specific books, articles, pamphlets, advertisements, and archival documents concerning cowboys and cowgirls

Adams, Ramon F. *Come an' Get It: The Story of the Old Cowboy Cook.* Norman: U of Oklahoma P, 1952.

Adams, Ramon F. *Western Words: A Dictionary of the American West.* Norman: U of Oklahoma P, 1968.

Aikman, Duncan. *Calamity Jane and the Lady Wildcats.* Lincoln: U of Nevada P, 1980.

Amaral, Anthony. *Will James: The Last Cowboy Legend.* Reno: U of Nevada P, 1980.

Animal Health Technician. Laredo: United States Department of Agriculture, 1988.

Armitage, Susan, and Elizabeth Jameson, eds. *The Women's West.* Norman: U of Oklahoma P, 1987.

Arnold, Oren, and John P. Hale. *Hot Irons: Heraldry of the Range.* New York: Macmillan, 1940.

Atherton, Lewis. *The Cattle Kings.* Bloomington: Indiana UP, 1961.

Aveling, Edward, and Eleanor Marx Aveling. *The Working-Class Movement in America: From Conspiracy to Collective Bargaining.* New York: Arno, 1969.

"Baldrige Recalled as Honest Cowboy." *Gazette Telegraph* [Colorado Springs, CO] 30 July 1987: A5.

Barker, Warren J. "The Stereotyped Western Story: Its Latent Meaning and Psychoeconomic Function." *Psychoanalytic Quarterly* 24 (1955): 270–80.

Branch, Douglas. *The Cowboy and His Interpreters.* New York: Cooper Square, 1961.

Brown, Mark H., and W. R. Felton. *Before Barbed Wire.* New York: Bramhall, 1956.

Brown, Richard Maxwell. *Strains of Violence: Historical Studies of American Violence and Vigilantism.* New York: Oxford UP, 1975.

"Bucking Horse in Mexico Throws Reagan." *Gazette Telegraph* [Colorado Springs, CO] 5 July 1989: A1.

"Bush Eulogizes Baldrige as 'Noblest Work of God.'" *Gazette Telegraph* [Colorado Springs, CO] 31 July 1987: A5.

Butler, Anne M. *Daughters of Joy, Sisters of Misery: Prostitutes in the American West, 1865–90.* Urbana: U of Illinois P, 1987.

Carrier, Jim. "Ralph Rides the Range: Designer Lauren Puts His Brand on His Colorado Ranch." *Washington Post* 10 March 1987: D11.

Casey, Betty. *Dance Across Texas.* Austin: U of Texas P, 1985.

Cattle Call: News for Cattlemen. Terre Haute: Pitman-Moore, 1987.

Chin, Frank. "Confessions of the Chinatown Cowboy." *Bulletin of Concerned Asian Scholars* 4 (1972): 58–70.

Colorado Brand Book. Denver: Colorado State Board of Stock Inspection Commissioners, 1972.

Colorado Wild Horse–Inmate Program. Cañon City: United States Department of the Interior and Bureau of Land Management, 1988.

Dahlburg, John-Thor. "It's Just 'Glasnost,' Soviet Says of Anti-American Publications." *Philadelphia Inquirer* 11 March 1989: A3.

Dale, Edward Everett. *Cow Country.* Norman: U of Oklahoma P, 1965.

Dary, David. *Cowboy Culture.* New York: Avon, 1981.

Dittmer, Steve. "Tailoring Cattle for Today's Consumer." *Calf News* May 1987: 1–4.

Dobie, J. Frank. *Cow People.* Boston: Little, Brown, 1964.

Drago, Harry Sinclair. *Great American Cattle Trails.* New York: Dodd, Mead, 1965.

Duke, Cordia Sloan, and Joe B. Frantz. *6000 Miles of Fence: Life on the XIT Ranch of Texas.* Austin: U of Texas P, 1961.

Durham, Philip, and Everett L. Jones. *The Adventures of the Negro Cowboys.* New York: Dodd, Mead, 1965.

Durham, Philip, and Everett L. Jones. *The Negro Cowboys.* Lincoln: U of Nebraska P, 1983.

Dykstra, Robert R. *The Cattle Towns.* New York: Atheneum, 1970.

" 'Elite' Horse–Inmate Program Enlarged." *Daily Record* [Cañon City, CO] 26 March 1987: 1.

Ensminger, M. E. *The Stockman's Handbook.* Danville: Interstate Printers, 1983.

Fifty-Fourth Annual Texas Prison Rodeo Program. Huntsville: Texas Department of Corrections, 1985.

Fifty-Third Annual Texas Prison Rodeo Program. Huntsville: Texas Department of Corrections, 1984.

Frantz, Joe B., and Julian Ernest Choate, Jr. *The American Cowboy: The Myth and the Reality.* Norman: U of Oklahoma P, 1955.

Frink, Maurice, W. Turrentine Jackson, and Agnes Wright Spring. *When Grass Was King: Contributions to the Western Range Cattle Industry Study.* Boulder: U of Colorado P, 1956.

Funke, Gail S., Billy L. Wayson, and Neal Miller. *Assets and Liabilities of Correctional Industries.* Lexington: Lexington, 1982.

Gann, Walter. *Tread of the Longhorns.* San Antonio: Naylor, 1949.

Gard, Wayne. *The Chisholm Trail.* Norman: U of Oklahoma P, 1954.

Goff, Richard, Robert H. McCaffree, and Doris Sterbenz, eds. *Centennial Brand Book of the Colorado Cattlemen's Association.* Denver: Colorado Cattlemen's Centennial Commission, 1967.

Goodwyn, Frank. *Life on the King Ranch.* New York: Crowell, 1951.

Haley, J. Evetts. *Charles Goodnight: Cowman and Plainsman.* Norman: U of Oklahoma P, 1949.

Haley, J. Evetts. *The XIT Ranch of Texas and the Early Days of the Llano Estacado.* Norman: U of Oklahoma P, 1929.

Hall, R. M. Telephone Interviews. 12 July and 14 September 1988.

Harris, Charles W., and Buck Rainey, eds. *The Cowboy: Six-Shooters, Songs, and Sex.* Norman: U of Oklahoma P, 1976.

Hoagland, Edward. "Buckaroo Poets: Whoop-ee-ti-yi-yo, Git Along, Little Doggerel." *New York Times Book Review* 8 January 1989: 3.

Hollon, W. Eugene. *Frontier Violence: Another Look*. New York: Oxford UP, 1974.

Hough, Emerson. *The Story of the Cowboy*. New York: Appleton, 1898.

Hunter, J. Marvin, ed. *The Trail Drivers of Texas*. Austin: U of Texas P, 1924.

Jeffrey, Julie Roy. *Frontier Women: The Trans-Mississippi West, 1840–1880*. New York: Hill and Wang, 1979.

Jordan, Teresa. *Cowgirls: Women of the American West*. Garden City: Anchor, 1982.

Katz, William Loren. *The Black West*. Seattle: Open Hand, 1987.

Kauffman, Sandra. *The Cowboy Catalog*. New York: Potter, 1980.

Kohn, Linda. Telephone Interviews. 12 August and 9 September 1988.

Krakel, Dean F. *The Saga of Tom Horn: The Story of a Cattleman's War*. Lincoln: U of Nebraska P, 1988.

Kuehlthau, Margaret. "Plaited Horsehair Bridles." *Western Horseman*. August 1967: 65, 114–15.

Lemons, John. "Inmate Paints History Lesson on Wall of Centennial Facility." *Daily Record* [Cañon City, CO] 29 April 1987: 3.

Lomax, John. *Adventures of a Ballad Hunter*. New York: Hafner, 1971.

"Magnum CP-20: New Controlled Pressure Design, Implants Right the First Time." *National Cattlemen* 3 (1988): 41.

McCallum, Henry D., and Frances T. McCallum. *The Wire That Fenced the West*. Norman: U of Oklahoma P, 1965.

McCarty, Tara. "Audience Polled During 1989 Cowboy Poetry Gathering." Elko: Western Folklife Center of Nevada, 1989.

McClure, Grace. *The Bassett Women*. Athens: Swallow, 1985.

McCoy, Joseph G. *Historic Sketches of the Cattle Trade of the West and Southwest*. Kansas City: Ramsey, Millet and Hudson, 1874.

McGinn, Elinor M. "Trying to Profit: Inmate Labor at Cañon City, 1872–1927." *Colorado Heritage* 2 (1987): 14–21.

McMurtry, Larry. *In a Narrow Grave: Essays on Texas*. New York: Touchstone, 1989.

Mitchell, Lee Clark. "'When You Call Me That . . .': Tall Talk and Male Hegemony in *The Virginian*." *PMLA* 102 (1987): 66–77.

Montana Prison Description Sheets, 1880–94. Helena: Montana State Prison, 1880–94.

Montana Prison Record Sheets, 1871–85. Helena: Montana State Prison, 1871–85.

Montana Prison Record Sheets, 1892–96. Helena: Montana State Prison, 1892–96.

Myres, Sandra L. *Westering Women and the Frontier Experience, 1800–1915*. Albuquerque: U of New Mexico P, 1982.

Nevada's Annual Report of the Warden of the Nevada State Prison, 1865. Carson City: State Printer, 1866.

Nevada's Annual Report of the Warden of the Nevada State Prison, 1866. Carson City: State Printer, 1867.

Nevada's Biennial Reports of the Warden of the Nevada State Prison, 1867–68 through 1917–18. Carson City: State Printer, 1869–1919.

New Mexico's Biennial Reports of the Board of Commissioners and Superintendent of the New Mexico Penitentiary, 1893–94. Sante Fe: New Mexican Printing, 1894.

New Mexico's Report of the Board of Penitentiary Commissioners, 1902. Santa Fe: New Mexican Printing, 1902.

New Mexico's State Penitentiary Report of the Board of Commissioners and Superintendent to the Governor of New Mexico, 1912–13. Santa Fe: New Mexican Printing, 1913.

New Mexico's State Penitentiary Reports of the Board of Commissioners and Superintendent to the Governor of New Mexico, 1916, 1919, 1921, 1922, 1928. Santa Fe: New Mexican Printing, 1916, 1919, 1921, 1922, 1928.

Noreen, Barry. "Mustangs Shipped East After Stay at Prison." *Gazette Telegraph* [Colorado Springs, CO] 9 May 1988: A1, 3.

Norris, Frank. *The Literary Criticism of Frank Norris*. Ed. Donald Pizer. Austin: U of Texas P, 1964.

"On the Range." Narr. Bob Brown. Prod. Rob Wallace. "20/20." ABC. 30 July 1987: 11–14.

Osgood, Ernest Staples. *The Day of the Cattleman*. Minneapolis: U of Minnesota P, 1929.

Palen, J. S. Telephone Interview. 17 July 1988.

Pattie, Jane. Telephone Interview. 17 July 1988.

Porter, Kenneth Wiggins. *The Negro on the American Frontier*. New York: Arno, 1971.

"Ralgro. Because No Other Implant Triggers a Better Investment." *National Cattlemen* 3 (1988): 34.

Ralgro Implants. Terre Haute: Pitman-Moore, 1988.

Report of the Industrial Commission on Prison Labor. Washington, D.C.: Government Printing Office, 1900.

Rice, Lawrence D. *The Negro in Texas 1874–1900*. Baton Rouge: Louisiana State UP, 1971.

Riley, Glenda. *The Female Frontier: A Comparative View of Women on the Prairie and the Plains*. Lawrence: UP of Kansas, 1988.

Rollins, Philip Ashton. *The Cowboy*. New York: Scribner, 1922.

Sandoz, Mari. *The Cattlemen*. New York: Hastings, 1958.

Savage, W. Sherman. *Blacks in the West*. Westport: Greenwood, 1976.

Savage, William W., Jr. *The Cowboy Hero: His Image in American History and Culture*. Norman: U of Oklahoma P, 1979.

Savage, William W., Jr. *Cowboy Life: Reconstructing an American Myth*. Norman: U of Oklahoma P, 1979.

Shaw, Lloyd. *Cowboy Dances: A Collection of Western Square Dances*. Caldwell: Caxton, 1948.

Sifford, Darrell. "Can Playing 'Girl' Games Turn a Boy into a Homosexual?" *Philadelphia Inquirer* 25 April 1989: E10.

Slatta, Richard W. *Cowboys of the Americas*. New Haven: Yale UP, 1990.

Slotkin, Richard. *The Fatal Environment: The Myth of the Frontier in the Age of Industrialization, 1800–1890*. Middletown: Wesleyan UP, 1986.

Smith, Henry Nash. *Virgin Land: The American West as Symbol and Myth*. Cambridge: Harvard UP, 1971.

Social Science Research Council, ed. *Theoretical Studies in Social Organization of the Prison*. Washington, D.C.: Social Science Research Council, 1960.

So You'd Like to Adopt a Wild Horse . . . or Burro? Washington, D.C.: United States Department of the Interior and Bureau of Land Management, 1988.

Steckmesser, Kent Ladd. *The Western Hero in History and Legend*. Norman: U of Oklahoma P, 1965.

Tatum, Stephen. *Inventing Billy the Kid: Visions of the Outlaw in America, 1881–1981*. Albuquerque: U of New Mexico P, 1982.

Thorp, N. Howard, and Neil M. Clark. *Pardner of the Wind*. Caldwell: Caxton, 1945.

Tick Eradication: A Program Chronology. Laredo: United States Department of Agriculture, 1988.

Tompkins, Jane. *West of Everything: The Inner Life of Westerns*. New York: Oxford UP, 1992.

Utah's Biennial Reports of the State Board of Corrections for the State of Utah, 1895–96, 1897–98, 1899–1900. Salt Lake City: Desert News, 1897, 1899, 1901.

*Utah's Biennial Reports of the State Board of Corrections for the State of Utah, 1901–02,
1903–04, 1905–06, 1907–08.* Salt Lake City: Star, 1903, 1905, 1907, 1909.

*Utah's Biennial Reports of the State Board of Corrections for the State of Utah, 1909–10,
1911–12.* Salt Lake City: Arrow, 1911, 1913.

Vestal, Stanley. *Queen of Cowtowns: Dodge City.* New York: Harper, 1952.

Vrazo, Fawn. "USDA's Cowboys Hunt a Deadly Little Outlaw." *Philadelphia Inquirer* 2
March 1988: A1, 12.

Walker, Don D. *Clio's Cowboys: Studies in the Historiography of the Cattle Trade.* Lincoln:
U of Nebraska P, 1981.

Ward, Fay E. *The Cowboy at Work.* New York: Hastings, 1976.

Webb, Walter Prescott. *The Great Plains.* Lincoln: U of Nebraska P, 1981.

Westermeier, Clifford P., ed. *Trailing the Cowboy: His Life and Lore as Told by Frontier
Journalists.* Westport: Greenwood, 1978.

Weston, Jack. *The Real American Cowboy.* New York: Schocken, 1985.

White, George Ransom. *Animal Castration: A Textbook for the Use of Teachers, Students
and Practitioners.* Nashville: privately printed, 1947.

White, John I. *Git Along, Little Dogies: Songs and Songmakers of the American West.*
Urbana: U of Illinois P, 1989.

Winzeler, Judith K., and Wilbur S. Shepperson. "Cowboy Poetry: The New Folk Art."
Halcyon 9 (1987): 195–205.

Wolfenstein, Manfred R. *The Manual of Brands and Marks.* Norman: U of Oklahoma P,
1970.

Wyoming's Annual Reports of the Board of Charities and Reform, 1892–98. Laramie: Wyoming
State Prison, 1892–98.

Wyoming's Biennial Report of the State Board of Charities and Reform, 1923–24. Laramie:
Wyoming State Prison, 1924.

Works not pertaining specifically to cowboys and cowgirls

Arendt, Hannah. *The Human Condition.* Garden City: Anchor, 1959.

Barthes, Roland. *Elements of Semiology.* Trans. Annette Lavers and Colin Smith. New York:
Hill and Wang, 1967.

Bettelheim, Bruno. *Symbolic Wounds: Puberty Rites and the Envious Male.* New York:
Collier, 1962.

Bloom, Harold. *The Anxiety of Influence: A Theory of Poetry.* New York: Oxford UP, 1973.

Certeau, Michel de. *The Practice of Everyday Life.* Berkeley: U of California P, 1984.

Eco, Umberto. *Semiotics and the Philosophy of Language.* Bloomington: Indiana UP, 1984.

Fiske, John. *Understanding Popular Culture.* Boston: Unwin Hyman, 1989.

Foucault, Michel. *Discipline and Punish: The Birth of the Prison.* Trans. Alan Sheridan. New
York: Pantheon, 1977.

Freud, Sigmund. *Civilization and Its Discontents.* Trans. and ed. James Strachey. New York:
Norton, 1961.

Freud, Sigmund. *Totem and Taboo: Resemblances Between the Psychic Lives of Savages and
Neurotics.* Trans. A. A. Brill. New York: Vintage, 1978.

Frye, Northrop. *Anatomy of Criticism: Four Essays.* Princeton: Princeton UP, 1973.

Geertz, Clifford. *The Interpretation of Cultures.* New York: Basic, 1973.

Hobsbawm, Eric. *Bandits.* New York: Delacorte, 1969.

Irwin, John T. *American Hieroglyphics: The Symbol of the Egyptian Hieroglyphics in the
American Renaissance.* New Haven: Yale UP, 1980.

Lévi-Strauss, Claude. *The Raw and the Cooked.* New York: Harper, 1975.

Lévi-Strauss, Claude. *The Savage Mind.* Chicago: U of Chicago P, 1966.

Lévi-Strauss, Claude. *Totemism.* Boston: Beacon, 1962.

Lewis, R. W. B. *The American Adam: Innocence, Tragedy and Tradition in the Nineteenth Century.* Chicago: U of Chicago P, 1955.

Lord, Albert B. *The Singer of Tales.* New York: Atheneum, 1978.

Said, Edward W. *The World, the Text, and the Critic.* Cambridge: Harvard UP, 1983.

Saussure, Ferdinand de. *Course in General Linguistics.* Trans. Roy Harris. Ed. Charles Bally and Albert Sechehaye. La Salle: Open Court, 1986.

Index